THE
WRONG STUFF

THE
WRONG STUFF

The Extraordinary Saga of
Randy "Duke" Cunningham,
The Most Corrupt Congressman Ever Caught

Marcus Stern
Jerry Kammer
Dean Calbreath
George E. Condon Jr.

 PublicAffairs / *New York*

Published in the United States by PublicAffairs™, a member of the Perseus Books Group.

Public Affairs books are available at special discounts for bulk purchases in the U.S. by
corporations, institutions, and other organizations. For more information, please contact
the Special Markets Department at the Perseus Books Group, 11 Cambridge Center,
Cambridge, MA 02142, call (617) 252-5298, or e-mail
special.markets@perseusbooks.com.

DESIGNED BY JEFF WILLIAMS

Cataloging-in-Publication Data for this book is available from the Library of Congress
ISBN-13: 978-1-58648-479-8
ISBN-10: 1-58648-479-6

10 9 8 7 6 5 4 3 2 1

To Lee, Marie, Sarah, and Heidi

"Show me a hero and I'll write you a tragedy."

—F. SCOTT FITZGERALD

CONTENTS

THE CORRUPTION OF A WAR HERO

N OBODY LOOKING AT THE SCENE IN GEORGETOWN COULD HAVE THOUGHT that anything unusual, important, or historic was happening. It was, it seemed, just a congressman and a defense contractor having lunch and going over some figures written on a small piece of congressional stationery.

The congressman was Randy Cunningham, a member of the U.S. House who was known more for what he did before he entered politics than for legislation he had pushed or any particular lawmaking wizardry. A staunchly conservative Republican from the northern parts of San Diego County, Cunningham was famous for his exploits in the skies above North Vietnam back in 1972; his piloting skills and personal bravery made him the Navy's only fighter ace of the war. One of the few heroes to emerge from that unpopular war, he came home to great acclaim. He seized that fame, turned to politics, and became a congressman who was regularly reelected by comfortably large margins. He seemed—as he never tired of telling audiences—the real life embodiment of the "Maverick" character played so memorably by Tom Cruise in the movie *Top Gun*.

That was how the country viewed this man who wanted to be known simply as "Duke." Until, that is, a different picture emerged in 2005. This was the darker picture of a congressman on the take, a self-styled patriot forcing the Pentagon to spend limited funds more on enriching his friends than on protecting the troops in harm's way in Iraq and Afghanistan. It was a sordid tale of corruption unrivaled in the two centuries in which members of Congress have been tempted by those willing to pay them for favors.

And if there was a key moment in the entire saga of the biggest case of congressional corruption ever documented, it occurred, as important moments often do in Washington, over drinks and a meal at a restaurant, this time lunch for two at the Daily Grill in the Georgetown Inn, situated on bustling Wisconsin Avenue.

The men were haggling over the bribes that Wade would have to pay Cunningham for him to use his perches on the Appropriations and Intelligence Committees to steer lucrative federal contracts to Wade's company, MZM, Inc. As prosecutors would document later, Cunningham was quite willing to do Wade's bidding. He just wanted to make sure that Wade would pay him enough to finance the lifestyle he craved: nineteenth-century French antiques, yachts, Persian rugs, hunting trips, a Rolls Royce, and a $2.55 million house in one of San Diego County's most exclusive communities.

As Wade learned that day, Cunningham was not bashful at all about putting some pretty high price tags on his official services to pay for all this. And he was not reluctant to be up front about those price tags. So he took from his pocket a pad of official congressional stationery and started writing.

It was quite a scene, recounted by someone familiar with the details: "Duke just wrote this stuff out while they were talking. Mitch was there and saw him writing this stuff down but he didn't get a copy of it or anything like that," said the person who asked not to be identified. "He was using it as an aid while he was talking. He's talking and he's explaining, 'Here's what you get for this and here's what you get for that.'"

What he wrote ended up being the most damning piece of evidence against Cunningham, the one thing he could never explain away, the one document that forced him to drop his protestations of innocence and take the best deal he could get from prosecutors.

That piece of paper became known as the "bribe menu," an infamous document in the history of congressional corruption and the best refutation of Cunningham's later insistence that all he did was accept "gifts" in exchange for votes he would have cast anyway.

Oddly, it is not obvious at first glance what the cryptic numbers and letters mean. It is easy at first to miss the import and, in fact, investigators did just that. Unfortunately for Cunningham, when investigators took a second look at the document after a tip they realized that they had the "smoking gun." In effect, they now understood, this was an offer sheet for Wade. Directly beneath the Great Seal of the United States embossed at the top of his stationery, Cunningham had scribbled two columns of numbers.

The left column reflected the millions of dollars in federal contracts Cunningham would direct to Wade. The right column reflected the corresponding amount of bribe money Wade would pay Cunningham. It shows that Cunningham wanted a $140,000 yacht for the first $16 million in government contracts. Thereafter, he expected $50,000 in bribes for each additional million dollars in contracts. After Wade had paid Cunningham $340,000 in bribes for $20 million in defense contracts, the size of bribe for each additional million dropped from $50,000 to $25,000.

When the existence of the bribe menu was made public in a government sentencing memo on February 17, 2006, it stunned those who had known the congressman and had believed his protestations of innocence. It was almost more shocking than Cunningham's earlier guilty plea, and few were more shocked than his own staff and fellow congressmen, the people who thought they had been closest to him but had seen nothing to alert them to what their boss and colleague was up to. They were now at a complete loss to explain what had turned a hero to corruption and public shame. "We were all stunned. None of us saw any signs of this," said Rep. Edward Markey, a Democrat from Massachusetts who worked with Cunningham on housing issues. "The only thing we could think is that something happened and he just flipped."

But some who had served in the Navy with Cunningham decades earlier were not stunned to learn of his greed and his willingness to cut corners to put an extra buck in his own wallet. For some of them, that trait was memorably present when they watched Cunningham try to make as much money as possible from his status as the first ace of the Vietnam War. There had been the speaking fees and the ghost-written book, but Exhibit No. 1 in making that case came on what should have been a great day, October 14, 1972.

It was a Friday afternoon and the commanding officer at Miramar's Top Gun fighter pilot school was a busy man. He had the secretary of the Navy coming to the base to welcome into the Navy's war-fighting arsenal a new fighter jet, the F-14 Tomcat, and to bestow the Navy's top honor—the Navy Cross—on two aviators. On that afternoon he had less than twenty-four hours to make sure everything was ship-shape and sparkling for Secretary John Warner. So Ron McKeown, a former fighter pilot himself, was not in a conciliatory mood when Lt. Randy Cunningham and Lt. (jg) Willie Driscoll confronted him in the ready room with an ultimatum.

"Willie and I have decided we're not going to accept the Navy Cross," Cunningham declared to his stunned commander, recalled McKeown. "I said, 'I'm sorry, Duke. I wasn't listening right. I could have sworn you said you weren't going to accept the Navy Cross.'" Cunningham said he had heard correctly, adding that he and Driscoll were "going to hold out for the Medal of Honor."

At that, McKeown went from stunned to downright angry. Standing before him were two men whose combat skills he admired. They were aces, the only ones the Navy had produced since the Korean War. But here they were threatening to embarrass him, to snub the secretary of the Navy, and to dishonor the memories of the four thousand men who had received the Cross in its history. The Navy

Cross is not some trinket loosely awarded; it is the most prestigious medal the Navy could bestow. It had been good enough for the likes of Admiral "Bull" Halsey and Generals "Chesty" Puller and Lew Walt, some of the bravest to ever wear the uniform. But it was not good enough for Duke Cunningham?

McKeown could not believe it. And he was aware that everybody in his office was waiting to see how he would handle such incredible insubordination. He chose his words carefully: "The way you get the Medal of Honor is you don't hold out for it—you die for it." Then he firmly "invited" the two aviators into his inner office—though he intentionally left his door open a little bit so others could hear him dress down Cunningham and Driscoll.

"I said, 'Are you serious?' and they said, 'Well, they promised us the Medal of Honor.'" Cunningham was doing the talking while Driscoll, his back-seater in combat, listened. Pressed by McKeown as to who had done this alleged promising, Cunningham mentioned an aide to Admiral Elmo Zumwalt, the Chief of Naval Operations (CNO). Cunningham seemed unperturbed that this "nomination" he kept talking about—and made a fixture on his later political bio—had come from a Washington bureaucrat and not from someone involved in the dogfighting on May 10, 1972. He also seemed unswayed when McKeown informed the aviators that he had already spoken to this aide and had heard a much different story. According to McKeown, this aide—who has since died—told Cunningham what he should have known already, that the Navy itself cannot award the Medal of Honor, that the highest medal the Navy can bestow is the Navy Cross.

But McKeown had too much to do and was too perturbed with the two men to play nice with them. "You ain't going to get the Medal of Honor," he said flatly, and he added: "Here's what's going to go down: First, both of you are going to go get a haircut. Then you're going to get your blues cleaned and pressed with gold braid and make sure you've got a good shine on your shoes. And tomorrow, at ten o'clock, a grateful nation is going to heap its praise on two of its lofty heroes and give you the Navy Cross. And you're going to accept them and be gracious and charming. Anything less than that and I will personally rip your tits off. Now get out of my office."

From McKeown, this was no idle threat. The hard-nosed McKeown after all was a pretty imposing presence with an even more impressive athletic resume. At two hundred pounds, he had won the Naval Academy's light heavyweight boxing title three years in a row. And as the fullback on the most successful Navy football team in memory he had gained renown for his ability to throw devastating blocks that cleared running lanes for Joe Bellino, the academy's first-ever Heisman Trophy winner. So when McKeown threatened to "rip your tits off," you listened—even if you were a hotshot aviator.

McKeown has told that story before. But before now he has not talked about what really amazed him about Cunningham's actions that day. It was bad enough that Cunningham had persuaded himself that he deserved the Medal of Honor, that somehow it was owed him. And it was bad enough that he then twisted the words of a Pentagon bureaucrat to suggest he really had a chance. But McKeown could not believe it when Cunningham gave the reason for his anger over not getting it: "Duke said, 'Well, I was counting on getting that money.'"

To McKeown, here was evidence of almost incomprehensible greed because the money Cunningham was "holding out for" was pretty paltry. Although some states do give small tax breaks to Medal of Honor winners, all that Cunningham would have been eligible for would have been a stipend paid out by the Veterans Administration. In 1972, that would have totaled only $100 a month. As McKeown dryly observed: "We're not talking about a hell of a lot of money." But it was still money Cunningham felt was his. "He felt cheated. He said, 'I earned it and I deserve it,'" according to his wife, Nancy.[1]

From today's perspective, it is clear that a strong and growing sense of entitlement had already taken root inside Cunningham. It was a sense that would dominate the rest of his military career and reach historic proportions when he entered politics and gained positions of influence in Washington. But it was already evident to Cunningham's friends and fellow pilots back in 1972. They just weren't sure whether to laugh at it or try to shame him. They tried both.

It was the tough approach that worked on the Navy Cross ceremony—which came off smoothly. Cunningham and Driscoll, as ordered, did, indeed, look freshly shorn, polished, and buffed. Their tits survived the day. And Cunningham now proudly wore the Navy Cross along with his other medals—two Silver Stars, fifteen Air Medals, and one Purple Heart for injuries sustained while ejecting on May 10, 1972. But the other aviators knew about his session with McKeown. "Aviators resented him for it," said Pete "Viper" Pettigrew, another MiG killer. "Randy was a legitimate war hero. In one sense he was bigger than life. But he exaggerated everything. He destroyed his own stature by trying to make himself bigger than bigger than life."

What no one could have guessed back then was that this battle over a $100-a-month stipend would foreshadow a scandal over mansions, yachts, and antiques that truly was bigger than life. In 2005, everything—an undisciplined lifestyle, the oversized sense of entitlement, the personal indiscretions, the moral blindness, the loose dealings with lobbyists and contractors—caught up with Cunningham. By then, the spit-shined and polished Navy aviator who had cut such a dashing figure for the Navy Cross ceremony was supplanted by the decidedly less-cocky congressman who stood before a federal judge. Through his tears, he admitted he had betrayed the voters' trust and sold his official actions to the highest bidder. And he was even more chastened in 2006 when he faced the same federal judge to hear himself sentenced to prison.

Cunningham was haggard, pale, and noticeably thinner when he showed up for his sentencing on March 3, 2006; he told U.S. District Judge Larry Alan Burns that he had gone from 265 pounds to 175 pounds in the 264 days since his life had been turned upside down and his corruption revealed in a story in the hometown *San Diego Union-Tribune*. His uniform at the beginning of the day was a charcoal gray suit and dark-striped tie. By the end of the day, it would be a prison jumpsuit and shackles; his home would be San Diego's Metropolitan Correctional Center.

Before that week was over, the now-former congressman would find himself once again shackled and under heavy guard as a passenger on what has become known as "Con Air," the airline operated by the U.S. Marshals Service to move federal prisoners to new locations.

At year's end, he would be wearing still another uniform, one not even slightly reminiscent of the aviator's gear featured in the glossy photographs Cunningham liked to hand out to people when he first met them. This uniform was sadder—the khaki-colored shirt and coarse khaki pants of an inmate at the Butner Federal Correctional Complex in North Carolina. There, Cunningham slept in a dormitory-style room penned in by double fences, and he worked in the prison library while being evaluated for assignment to a permanent prison where he would serve the remainder of his sentence. That prison turned out to be a minimum-security work camp attached to the Federal Correctional Institution at Tucson.

At eight years and four months, it is the longest prison sentence ever meted out to a member of Congress, far longer than the thirty months facing his colleague Ohio Rep. Bob Ney. Ney in 2006 admitted that he had accepted thousands of dollars in trips, gambling chips, meals, sports and entertainment tickets, campaign contributions, and other benefits from Jack Abramoff and other lobbyists in exchange for his official help.

The sentence was also considerably longer than the one received by Abramoff himself. Abramoff was the person most identified with congressional scandals in the early part of this century. Memorably attired in his fedora and too-tight trench coat, he was sentenced to almost six years in prison for fraud related to the 2000 purchase of the SunCruz Casinos gambling fleet. The wide-ranging investigation of Abramoff's favors at one point threatened to include up to twenty members of Congress, though Ney may end up being the only one snared by prosecutors.

But Congress in its long history has seen many men like Abramoff, lobbyists fishing for weak congressmen willing to sell their official offices. What was notable about Abramoff was how far he was willing to go and how much money he was willing to spend. Abramoff made sure that his clients funneled huge amounts of cash into the campaign committees of selected members and to conservative think tanks and charities. His entertainment was lavish even by Washington standards. It was notable as well that the ponds he most liked to fish in were the Appropriations Committees, which he labeled the "favor factories." It is a description that was certainly apt for Cunningham. For unlike Abramoff, Cunningham, in the long history of congressional wrongdoing, was one of a kind.

There have been more colorful rogues and scoundrels in the two centuries in which unscrupulous contractors and office seekers have been tempting members of Congress. It would be hard to forget hapless Senator Herman Talmadge of Georgia trying to explain how he kept finding thousands of dollars of cash in that old torn overcoat of his in 1978. And no bribe was ever more memorable than the 1980 videotape that showed Rep. Richard Kelly stuffing $25,000 in Abscam cash down his pants and then worrying about a telltale bulge as he earnestly asked an undercover FBI agent, "Does it show?" In more recent years, scandals landed a powerful congressional king—the Ways & Means chairman, Rep. Dan Rostenkowski—and a House court jester—Ohio Rep. Jim Traficant—in prison. Rostenkowski was nailed for improperly taking $700,000 over three decades, and Traficant took no more than $100,000—ill-gotten gains that pale in comparison to Cunningham's take in cash, yachts, luxury cars, and French antiques.

Cunningham was not just another venal politician. His story was both an interesting personal saga and a warning of something crying out to be fixed in Washington, something much bigger than one man. Personally, here was a man who soared to the heights only to plummet to unforeseen depths. Born under humble circumstances, he became a hero in combat but succumbed to personal blandishments and easy fortune. His rise and fall struck notes that were almost Shakespearean in their giddy highs and tragic lows.

But if that was all he represented, his story would be no more worth the telling and retelling than that of any other member of Congress who has disgraced the office and then faded into deserved obscurity. The Cunningham saga is one for the history books because it is more than the tale of a lone corrupt man. Instead, it is one of those rare political scandals important because it exposes a fundamental flaw in the way Congress adopts its laws and spends its treasure in protecting America. And scandals like that come along infrequently.

This time, the flaw is the way Congress orders the administration to spend money on projects that may be supported by only one congressman—and the almost complete lack of controls in this system. Often, what matters is only the committee clout of that congressman, and no one even has the chance to ask him to justify the spending. Compounding the flaw, in the wake of the September 11, 2001, terror attacks, is that much of the spending is never revealed to the public. "Follow the money" helped break the Watergate scandal, but there was no easy or clear path for following this money because so many of the programs are classified and unknown even to other congressmen.

It was Watergate, of course, that laid bare the role of big money in presidential campaigns. And even earlier—in what was before Cunningham perhaps the worst scandal in congressional history— there was the Credit Mobilier drama. That came in the decade after the Civil War when big money and high stakes combined in the ambitious plan to extend the railroad to the West Coast. That 1872 scandal captured the excesses of the Gilded Age when the Union Pacific Railroad, in effect, bought several members of the Congress. The railroad set up a company called Credit Mobilier and gave shares in the new company to influential members of Congress who then enriched themselves by voting federal subsidies for railroad construction.

That scandal not only revealed something more than just individual corruption but also ushered in the Progressive Era of fundamental reform. So, too, with Cunningham. His fall contributed to the

Republican loss of the House and Senate in 2006. And reformers continue to cling to the hope that it—along with companion scandals—may be enough to shame Congress into enacting genuine reform, though they have been disappointed with the reluctance of the now-ascendant Democrats to get truly tough on the abuses.

The nation has often been warned—first by President Ronald Reagan in a memorable address in 1987, and more recently by money spent on a "bridge to nowhere" to get commuters from Ketchikan, Alaska, to an undeveloped island. In his 2007 State of the Union address, President George W. Bush cautioned about the evils of what has proved to be one of the greatest invitations to corruption ever devised by Congress. It is called the earmark, and through Cunningham's tenure it permitted individual congressmen, under cover of anonymity, to insert appropriations into bills even though the spending was not requested by the executive branch or vetted in hearings.

At the same time, other changes in the way the government spends its money made it easier for the system to be subverted. Just as Cunningham was gaining seniority and clout, the Pentagon procurement process was streamlined during the 1990s in a way that reduced transparency and oversight. Then, after the terrorist attacks of September 11, 2001, the volume of programs funded through the so-called and highly secretive "black budget" soared amid only feeble attempts by the Bush administration to monitor them. All this combined with Cunningham's own hubris and unchecked sense of personal entitlement to bring shame to a war hero and to contribute to the end of Republican rule of Congress.

With Cunningham's friends no longer in control of the House committees, there is some hope that genuine investigations will determine the full extent of his corruption, which today can only be surmised. At least four investigations were still underway at the beginning of 2007. Almost certainly the corruption was more extensive than what the prosecutors tried to prove. The question of when it started and what turned a war hero admired by thousands into a corrupt felon condemned publicly by the president of the United States—that still is being debated by those closest to Cunningham.

What is known is that this proud fighter pilot and American hero was too weak to resist the allure of earmarks, the blandishments of big-spending lobbyists, and the shot at living the country club life he envied as a teen. In retrospect, the earmark seemed to be invented just for Randy Cunningham. For even though he was taught by his parents in Missouri that nobody owed him anything, he proved to be a man vulnerable to being seduced by awards and standing ovations into believing that everybody owed him everything.

chapter one

GROWING UP IN MIDDLE AMERICA

E VEN AFTER FIVE DECADES, FOLKS IN SHELBINA, MISSOURI, STILL REMEM-
ber how cocky the thirteen-year-old Randy Cunningham was
when he arrived in town in early 1955.

"When he first got here, it was like he thought everybody here
was a hick," said Sam Hawkins, who was a year behind Cunningham
at Shelbina Elementary. "He had to learn different." Randy was a
lean and athletic seventh grader when he arrived from Northern
California, but many of the kids didn't like his attitude or the way he
looked, and they made fun of him for his close-set eyes. "They called
him a Jap," said Hawkins, remembering that the era was still thick
with anti-Japanese hostility from World War II.

Complicating things was Randy's discontent with the move that
had taken him away from friends and family back in Fresno. It made
for a difficult introduction to the nation's heartland for the homesick
boy. He had been uprooted along with his younger brother, Rob, by
his father, thirty-seven-year-old Randall Cunningham. A tall, broad-
shouldered man, at six feet one and 230 pounds, Randall towered

over his wife, Lela. Both Randall and Lela had been born in Oklahoma and had joined the 1930s Dust Bowl migration to California.

Lela gave birth to their first child on December 8, 1941. Randall H. Cunningham entered the world in a Los Angeles hospital whose windows were covered as part of a blackout against a feared attack on the mainland after the previous day's Japanese attack on Pearl Harbor.

The elder Randall operated a gasoline station near Beverly Hills before moving to Fresno in 1948 to allow Lela to be closer to her large family, including eleven uncles for the boys. There, Randall ran a Union 76 station until he was offered the chance to run a variety, or "dime," store in Shelbina, a northeastern Missouri town of about two thousand residents. His brother Winford, who already owned a similar store sixty miles away in Fulton, had just bought the store in Shelbina and asked Randall to run it.

At that time, Shelbina was but a tiny town of about two thousand. "We plan on putting in a complete line of Babies' and Ladies' dry goods and will broaden the assortment in all departments," the Cunninghams said in an ad in the weekly *Shelbina Democrat*. "We solicit your good will and continued patronage." It had sprouted from the prairie in 1857, when the railroad came through. Forty miles to the east lay Hannibal, the Mississippi River town where Mark Twain had grown up as Samuel Clemens. The Shelbina that welcomed the Cunninghams in 1955 was a town whose fortunes depended upon the market for the livestock, corn, and soybeans brought in from the fields. The business district was thriving back then, and Cunningham Variety shared a handsome commercial block of gray stone buildings that housed a drug store, a hardware store, and a dress shop.

Politically, the family fit right in with their new neighbors. They were staunch Democrats and backers of Adlai Stevenson in 1956 even while President Dwight Eisenhower was sweeping to an easy reelection.

"My parents moved us there because they saw an opportunity to raise Randy and me in a small, safe community," recalled Rob much later. "It was a place where kids could stay out late to play without their parents needing to worry." It took Randy a while to adapt to the move, but one thing that made it easier was his obvious athleticism. And what the boys saw as cockiness some girls saw as self-confidence. "I thought he was full of life," said Betty Brown. "He could do back flips, and that wasn't something you saw much back then."

Randy often rode his younger brother to school on his bike and took him to the movies. "I always thought of him as my protector. Nobody would mess with me when Randy was around," said Rob. Even though Randy would later claim in his own book to be an Irish Catholic, he was never a Catholic. He was raised Baptist, and he often walked with the rest of his family to the Baptist church just a block from his home.

Of course, at such a small school—his senior class had just nineteen boys and twenty-one girls—there is plenty of opportunity to participate in team sports. Randy played football and basketball all four years of high school for the Shelbina Indians. The 1960 school yearbook reported that Randy won the award as the team's best free-throw shooter. The yearbook also teased Cunningham about his enthusiastic interest in girls. The Class Prophecy anticipated that Randy would coach high school basketball at Stoutsville, a tiny burg over toward Hannibal, and indicated that he took a lot more interest in the girls' team, which was undefeated, than the boys', whose record was three wins and forty losses: "He is thinking seriously of having his boys team dropped from the conference and concentrating on the girls." For the quotation to accompany his senior picture, Cunningham chose: "I like a girl with a good head on my shoulder."

For most of his senior year, Randy dated a pretty cheerleader named Linda Parker. To pick Linda up for a date, Randy would drive the family's Chevy station wagon the six miles to the farm north of town, where the Parkers grew corn, wheat, and soybeans and raised a few hogs and Black Angus cattle. But the romance did not survive graduation and Linda left him for someone else. "He got upset and said he was going to beat the poor guy up," Linda Parker Dye laughingly recalled in an interview forty-six years later. "But he didn't. He cooled off."

Others state that Randy often had difficulty accepting the rules and did not like to have anyone tell him no. Randy had "a chip on his shoulder a little bit," remembers Wes Sanders, the basketball coach. "He had some problem accepting authority. . . . If I took him out of the game, he'd get upset. . . . He liked the glory of being on the team. You could see that. But sometimes he wouldn't want to pay the price for the team. It seemed like he was more concerned with being an individual than he was for the team."

When he was a senior, Randy made a big impression on Sandy O'Donnell, who was then in seventh grade. Now Sandy Requet, she recalled that one of the older boys was making a habit of tormenting her and other girls. "I hated it," she recalled. "Then one day Randy came over and grabbed him by the front of his shirt and said, 'You leave these little girls alone!'" She said the bully "never bothered us again after that." But Sam Hawkins remembers other times when Randy himself was the bully. "Randy was basically a nice guy," he said, but sometimes he picked on the smaller kids. "He would just haul off and hit you." One of Sam's sisters said flatly: "He was a bully."

Randy was a very good friend to Ronnie Cullers, the buddy who joined him catching catfish in the Salt River and hunting for squirrel and rabbits. "We did everything together," said Ronnie's brother, Rick. In high school, the three would hire out to farmers who needed help to bring in the hay. "We'd buck bales all day," Cullers said, recalling that fresh bales that had yet to dry sometimes weighed more than a hundred pounds. "And the pay was a dollar an hour. It helped us realize that we needed to get an education and go to college."

For Cunningham, this meant a year at Northeast Missouri State Teachers College before he was ready for the big time—the mammoth University of Missouri campus at Columbia, fifty-three miles from his home. It was the fall of 1961 when Cunningham enrolled at what they all called Mizzou. He quickly learned that the distance he had traveled was much, much more than just those fifty-three miles. He was now in a different world. The biggest crowds he had ever seen were at St. Louis Cardinals' ballgames. Now he was but one of almost thirteen thousand students on campus.

It was time for him to find out whether he could cut it outside the sheltered confines of Shelbina. It was also—though he didn't know it then—time for him to cast aside the youthful innocence of his hometown and begin to take on the adult responsibilities that went with a wife, a child, and the job that soon were to come his way—all under the gathering storm of a war across the ocean in a place some still called French Indochina. This was a war that soon enough would change his life even more dramatically than the wife and son and job.

Even from the beginning, and even on a campus in the middle of the country, there were hints of Vietnam. Cunningham's arrival on campus coincided with the arrival in Washington of John F. Kennedy, a politician Cunningham welcomed as a fellow Irishman and fellow Democrat. Kennedy used his Inaugural Address to pledge to "pay any price, bear any burden, meet any hardship, support any friend, oppose any foe" for the cause of freedom. But for Randy, all that would come later.

Cunningham majored in physical education: His dream was to become a coach and phys-ed teacher. At six foot one and about 180 pounds, he was lean and athletic and he took quickly to the level of competition offered by intramurals. Former dorm mates in Stafford Hall remember him as one of the best athletes on their championship teams. "Randy was good at about everything—football, basketball, volleyball," recalled teammate Barry Billings. "He was a very self-confident, self-assured guy," said Billings. "I'd say he exuded self-confidence. He was a little cocky, but not to the point that you thought it was obnoxious."

He also loved to have a good time now that he was away from his strict parents. "We partied together. We'd get a keg and drive out to Hinkson Creek on a Friday or Saturday night," Billings said. Hinkson was the all-but-official "make-out" spot near campus and a keg was a favored way to get around the laws in Missouri. In those days, students not yet twenty-one could buy only 3.2 beer, a remnant of Prohibition, so-called because of the low percentage of alcohol.

One of Cunningham's electives was a course in government, where, as classmate Gary Dye recalled, "he definitely wanted to be part of the conversation." Across the distance of more than four decades, Dye vividly remembers Cunningham: "He was the kind of guy you'd remember. I think he liked to draw attention to himself . . . I thought he was really neat. He had a big smile all the time. He was as close to being a BMOC [Big Man on Campus] as you could be without being a varsity athlete."

In the second semester of his junior year, he enrolled in a water safety instruction class. It was there by the pool that he met a pretty, shy freshman girl from St. Louis. Sue Albrecht hadn't wanted to go to college. She enrolled at Missouri at the behest of her parents. Even though she had thought of becoming a physical therapist, what she really wanted was to have a family. Now she had found a man to help her start that family.

Sue easily recalled her first impression of Randy in that pool: "He had a good physique. And he had a sort of swagger," she said. "He had a lot of self-confidence and I didn't. That's probably why I was drawn to him." And the attraction was very much mutual. Cunningham was smitten.

The young couple began dating, often going out for rides in Randy's leaky Ford convertible. They enjoyed dinners at the Shack and fall afternoons in Memorial Stadium. Like most fiancées, Sue did not recognize the warning signs that could have told her Randy might not be her perfect match and lifelong partner. One of those signs came when they shopped for wedding rings. Mindful of their financial status, repeatedly she told Randy that she just wanted a simple band to symbolize their engagement. But Randy would not have it. Instead, he went into debt to purchase a marquis diamond.

Sitting for an interview in her St. Louis home thirty-three years after her divorce from Cunningham and twenty-nine years into her second marriage, Sue ruefully acknowledged that this was a marriage that never should have happened. But she didn't see that in time, and the wedding went forward. It was 1964 and the newlyweds thought they knew what life held in store for them—a teaching job for Randy, children for Sue. But that year turned out to be a turning point not just for them but for the entire country. In June, three young civil rights workers were brutally beaten and then shot to death in Mississippi, condemned for their sin of trying to register black voters. In August, Congress passed the Gulf of Tonkin Resolution, which gave the president broad powers to expand American involvement in the Vietnam War. It was a key step along the path to all-out war.

Randy was working on a master's degree and had found a job that matched his love of swimming. The university was starting its first varsity swim program and Cunningham got the job as assistant to Tom Hairabedian, the new coach. In 2006, a year after he won three gold medals in the diving competition at the World Masters Games in Edmonton, Canada, the eighty-two-year-old Hairabedian enthusiastically recalled: "Everybody liked Randy. He had a lot of enthusiasm and he did a good job."

Randy worked as a lifeguard as he finished his masters work and a chance poolside conversation led to another job. He took his bride up storied Route 66 to suburban Chicago, where he became assistant to Don Watson, Hinsdale Central's now legendary swim coach. Hinsdale was a new world for Cunningham, a world of affluence and big city success. By all accounts, Cunningham was a popular figure during the year and a half he spent there. As an assistant to Watson, he worked not only with the freshman swim team but also with younger boys in a community-based feeder program. "He was gregarious and outgoing and really seemed to like us kids," recalled Loren Druz, who was nine years old in 1965. Druz also recalled nights when his parents dropped him and his brother off at Cunningham's small rented house, near the center of the prosperous community, about twenty miles outside the Chicago Loop.

"I really liked both of them," said Druz. "I think they were the first cool, young married couple that I knew. We'd eat popcorn and watch movies on television." Druz's mother was even more taken with Cunningham. "We thought Randy was the cat's meow," she said. "He was full of good will and he would tease the kids, in a good way, so they'd relate to him."

The 1967 Hinsdale Central yearbook had a picture of a smiling Cunningham, in street clothes, standing in the pool along with other coaches and swimmers on the team at the meet where Hinsdale won the Illinois State championship. It was the first of twelve consecutive state titles the school won under the direction of Coach Watson, a man whose name still evokes reverence both at the school and in national swimming circles.

Cunningham always joined in the chorus of praise for Watson—but he irked others by seeming to try to take more credit than he himself deserved. The students generally liked Assistant Coach Cunningham. But they were openly annoyed when he used his 1984 book and his political speeches to claim that he "produced thirty-six high school All Americans in 1965–67, three of whom went on to win gold or silver medals" in the Olympics.

"That is a fantasy. It has nothing to do with reality. That program wasn't the Randy and Don show. It was the Don Watson show," said John Kinsella, the bluntest of the swimmers who were there when Cunningham was the assistant. "Randy was basically a go-fer for Don. He had about as much right to claim responsibility for our success as Clarence did—the guy who maintained the pool." Kinsella was a swimming phenom—making the varsity as a freshman in 1967 and bursting onto the international scene with a silver medal at the 1968 Olympics in Mexico City. In 1970, after he had broken several American and world records, he was named winner of the Sullivan Award as the nation's outstanding amateur athlete. In 1972, he won a gold medal as a member of the eight-hundred-meter freestyle relay team.

Kinsella's rejection of Cunningham's claims to swimming glory were seconded by other members of the team, almost all of whom spoke fondly of their former assistant coach but were incredulous of his boasts. "Randy Cunningham was a nice guy, but he wasn't an integral part of the success of that team. That's just talk from a guy trying to prove that he was the best at something when he wasn't," said Bob Nieman, a member of the Class of '66 who went on to win the 1979 world Pentathlon championship.

Coach Watson himself is proud of what he has accomplished. But he is not a man given to bragging. The trophies and the championships and titles pretty much do that for him. And he doesn't like to be kicking Cunningham, who is already down. But even Watson stepped out of character when he saw what Cunningham's lawyer claimed in one court document seeking a more lenient sentence after the congressman had admitted to taking bribes. In the pre-sentencing memo, attorneys cast Cunningham as a far-sighted pioneer at Hinsdale, contending that he had "immersed himself in coaching and developed a system to keep computerized records of each swimmer's performance—a technique that was nearly unheard of at the high school level in the mid-sixties."

"I wonder what Randy was smoking when he came up with these statements," Watson said. "He never shared these computerized records with me." He added, "There wasn't anything computerized in swimming in 1967—or in anything else, as far as I can remember."

What many of those he coached did remember about Cunningham was his love for fast cars whose cost far exceeded what an assistant coach in both football and swimming could prudently afford. When Congressman Cunningham got into trouble, some of his students thought back on the Corvette Coach Cunningham bought over his wife's objection. "I never really thought about the idea of having a Corvette on a high school coach's salary, until Coach Cunningham became nationally famous," said Mike Flynn, the freshman quarterback who is now a linguistics professor at Carleton University in Minnesota. "Maybe he had ambitions and ways of fulfilling them long before public office appeared on his agenda."

Others remember that car. It was a slick metallic green number that cost, as his then-wife Sue remembers, $5,200—quite a stretch on a teacher's salary. It was the second new car in two years, following the 1965 Chevrolet Impala Super Sport. Looking back, some friends wondered whether maybe even then Randy was struggling to become the oversized personality he called "Duke."

But a raging war soon overtook football and swimming and fast cars. While Coach Cunningham was toughening up high school freshmen, the war in Vietnam was becoming impossible to ignore—even for a young man whose marriage provided him a draft deferment. It was barely a year earlier—May 3, 1965—that the first U.S.

Army combat troops arrived in Vietnam. By the year's end, the troop level was at 184,300 and rising.

One of those men was Cunningham's best friend from back in Shelbina. Now an Army first lieutenant, Ronnie Cullers was a combat engineer officer commanding the 1st Platoon, A Company, 1st Engineer Battalion. Cunningham had stayed in touch with friends for news about his buddy, but he was ill prepared for the news of July 15, 1966. Operating over Quang Tri Province at something called Landing Zone Crow, Cullers's helicopter was hit by enemy fire at about fifteen hundred feet. Marines on the ground were horrified to see smoke billow from the chopper's windows and flames shoot out of its rear just before it crashed. All fifteen aboard were killed.

Nothing was to be the same for Cunningham. His friend was dead. A war he supported was growing. And his doubts about how long married men and teachers would be deferred were building— especially when the Pentagon announced on August 3 that it now needed thirty-six thousand men a month from the draft. "I wasn't paying too much attention to the war," Cunningham admitted. But events "hit me really hard," he told an interviewer in 1992. "When Ronnie died, the war got really close to me. I felt bad because I hadn't lived up to the things my mom and dad believed in."

Until Cullers's death, Cunningham's life in Fresno, Shelbina, and Hinsdale had been largely isolated from the bigger issues roiling American public life. He had paid little attention to current events and had shown no interest even in voting. His life was sports, hunting, family. Although he had been criticized for cockiness, he had lots of friends. Nothing in his life suggested that he felt he was "owed" special treatment or "entitled" to a good life. When Cullers died and the violence in Southeast Asia escalated, Cunningham felt it was time to act. To the surprise of his wife and family, Randy Cunningham enlisted in the U.S. Navy.

chapter two

MAY 10, 1972:
THE DAY THAT MADE DUKE

IT IS NOT CLEAR EXACTLY WHEN RANDY CUNNINGHAM TOOK "DUKE" AS HIS call sign. But there is no question about when Cunningham actually became the Duke and fully took on the persona that was to carry him to stardom, wealth, fame, political power, and—ultimately—shame, dishonor, and prison. That happened on May 10, 1972.

On that day, in a matter of just a few life-and-death minutes in the skies above North Vietnam, Cunningham was the pivotal player in an aerial drama still celebrated and studied more than three decades later as the most famous dogfight of the Vietnam War, and one of the most intense of the jet age. With three "kills" to go along with two he had collected earlier that year, it made the boy from Shelbina an ace—the designation, first made famous by Baron Manfred von Richthofen in World War I, for any pilot who has made five enemy kills.

This was what Cunningham had dreamed of from his first flying lesson at an airfield in Illinois. "When I flew an airplane . . . I would will the airplane to do something and that's what it would do," he said. "It actually becomes part of you."[1] That command of the air did not come easily to Cunningham. Others in training were graded higher; others got tapped first to go to Top Gun—the Naval Fighter Weapons School—at Miramar in San Diego.

But no one out-worked Cunningham. Jim Laing, one of his tactical flight instructors, once marveled at his willingness to study. "I think what stood out most was that you couldn't give him enough information," Laing told the author Robert K. Wilcox. "He always wanted more. 'What should I read? Where do I study more?'"[2] Willie Driscoll, who rode the back seat of Cunningham's fighters as his radar intercept officer (RIO), saw the same thing. "I was with Duke Cunningham during the entire combat cruise and he was up twenty-four hours, seven days a week. He would just as soon skip lunch and go read up something in the book. Very dedicated to his craft."[3]

Cunningham forced himself to become an expert on the capabilities both of his own plane—the F-4 Phantom, the twin-engine supersonic workhorse for both the Navy and the Air Force during Vietnam—and that of the enemy—the Russian-built MiG-17, MiG-19, and MiG-21. And he read everything he could about the lives and tactics of the great aces in history: Germans von Richthofen, Oswald Boelcke, Max Immelmann, and Ernst Udet; and Americans Eddie Rickenbacker, Frank Luke, Joe Foss, Pappy Boyington, and Chuck Yeager.

On his first combat assignment, a rather uneventful cruise aboard the carrier USS *America,* and then during his very eventful stint on the carrier USS *Constellation* (the "Connie"), Cunningham, despite his amiable manner, often rubbed the other pilots the wrong way. He was all business. Flying and fighting were all he cared about "every second of my life," Cunningham said of his time on the carriers.[4] He became famous for his saying "You fight like you train," and few trained any harder.

On October 1, 1971, Lt. Cunningham joined the squadron known as the "Fighting Falcons," setting out from homeport San Diego. It was on the Connie that "Duke" was born. His call sign had been "Yank," but he switched it to Duke. He also began wearing an all-black flight suit, tailored in Hong Kong, that he had designed for himself. The other pilots kidded him because of the number of weapons he strapped on. "He liked the Hollywood shot too—big guns, knives . . . I always accused him of carrying so many weapons . . . that if he ever ejected, he'd sink," said his Top Gun roommate Jim McKinney.[5]

Less clear was the reason—or timing—for the change in his call sign. In almost all his interviews after 1972 he stated that it was done in homage to his movie hero John "Duke" Wayne. But in his court-ordered interview on February 6, 2006, with Saul J. Faerstein, a Beverly Hills psychiatrist, Cunningham added an important layer—and a different time sequence—to the story. To the doctor, Cunningham said he took on the call sign Duke because he felt the North Vietnamese were gunning specifically for him after he bagged his first enemy MiG on January 19, 1972. In a report to the court, Dr. Faerstein wrote:

> Because of his expertise as a pilot, he was targeted by the North Vietnamese who listened for his call names "Yank" and "Maverick" to try to shoot him down. He changed his call name to "Duke" because he admired John Wayne and he has been "Duke" ever since.[6]

Cunningham's mention of "Maverick" as his call sign is baffling unless seen in the context of many years of contending—wrongly—that he was the model for Tom Cruise's character in the popular 1986 movie *Top Gun*. The timing of the switch also seems improbable since Cunningham's second kill—the one that would have drawn increased enemy attention—came only two days before the big dogfight of May 10.

Jack Ensch, a fellow pilot who later was shot down and spent seven months as a POW, said Cunningham himself tried to sell the "Duke" handle. "That was not his call sign in the squadron," said Ensch. "He tagged himself Duke and it stuck after he was the ace. . . . Usually a call sign is assigned to you."[7]

Whenever he adopted the new call sign, Duke woke up on the Connie on May 10, 1972, wondering whether the war would end before he could get his third kill. Two days earlier he had even watched John Wayne's Vietnam movie *The Green Berets* to inspire him. But Cunningham and the other aviators knew that they were entering a new and final phase of the war. U.S. forces were racing to the exits. American troop levels were down drastically, to fewer than 69,000 from a peak of 543,000. In only three months, the last U.S. combat troops would be gone from Vietnam, leaving only a few thousand Army advisers, some Marine Corps security guards, and administrators to assist the embattled and doomed regime in Saigon. But there was still fighting to be done. Just the day before—May 9— President Richard Nixon authorized the mining of Haiphong Harbor amid the heaviest aerial combat of the entire war.

For Duke Cunningham, the sudden furor in the skies matched the turmoil in his personal life. He had just received a letter from Sue. He called it a "Dear John" letter. "She wanted out of the marriage. The strain was almost unbearable," he wrote in his book.[8] In a later interview, he elaborated: "I fought back tears and a lump in my throat often. This brooding had come over me on the morning of the tenth, only more consuming."[9] His ex-wife to this day still is baffled by his characterization of her letter, which she insists was a letter urging him to work with her to save the marriage.

So there was this brooding pilot, filled with questions as dawn broke May 10: Would the war end before he could get more kills or become an ace? Would his marriage survive? And, of course, the question no fighter pilot wants to face but can't escape: Will I live through the day?

Death is not something an aviator can afford to contemplate and still retain the instinct and reflexes so critical to success in aerial combat. Cunningham himself was almost grounded after he let those thoughts get to him in the wake of his first kill back in January. Then, flying over Quan Lang near the Laotian border, he had downed a MiG-21 with a Sidewinder heat-seeking missile. He was jubilant until, at a shipboard celebration, another crewman asked him what it was like to kill another human being.

Until then, Cunningham had preferred to dismiss the North Vietnamese as a bunch of "Gomers," a disparaging word drawn from *Gomer Pyle,* a popular television show on CBS from 1964 to 1970. But now the question forced him to think of the enemy pilots as real human beings. "The words hit me full force, as if I were being knocked to the floor," Cunningham later wrote. "I looked at my questioner, unable to reply. I turned and went straight to my room feeling as if the whole world had blown up. Always thinking of myself as a hard-core professional, I had believed that such a question would never faze me."[10]

But it very much had, leaving him with "a sickening feeling" and a late-night need to seek the help of a Catholic priest serving as the Connie's chaplain. His doubts were eased by the priest's counsel—though he was furious with him for reporting what Cunningham thought were confidential comments to the ship's commanding officer. The CO decided not to ground him, but did order him to take a few days of rest in the Philippines. Though relieved to be back in the cockpit, Cunningham wrote in his book that he never got over that night's unease. "The act of killing someone was never a pleasant experience for me," he said. "The after-effects remain with me to this day."

In the macho world of fighter pilots, though, doubts like these are to be shared only with priests and wives. The public face has to be one of confidence. Pilots well know that there may be men on each mission who won't come back; but they are all convinced it will be the other guy. Cunningham's back-seater, Willie Driscoll, his RIO, has spoken eloquently about that world. "I liken it to gladiator work," said Driscoll. "These are fights to the death. They only end when you kill him or he kills you. And they are vicious, violent, and they end in a big explosion, lot of fire when the plane burns and that's what it's all about."[11]

When Driscoll lists the traits necessary in a good fighter pilot, he includes a "great ability to compartmentalize and focus only on the task at hand."[12] And that's what Cunningham did the morning of May 10. He easily could have avoided flight duty—with a shortage of planes he and Driscoll originally were not included in the attack plans. But he got himself added to the afternoon strike when he located another plane.[13] So, with Driscoll in his back seat, his old friend Brian Grant as his wingman, and a lucky rabbit's foot in his pocket, Cunningham focused on the target—the rail center at Hai Duong, between Hanoi and Haiphong. The mission was to protect the bombers from enemy MiGs almost certain to be there since the target was right in the middle of several enemy airfields.

No other dogfight in the entire war has been celebrated as much as the one that followed. It is featured in a History Channel documentary that is one of the channel's best-selling DVDs and is re-aired to a sizable audience every year. It has been examined in multiple news articles and analyzed in at least four books. Those analyses and books are filled with minute-by-minute breakdowns of the action, rich color, and endless talk of Immelmann maneuvers and double-scissors rolls, G-forces, and afterburners.

The play-by-play would excite even the most amateur of aviator buffs. But it has also triggered lively debates over the actions of the pilots—including Cunningham. Even with the benefit of recordings of the cockpit chatter, several of those debates are still raging more than three decades later. But the main points are inarguable—Navy pilots, including Cunningham, displayed commendable courage, remarkable skill, and the tactical tenacity to deliver a deadly blow to a MiG force that badly outnumbered them.

Considering all that happened—all the maneuvering, the dodging of anti-aircraft fire, the plane-to-plane dogfighting, and the firing of missiles on both sides—it is striking to someone not trained as a pilot or not expert on the art of dogfighting just how little time the battle took. But that is the nature of aerial warfare—brief encounters where the pilot has to decide in a split second how to respond and how to maneuver the powerful jet in his control.

The stage was set for this particular battle when thirty-two planes were catapulted from the deck of the Connie shortly before noon. At 12:54 P.M., the planes crossed the coast of North Vietnam not far from the mouth of the Red River. They were heading for Hai Duong, an agricultural town located in the Red River Delta. Hai Duong was important to the war effort because it lies along the

Haiphong Railway, which was essential for getting supplies down from Hanoi. As they neared the target, they encountered heavy flak from anti-aircraft guns hidden in the jungle below.

Cunningham's plane was loaded with four cluster bombs, four Sidewinder heat-seeking short-range missiles, and two Sparrow radar-guided missiles. But he needed none of these at first as he circled above, watching the attack planes hit their targets. He then dropped his cluster bombs on warehouses alongside the target. Later, he confessed he made a mistake by pausing to admire the explosions he had triggered with those bombs. Luckily, he looked up in time to see two MiG-17s shooting at him. "I don't know why they didn't hit me," he said. "I could see tracers flying by the canopy."[14] But miss they did.

Given time to recover, Cunningham did not miss. One of his Sidewinders sailed up the tailpipe of one of the MiGs and exploded. Kill No. 3 for the team of Cunningham and Driscoll. But there was no time to celebrate. The skies had suddenly grown crowded. By one estimate, there were now forty planes, all flying at about five hundred miles per hour and operating inside no more than a three-mile circle. And one of those planes, another MiG-17, was on their tail. Using his afterburner, Cunningham outdistanced the slower MiG and shot skyward. But from above, Cunningham and Driscoll saw that Cmdr. Dwight Timm, their executive officer, was in trouble amid eight enemy MiGs.

To come to Timm's rescue would be dangerous, and Cunningham hesitated for a second. But his desire to get Timm out of there overrode the fear. "I said, 'If I leave him, he's going to die.' And I said, 'I don't know how I'm going to live with myself and look his family in the eyes when he doesn't come back.'. . . I just went 'Damn,' you know, and I . . . made the decision, so I've got to go back. And at that point, I thought I was going to die," recalled Cunningham later.[15] The situation quickly grew even more perilous for Timm because he was unaware of a MiG-17, hidden from his view, under his wing.

With a MiG-19 now bearing in on him and Driscoll, Cunningham shouted into the radio: "Reverse starboard . . . goddamnit, reverse starboard!"[16] Timm got the message, making his turn and giving Cunningham a clear shot at his pursuer. The missile found its mark. It was Kill No. 4 for Cunningham and Driscoll. But now they were badly outnumbered by enemy aircraft. It was time to head back to the coast and the safety of the Connie. Fewer than five minutes had passed since they had entered North Vietnamese airspace and the dogfighting had been going on for only about two minutes. But the intensity of the battle had made it seem much longer—and their day's fighting was not yet over.

Racing toward the coast, Cunningham spotted a MiG-17 heading toward him. "He decided to play a game of chicken with the MiG, as he had often done to rattle other pilots at Miramar, and turned into it," wrote the British aviation historians Peter Davies and Brad Elward.[17] As Cunningham later ruefully acknowledged, that turned out to be a "near-fatal mistake." He had forgotten that MiG-17s have guns in the nose.

"Pumpkin-sized BBs went sailing by our F-4," Cunningham wrote in his book. To escape, he pulled his plane into an abrupt and rapid straight-up climb, placing himself and Driscoll under six Gs of pressure. One G is the force of Earth's gravity; six Gs is a force equal to six times your weight. That sounds very clinical. But, as Driscoll noted in his 2006 letter to the judge, it was anything but routine. "Pulling Gs in combat is a bone-crushing experience," Driscoll wrote. "You are constantly grunting and rigorously flexing your entire body to stay conscious. The sweat coming off your body feels like it's being shot from a gun. Your face feels like it's being stretched and nailed to the floor."[18]

Cunningham thought this would get him away from those guns. But, instead, he got what he called "the surprise of my life"—the MiG was following him and was only three hundred feet away. "Close enough I could look in and see a little set of Gomer goggles, a little Gomer scarf that he had on his neck and we're going canopy-to-canopy with a MiG-17," said Cunningham.[19]

Cunningham shot above the MiG, only to find out he had made his second near-fatal mistake in the last few seconds. The MiG was now in a better firing position and ready to take him down. He rolled to the side to narrowly avoid the guns. At this point, Driscoll was nervous, calling the ensuing battle "a knife fight in a telephone booth."[20] What followed over the next two and a half minutes was a series of intense maneuvers that pushed the capacity of both planes and tested the mettle of both pilots.

Cunningham was irked—and impressed—by the skill of the enemy pilot. Twice, Cunningham tried the same maneuver that had always worked against other pilots; twice this pilot had out-flown him. Cunningham was not accustomed to one who could fly as well as he could. In his book, he wrote, "This almost put me into a blind rage. To think some Gomer had not only stood off my attacks but had gained an advantage on me twice!"[21] But there wasn't time to ponder—he had to find a way to kill the enemy pilot. Again, he pulled straight up, then tried something new: "So I pulled the power, hit the speed brakes, dropped the half-flaps and this guy went whoosh right out in front of me."[22]

It was as if he had been drag-racing on a highway and suddenly jammed on his brakes to let his opponent get in front of him. The North Vietnamese pilot tried to flee. But it was too late. A Cunningham-fired Sidewinder found the MiG, exploding near its tail. The pilot—whose identity even decades later is the topic of intense debate—did not eject and was killed.

It was Kill No. 5 for Cunningham. He was now an ace, the first for the United States since the Korean War. His life would be forever changed. But, still amid North Vietnamese fighters and low on fuel, first he had to get out of enemy air space and back to the safety of the Connie.

It was now 1:06 P.M., less than six minutes after the first part of the dogfight began, and Cunningham's Phantom was racing toward the coast. Not everybody is in agreement about the details of what happened next. Cunningham insists that his fellow pilot Matt Connelly warned him about four MiGs on his tail. But Connelly—backed up by the cockpit tape—said there was only one MiG-17 and that he told Cunningham he would be able to outrun him easily.

Believing that Cunningham was acting on his warning, Connelly headed to the coast, last seeing Cunningham's Phantom climbing to a higher altitude.[23]

According to Cunningham and Driscoll, they suddenly had a SAM—surface to air missile—explode only about five hundred feet from their plane. Inexplicably, there had been no warning from the plane's defensive devices; Cunningham admitted he was puzzled, and that led other pilots to question Cunningham's version of events. Still, Cunningham had to find a way to recover from the severe damage done to his Phantom and—most important at the moment—keep the plane in the air until he could get another twenty miles. Those twenty miles meant the difference between ejecting over North Vietnam and spending the rest of the war as a prisoner or ejecting over water and being rescued by friendlies.

"The airplane kind of rolled and went out of control upside down," recalled Cunningham. "I remember thinking at this time, 'I'm going to be a prisoner.' And I said, 'God, get me out of this. I don't want to be a prisoner of war.'"[24]

He had lost his hydraulics, which meant he had lost the ability to fly the plane with the stick. The situation was made more dire by a fire on the left wing and fuselage of the plane. "Duke, it's getting hot back here," warned Driscoll. But Cunningham was busy trying to figure out how to fly the plane to the coast without the use of the stick. All he had left were the rudders, which he hoped he could use to put the plane in a series of rolls to keep it aloft.[25]

With the fire spreading and other pilots screaming into the radio for the two men to eject, Cunningham repeated these rolls over and over again until finally the coast came into sight. None too soon because now the plane had flipped on its back; next, a small explosion cost Cunningham the last of his control. The Phantom was now in a fatal spin.

"Eject! Eject! Eject!" commanded Cunningham and, with great exertion, Driscoll pulled the handle that sent both men hurtling into the air. When they separated from their seats and their parachutes opened, they could see their plane as it disappeared into the sea. They could also see North Vietnamese patrol boats racing to capture them. Cunningham later boasted that he fired his handgun all the way down, just to show them he was armed. He said he fired so many shots he had to reload at least twice during the long float downward—though other aviators were skeptical of this account, wondering how that would be physically possible in the parachute harness and with all the tasks he had to perform during the short descent, such as readying his raft. Regardless, Cunningham did not need the gun because plenty of American planes were there to protect them until the rescue helicopters could arrive.

Those choppers would take only a few minutes to get there. But in this short time, Cunningham suffered the trauma he said triggered nightmares many years later. After dropping from his chute and trying to claw his way back to the top of the water, he said, his hand struck something fleshy. He was horrified to discover it was a rotting North Vietnamese corpse washed in from the Red River.

Once rescued, the two men were taken for medical treatment. Before the end of the night they were returned to the Connie, where the celebrations of America's freshly minted aces began.

Even amid that celebrating—and perhaps even more in the decades since—two aspects of that historic day have been debated. The first controversy swirled around the identity of the North Vietnamese pilot who matched Cunningham maneuver for maneuver in the air before finally becoming his fifth victim. Cunningham and his supporters insisted that this man was so skilled that he could only be the legendary Col. Toon or "Tomb." Tomb, they believed, was the best that North Vietnam had to offer; their ace of aces, the pilot who had downed thirteen American planes during the war.

This myth was not debunked for years. Only after both the United States and North Vietnam declassified documents from the war was it agreed that there was no such man. "Col. Tomb" was a composite. When Cunningham's book came out in 1984, it continued to push the myth. But Jeffrey Ethell, who wrote that book, corrected the record in 1989 when he took a more exhaustive look at the fighting of May 10, 1972. "If all the stories about the colonel are to be believed, he was in action three times on May 10, flying a different type of MiG on each," he wrote then, calling the Tomb figure "unlikely in the extreme." He said that he and his co-author "believe there was no Colonel Tomb or Toon, and no North Vietnamese pilot achieved thirteen victories."[26]

Yet two decades after this consensus was reached, "Col. Toon" resurfaced in Willie Driscoll's letter to U.S. District Judge Larry Alan Burns in 2006.

In part, this stubborn refusal to accept the evidence is nothing more than an age-old tendency to exaggerate the skills and threat posed by an enemy. President George H. W. Bush showed this tendency in the first Gulf War when he couldn't just state that Saddam Hussein was a thuggish dictator who was a threat to his region. In order to whip up support for the war, Saddam Hussein suddenly became another Adolf Hitler. The second part of the equation with Col. Tomb is the ego of the fighter pilot. If Cunningham couldn't out-fly an enemy, it was hard for him to accept that an ordinary North Vietnamese pilot was in that other cockpit. It just had to be the best ever seen, a legend even.

The other unanswered question left from May 10, 1972—still unsettled for some of the pilots there that day—is the issue of what brought down Cunningham's Phantom. Was it a SAM, as he insisted? Was it running out of fuel, as several of the other pilots privately thought? Or was it a missile or gunfire from that MiG-17 that Matt Connelly had warned Cunningham about?

This last question infuriates Cunningham, who is quick to challenge anyone who suggests he could have been shot down by another pilot. Once, he threatened an author who was going to explore that possibility. "If you print that, I'm coming after you," he told Robert K. Wilcox.[27] But the question will not go away. It was raised anew in 2002 by Elward and Davies in their exhaustive examination of naval combat in Vietnam. The first researchers given full access to both the U.S. Navy after-action intelligence reports and the Vietnamese People's Air Force accounts, they give Cunningham's version. But they note as well that the Vietnamese insist that Cunningham's Phantom was brought down by a missile fired by a MiG-21.[28] Some reports have even named the MiG pilot involved as Le Than Dao, who supposedly spotted Cunningham's plane, sneaked in behind, and fired the missile up his tailpipe.

Matt Connelly said he was stunned when he read Cunningham's book and found himself scribbling "ridiculous" and "never happened" in the margins. He not only believes that a MiG-17 shot Cunningham down but particularly disputes the notion that Cunningham was downed by a SAM. "No one ever believed that," he said of the other pilots.[29] Another skeptic among the pilots that day was Pete "Viper" Pettigrew, who said he thought Cunningham had been downed by a MiG and that he invented the SAM story because he could not handle being shot down by another pilot. "That has to do with his ego," said Pettigrew. "But to me that makes no sense. If you shoot down three airplanes and you get shot down—no matter how you get shot down—it doesn't mean a thing. . . . That doesn't take away from what you accomplished."[30]

Cunningham has no answer for why this particular SAM would set off none of the plane's alarms or be seen by any other pilot. His attitude, though, is hardly surprising in the world of fighter pilots, who never—ever—want to admit that they could be bested by another pilot. It was seen, for example, when the U.S. Navy insisted for years that no American pilot had been downed by any Iraqi pilot when the record clearly indicates that there was one such downing in Operation Desert Storm in 1991.

It is also not surprising that other pilots would have differing recollections of the actions that day. Eyewitness testimony is always suspect, and never more so than in wartime. Senator John Kerry learned that painfully when comrades-in-arms and fellow veterans had radically different memories of his Swift Boat days in Vietnam. Reporters even found that when chronicling Senator Robert Dole's heroism in the Italian campaign in World War II. Some of those involved in that battle could not even agree whether it was day or night when Dole was wounded.

The clashing recollections and the questions, however, do not detract from what Cunningham achieved that day. He showed surpassing skill in the cockpit and unwavering courage in the face of extreme danger. No matter what else happened, he would always have May 10, 1972. That was his blessing. But it also was his burden, one that would become heavier than anyone could imagine when he returned triumphantly to the United States less than a week later.

chapter three

THE BOYS OF HILLTOP HIGH

At THE AGE OF SEVENTEEN, BRENT WILKES WAS TALL AND LEAN, WITH A shy, awkward grin playing on his face. He had a slimmer build than most of the other members of his high school football team, but what he lacked in heft he made up for in determination. When the season ended, he was voted Most Inspirational Player, which was not necessarily because he played all that well (none of them did), but because his teammates were impressed by how such a lanky guy could push through the opposition with such gritty determination.

"You knew that he was going to be somebody someday, but you didn't know exactly what," says Rick Foss, a high school buddy. Other schoolmates remember him differently—as "the quiet type," "inconspicuous," or "in the shadows." "Some people misunderstood his personality," says his high school sweetheart, Edie Hartin. "Brent was very serious about anything he really focused on. He was very intense. A lot of times, that might have made him appear aloof."

In May 1972, as Duke Cunningham was in aerial combat against North Vietnamese fighter pilots, Brent Wilkes—who three decades later would be identified as co-conspirator number one in the Cunningham corruption case—was entering the final month of his senior year at Hilltop High School in Chula Vista, a town of seventy-one thousand people about halfway between San Diego and the Mexican border. Chula Vista has since tripled in size, but in 1972 it was a sleepy backwater getting its first high-rise, a sixteen-story tower rising out of the downtown flatlands. The hills of Chula Vista—where Brent lived—were dotted with ubiquitous Spanish-style dwellings complete with red-tiled roofs and stucco walls and inhabited mostly by middle-class naval officers, defense contractors, and armament workers. Like most towns lining San Diego Bay at that time, Chula Vista was dominated by the military.

Brent's father, Navy Lt. Cmdr. Gaylen Wilkes, had brought the family to Chula Vista in 1953, two years before Brent was born. Gaylen, an Idaho-born veteran of World War II and the Korean War, headed a fighter jet attack squadron on the aircraft carrier *Lexington*. On May 1, 1959, three weeks before Brent's fifth birthday, Gaylen's Fury Jet stalled during a catapult takeoff from the carrier and plummeted into the sea off the coast of Hawaii. His body was never recovered.

After Gaylen's death, his thirty-seven-year-old wife, Elizabeth, was left to care for their children—one girl and six boys, including a four-month-old baby. Elizabeth never remarried; she raised the children under the strict precepts of the Mormon Church,* bringing them to worship services each Sunday, teaching them the words of Jesus Christ and Joseph Smith, and warning them against the evils of tobacco, alcohol, and illicit sex. "Brent's mom is the classiest woman I've ever met," says Tim Richardson, a high school buddy.

Without a father, Elizabeth's sons formed their own vision of what the male role within a family should be. High school friends use words such as "cult" and "clan" to describe them, saying they stuck together so tightly that it was hard for outsiders to penetrate

---

*Before his death, Gaylen served as the church's regional athletic director, Sunday School counselor, and superintendent of the church-run Young Men's and Young Women's Mutual Improvement Association.

the inner circle. One of the few outsiders to enter was a boy named Kyle Dustin Foggo, better known as "Dusty."

When Brent and Dusty first met in grade school, they immediately clicked. And thirty-five years later—while Wilkes was struggling against the Cunningham prosecutors and Foggo was fighting his own legal battles over his actions as the third-highest ranking official in the CIA—they were still buddies. One thing they had always had in common was growing up without a father. Dusty's dad, William, a World War II submarine veteran, had left the family and moved out of state when Dusty was a young boy. Somehow the rumor spread among some of Dusty's friends that William Foggo had died instead of divorced. Others thought he was a CIA agent, off on some secretive mission. Dusty did not go out of his way to dispel the rumors. As his mother's only son, he was extremely protective of her and rarely mentioned his father's name.

Like Brent, Dusty was a lineman on the football team. A curly-haired blond with sideburns that nearly stretched down to his chin, Dusty was by far the more outgoing of the two. He won a seat on the student senate and buddied up to as many girls as he could. At the local Dairy Queen, where he worked part-time, girls would often come by just to flirt with him. "Dusty had a knack for getting girls," says one Dairy Queen coworker. "He was like flypaper."

Brent's friendship with Dusty continued through their college days at Southwestern Community College in Chula Vista and San Diego State University. Their favorite pastime was to play long rounds of poker that sometimes stretched from nightfall to daybreak. "The games would start out small, with nickel, dime or quarter raises," says Richardson, who also went from Hilltop to Southwestern. "But then we'd drink some beer and the next thing you know the checkbooks would start coming out. The biggest pots got to around $150, which was big money at that time."

For spending money, Foggo, Wilkes, and several of their friends took jobs as security guards at the local Sears Roebuck, where they spent as much time chasing after female clerks or customers as trying to nab shoplifters. "We were typical teenagers and there were all these young girls working there. It was almost like a dating service," says Foss, the high school buddy who also worked at Sears. The guards would also try to catch thieves, and nobody was quite as zealous as Foggo. In one incident in 1977, a Sears customer, Carlos Carmona, said that Foggo and another guard threatened and assaulted him within the view of his wife and children after accusing him of shoplifting. After a jury found Carmona not guilty of theft, he sued Sears and the two guards. The case was settled out of court.

In another incident the same year, Foggo nabbed young Adam Landa and accused him of shoplifting a wrench. Landa protested, showing a receipt and insisting that he had paid for the wrench. But Foggo was unswayed.[1]

"You're talking to the best security guard in the business," boasted the twenty-two-year-old Foggo. "I've got an exceptionally good record of obtaining convictions in any case I initiate."

According to a court filing, even before the police arrived, a Sears clerk told his supervisor that he had sold Landa the wrench. Sears officials still let the police take Landa downtown. It was only after he was booked for shoplifting that the charges were dropped. Again, there was a lawsuit against Sears. And again it was settled out of court.

The part-time work at Sears gave Foggo a clear career path; he was hooked on law enforcement. When he and Wilkes entered San Diego State University in 1975, Foggo switched his major from political science to criminal justice; Wilkes gravitated to accounting and finance. After graduation, Wilkes took a job with Arthur Andersen & Co. as a tax accountant and Foggo entered the San Diego Police Academy. "Lawyers are great, judges are fine, but without the cop on the street nothing would work," he would later explain.[2]

Foggo asked to be assigned to one of the roughest neighborhoods in San Diego. In just three months on the beat, he and his partner Rick Martin made more than sixty felony arrests; these included two for murder, two for attempted murder, one for rape, and one for arson. And they seized half a gallon of PCP, "enough to blast half the heads of San Diego off into orbit," Foggo boasted. The young patrolman earned two commendations from the police department and was named Officer of the Month by San Diego's Stamp Out Crime Council.

"Dusty was a very hard charger, full of piss and vinegar," says Bill Howell, his former sergeant at the police department.

Foggo enjoyed the cop persona. When he came to play poker with Wilkes and his other friends, he would saunter in wearing his badge and gun, and then with a great flourish unstrap his holster and slap it onto the table before he anted up. "He loved to show that kind of stuff off," said high school buddy Tim Richardson, who had joined the police force in neighboring El Cajon. "We'd all look at him and say, 'Just sit down and shut up. Who are you trying to impress?' He loved to grandstand."

By that time, the nighttime games had changed. The cheap beers and smokes had been supplanted by fine brandies and aromatic Cubans from across the border in Tijuana. And occasionally, some poker players say, the games were enlivened by "rental girls" who would provide their own type of entertainment. During one game, following a bachelor's party at the Hyatt Islandia resort, a rental girl was at work in the bedroom of the suite while a dozen poker players—including Wilkes and Foggo—gambled in the living room, one of the players recalls. Periodically throughout the all-night game, the woman would emerge from the bedroom in an open bathrobe and invite another player to join her.

At one point in the evening, the player—an old friend from high school—says he turned to Foggo and asked: "Aren't you afraid the cops are going to find out about this?"

"Look around you," Foggo replied. "Half of these guys are cops."

In December 1979, Foggo left the department to take a job as an investigator for the Los Angeles district attorney. Then, in 1982, just as the Reagan administration was ramping up clandestine activities on the front lines of the Cold War, Foggo was hired by the Central Intelligence Agency as a presidential management intern. He was sent to the CIA station in Panama for a year. Then he pulled a stint at CIA headquarters in Langley, Virginia, before being sent back to

Central America—this time to Tegucigalpa, the capital of Honduras. It was in Tegucigalpa, friends say, that Foggo and Wilkes got their first lessons in the proper care and feeding of U.S. congressmen.

When Dusty Foggo arrived in Honduras in 1985, parts of Tegucigalpa looked little different from when the city served as a silver-mining center for the conquistadors. Donkey-drawn carts still rumbled along the cobblestone streets of the city's hilly suburbs. Locals lived in homes of brick and adobe and still worshipped—as they do today—at the Church of San Francisco, built less than ninety years after Christopher Columbus sailed past the coast.

At the time, the city was the nerve center of Ronald Reagan's attempts to block leftist movements that were rising throughout Central America. In the cloistered offices of the U.S. embassy, intelligence officials laid plans to overthrow the pro-Castro Sandinista government of Nicaragua and crush leftist guerillas in El Salvador. In forested terrain not far from the capital, dozens of U.S. Army officers trained Honduran troops in how to deal with insurgencies; during joint war games, as many as sixteen hundred U.S. soldiers were in a mock battlefield with four thousand Hondurans. There were so many U.S. soldiers, military advisors, intelligence officers, mercenaries, and adventurers that some observers began calling the country the USS *Honduras*.

Dusty Foggo was essentially a money manager for the CIA's operations in Honduras, attached to what was then known as the CIA's Directorate of Administration, which handled the agency's contracting, logistics, and financial dealings. The CIA station in the embassy was reputedly the largest in the world outside the agency's headquarters in Langley, so Foggo handled a sizable chunk of cash. Although little glamour or intrigue was involved in his job, he played an important role in the agency's operations in Honduras.

"The logistics guys made things happen," said Larry Johnson, who worked at the Honduras desk of the CIA in Langley in the mid-1980s. "They took care of everything. If somebody was moving to Honduras, they'd find you a house. If you needed electricity, they'd get you a generator. They'd get you running water, functioning toilets. They'd figure out how to get people paid. Everything that was handled there, from soup to nuts, the logistics guys would handle it."

During the day, Foggo would spend most of his time monitoring expenses and doling out funds to CIA contractors or agents. Since Honduras had few modern banks, the money was typically handed out in its rawest form: packets of dollars or thick stacks of Honduran *lempiras* instead of checks or money orders.

Once the working day was over, Foggo and his friends would migrate to the Maya Hotel, a twelve-story edifice on a hill overlooking Tegucigalpa's central plaza. The Maya was one of those deceptively peaceful havens that is often found on the fringes of a war zone. Spies, counterspies, gun-runners, journalists, terrorists, contractors, adventurers, and hangers-on brushed past each other in the lobby, dined together at the hotel's veranda restaurant, and kept a wary eye on each other as they sipped daiquiris at the bar.

"Counterrevolutionaries hatched bloody plots over breakfast beside the pool," wrote Stephen Kinzer, a journalist who stayed at the Maya in the 1980s. "You could buy a machine gun at the bar. Busloads of crew-cut Americans would arrive from the airport at times when I knew there were no commercial flights landing, spend the night, and then ship out before dawn. . . . Friends told me that death squad torturers stopped in for steak before setting off on their night's work."[3]

Attached to the Maya was the Casino Royale, Tegucigalpa's only fully fledged gambling hall, crowded with tables for baccarat, roulette, blackjack, and 21. To ensure discretion—and to keep out local gangsters and black marketeers—the Casino Royale catered to foreigners only. To enter, it was necessary to flash a passport. Sources say that Foggo was one of many expatriates who put money down at the casino's tables.

He also liked to visit Gloria's, a bar mainly known for its young prostitutes, according to several unnamed CIA sources quoted by Ken Silverstein, the Washington editor of *Harper's Magazine*. None of

Silverstein's sources said Foggo hired hookers there, but they said that upper-level CIA officials were concerned whenever any of their employees visited a place like Gloria's. "Gloria's was a ticking bomb," one CIA source told Silverstein. "There were a lot of Cuban women there and you had to be mindful that you might be set up."[4]

As Foggo launched his career in Honduras, Wilkes was one of his most frequent visitors, engaged in some type of business activity in the country that neither he nor Foggo has ever talked about in much detail.

In January 1983—during Foggo's hiatus between Panama and Honduras—Wilkes quit his job at Arthur Andersen and moved to Washington, D.C. By the age of twenty-nine, he had learned to be at ease in public. With his broad smile and a collection of off-color jokes that could be pulled out at the appropriate occasion, he was a friendly glad-hander. He was the quintessential salesman, although it was sometimes unclear what exactly he was selling.

For a brief period, Wilkes worked as a tax specialist in the D.C. office of the accounting firm then known as Deloitte Haskins & Sells. But by October 1984, Wilkes had left Deloitte and opened a business office at 1919 Pennsylvania Avenue, just three blocks from the White House. By December 1985, he had come up with an impressive-sounding name for his business: World Finance Group Ltd.

World Finance Group was a small firm that handled real estate transactions, equipment leasing, and aircraft leasing. One of its biggest clients was South Pacific Island Airlines, which ferried U.S. and allied military personnel on charter trips throughout the Pacific. At about the time Wilkes opened his business office, the airline was temporarily grounded after one of its planes strayed too close to Soviet airspace.

Perhaps by coincidence, Wilkes picked a name that was nearly identical to World Finance Corp., a reputed CIA front group in Miami founded by a CIA-affiliated veteran of the Bay of Pigs invasion. According to published reports, eight of that company's twelve directors were current or former members of the CIA.

In 1978, World Finance Corp. erupted into the headlines after federal prosecutors charged that it had been involved in money-laundering for cocaine smugglers from Colombia. After its brief, unwanted appearance under the glare of the public spotlight, the company faded out of existence in 1980, only to have its name resurrected—in slightly altered form—three years later by Brent Wilkes. But Wilkes denies that his firm had anything to do with the CIA or World Finance Corp.

Shortly after founding the company, Wilkes began taking business trips to El Salvador and Honduras, where he was involved in a congressionally backed program to import cattle embryos and bull semen from the United States as a way of boosting local milk production. Through his business dealings, he gained access to the upper ranks of Honduran society.

Because of his ties to Foggo, rumors began to spread that Wilkes was with the CIA. Wilkes allowed the rumors to grow, although he now says he was not working for the agency. Sources in the CIA confirm that he was never on the payroll. But that would not have prevented him from doing contract work for the agency.

"It wouldn't surprise me if Foggo was able to identify some business opportunities for his friend within the CIA," said former Honduras desk officer Larry Johnson. Although Johnson knew neither man personally, he was in contact with CIA staffers in Tegucigalpa who dealt with Foggo.

Wilkes's trips to Central America often coincided with those of U.S. congressional delegations—known as CODELs—whose members came for a first-hand look at how Reagan was prosecuting his wars. In the early 1980s, the tiny airport at Tegucigalpa was humming with congressmen on fact-finding missions. It took only four hours to fly from Washington's Dulles Airport to El Salvador, which was a mere forty-minute hop to Tegucigalpa—close enough to hit both countries during a long-weekend visit. As a result, on some weekends three or four CODELs would be visiting the countries at the same time.

Winning support from Congress was a top priority for the Reagan administration. Most of the Democrats who controlled the Congress—as well as a few Republicans—were skeptical of Reagan's covert operations in Central America. The House Appropriations Committee, which holds the purse strings on federal spending, often whittled down Reagan's requests for funding—much to the chagrin of Ambassador John Negroponte. In one angry telegram to the State Department, he warned that cutbacks at the Appropriations Committee "would give tremendous encouragement to adversaries of our policies."

Eager to gain congressional backing for the attempt to overthrow the Sandinistas, government employees pulled out all stops for the CODELs. And for some visiting legislators, sources say, that meant arranging meetings with hookers. "Hell, yeah," says Johnson. "Members of Congress would show up down there and expect to be lined up with women."

Johnson recalls how one of his buddies, a fairly low-ranking analyst at the CIA headquarters in Tegucigalpa, was asked to find a woman who could perform oral sex on a visiting Democratic senator who was one of the harshest critics of funding the Contras. The woman performed the service, Johnson said, but the senator didn't change his mind about the Contras.

On their occasional visits to San Diego during those days, Wilkes and Foggo boasted that they, too, helped arrange assignations between hookers and congressmen, according to several of their poker-playing pals.

"The Contra thing involved congressmen and underage girls," says one former high school friend, who bases his comment on the stories that Wilkes and Foggo used to tell. "It gets started with some congressmen saying, 'Hey we need to find out what's going on with the Contras,' and then they get down there and get plied with whiskey and colorful shirts and find that there are some girls around them and they say to themselves, 'Someone else is paying for this? This is sweet.'"

"Brent would talk about how easy it was to get prostitutes in Honduras," says another friend. "He said you could drive into a poor neighborhood and just honk your horn and fathers would bring their daughters to your car and you could just take your pick."

A one-time employer, Tom Casey, recalls that Wilkes and Foggo told him on several occasions the story of how they visited the home of a Central American general for a party late one night, accompanied by a congressman. The general reportedly told his troops to scour the nearby countryside for teenaged girls to provide the evening's entertainment.

"If Dusty Foggo had to provide women for legislators at some point in his career, it wouldn't surprise me at all," Johnson says. "But if that's something to indict him for, they'd have to shut down the whole CIA."

And the claim that a general rounded up young girls from the countryside? Todd Greentree, political officer at the El Salvador embassy at the time, confirms that such parties were a common practice for some military officers at the time. He says the officers would call up the police chiefs in nearby towns because they often controlled the local brothels. "These were prostitutes, not just people rounded up off the street," he said. But the official stresses that he is unaware that any congressman took part in such a party. He never met Wilkes or Foggo.

Rumors floated through the CIA: "My understanding is that Brent Wilkes would go down there from time to time, sometimes bringing a contractor or sometimes a congressman. And Dusty would procure girls, which wasn't too hard to do down there, frankly," says one CIA officer who declines to be named.

Through their attorneys, Wilkes and Foggo deny they were involved with prostitution in Central America. One source close to both men suggests that they were merely repeating stories they had heard—stories that involved other CIA operatives, not themselves. Another source writes it off to locker-room talk—"the kind of thing that guys say sometimes when they're drinking beer or playing poker." One of Foggo's defenders says that the rumors floating through the CIA about his activities might just reflect bureaucratic infighting in an agency with a reputation for internal strife.

But the guys around the poker table remain convinced that the stories are true. After all, they remember the parties with the rental girls in San Diego. If he could do this in California, it was not difficult to believe him when he boasted of doing the same thing in Honduras, where the laws were much looser. What's more, they say that Wilkes's days in Central America shaped his view of how to gain support from Congress.

"Brent figured that this was a way to do business with the government: maybe a little hooch, maybe a few women," one former friend said. "Once a guy uses a prostitute, of course, you've got some power over him."

"Wine 'em, dine 'em, and lay 'em," said another.

chapter four

HOMECOMING . . . AND FINDING POLITICS

RANDY CUNNINGHAM AND WILLIE DRISCOLL HAD NOT BEEN BACK ABOARD the Connie long enough to change clothes when it became clear that they were what the Navy had been praying for ever since this most unpopular of wars had begun: the first Navy aces since the Korean War. Aboard the carrier, the backslapping and congratulations kept the two men from getting to their quarters. And 8,300 miles away in Washington, there would be no waiting for details, debriefing, or decoding—no delay at all in delivering the delightful news.

Admiral Elmo Zumwalt, the chief of Naval Operations who so rarely had had good news to deliver about the Navy, could not wait to go on NBC's *The Today Show* to talk about his new aces—the aviators whose exploits were all over the front pages of most of America's newspapers on May 11. It was, proclaimed the admiral, a "great day for the Navy and the country."

Cunningham was a star. Even before his head hit the pillow on the night of May 10, 1972, it already was clear that nothing in his life would be the same. He had begun the day brooding about the state of his marriage and fretful that the war would end before he could reach the heights he craved, and he was going to bed with admirals singing his praises and plotting a campaign to introduce him to a war-weary nation.

For a brief time he played the role of the reluctant hero. After his first two "kills," Cunningham had refused entreaties from his superiors to meet with the press because he viewed it as unpatriotic and biased, an institution almost cheering for an American defeat. Now, as a freshly minted ace, he tried that same response again. But this time, with the CNO already bragging about his exploits and the Navy desperate to take a few bows, the chain of command would not accept Cunningham's demurral.

The Connie's commander, Admiral Damon Cooper, appealed to Cunningham's intense rivalry with the Air Force, noting that the Navy now had ace bragging rights. "He highly recommended that I attend the news briefing [in Saigon]. He said I could do the services some good in our divided nation, so I accepted," said Cunningham.[1] The next day in Saigon, Cunningham was a hit with the press. The United Press International dispatch described him as looking "like a young Paul Newman." And reporters lapped up his colorful quotes about "turkey shoots" and "a big circus . . . with plenty of MiGs for everyone." He and Driscoll were so smooth, one reporter wrote, that they were "like regulars on a television talk show."[2]

Suddenly, his picture was in newspapers around the country and the world. For him, the war was over and he and Driscoll found themselves on a plane home. The Navy had plans—big plans—for these aces, but they had nothing to do with flying and shooting and a lot to do with talking and posing for pictures. The Navy had planned a two-week speaking tour that ended up being a five-month, three city-a-day media blitz. But first, there was homecoming in San Diego, where Cunningham's very unsettled family situation was badly in need of attention and repair.

In his book, Cunningham said he spent most of the flight home "fighting back tears while wondering what was left of [his] marriage." Expecting no one on hand to greet him in San Diego, he said he was stunned to see Sue and their adopted son Todd, then two and a half. "I broke up completely at the sight of my wife and son," he wrote. "All I wanted to do was to hold Susie and Todd." But, he added, he was disappointed to find out that his wife was there only to share in the spotlight at the beginning of the tour. "She was meeting with a guy only a block away from our home," he noted with evident sadness. "It was more than I could take, so we filed for divorce."

With that, he used his book to sketch a vivid portrait of a man wronged while at war, a man deeply in love with his wife jilted under the worst imaginable circumstances. Poignant story if it were true. The reality was that Cunningham had been an indifferent father and an unfaithful husband who, by all accounts, had not felt particularly bound by his marital vows. His latest affair was with a woman who was younger and flashier than Sue. The reality further was that Sue did not consider her letter to Cunningham to be the end of their marriage. "To me, the letter was about the lack of family. I thought we weren't a family like I thought we should be. . . . He didn't seem to want to take into consideration the needs that Todd had," she said. "I wanted to make it a stronger marriage. I felt we could do that." And, despite what he wrote in his book, Sue accompanied him on much more than the first event of the media tour. The couple did not divorce or live separately upon his arrival; that did not happen until Cunningham left his wife seven months later.

That divorce was a crushing development for Sue because it meant she had to give up the baby girl, Kristi, whom she and Randy had adopted before he reported for duty in Vietnam. Even though the girl had been living as their daughter for months, Sue said "the adoption was never finalized" because her husband "wouldn't sign the papers." Decades later, Sue lamented that Randy had never really bonded with the little girl: "If she would cry, he would pick her up, take her upstairs and throw her in the crib. And I mean throw her. It got to the point where she would just look at him and start crying."[3] Although claims made after divorce are often suspect, Sue's contention here gains credence from the fact that Cunningham— incredibly—never even mentions Kristi in the sections of his book where he wrote about his family. To him, she was a nonperson. Or, as he told Todd—who was naturally dismayed to see his sister taken away from the home—she was just someone who lived with the family for a while.

But none of this turmoil was evident on May 16, 1972, when Sue and Todd threw their arms around Randy upon his televised arrival back at San Diego's Lindbergh Airport. The next day's *San Diego Tribune* showed a beaming Lt. Randall Cunningham closely holding his two-and-a-half-year-old adopted son. Todd had a smile big enough to match his dad's. The welcome itself was a sign of things to come for then–thirty-year-old Cunningham. Even though it was almost 11:00 P.M., there was a crowd of two hundred waiting for the aces, including the admiral who was commander of the Pacific Fleet Naval Air Force, the Miramar commander, and a representative of the San Diego Chamber of Commerce, who presented Cunningham and Driscoll with a scrap book of their press clippings of the past week.

Cunningham still voiced unease about going before a microphone, but once he started talking he seemed like an old pro. He drew laughter from the press—and a wince from Sue—when he was asked what he thought of the Phantom as an airplane. "It's sort of like your wife," he said. "It has its good points and it has its bad points, but you learn to love her."

Less than twelve hours later, Cunningham and Sue were on a plane on their way to the first event scheduled to showcase the aces—a Navy League speech in Charleston, South Carolina. Then one speech followed another as one city followed another. The highlight was a first-ever trip to New York City for dinner at the restaurant "21," a Broadway show, a helicopter tour of the city, and interviews on the *Today Show*—not even the chilly reactions by some opponents of the war could dampen the thrill of being there.[4] In June, Cunningham and Driscoll flew to Washington to meet with Navy Secretary John Warner and CNO Admiral Elmo Zumwalt. And there was Flag Day in Denver, the Rotary in Long Beach, an air show in Cleveland, the Fighter Aces Convention in San Antonio— too many stops for either ace to remember them all.

Sue had to skip most of these appearances—not because of marital friction, but because she had two children younger than three to take care of. But the man she still called Randy was thriving on it, exulting in all the stories about this hero named Duke. "He always had a big ego, but it really went on steroids," recalled Sue, now living in St. Louis with her second husband and about to celebrate their twenty-ninth wedding anniversary. "The Navy just helped to foster this. When they sent us on tour, we went to Charleston and Washington and got to meet with admirals and I got to go into the war room at the Pentagon. . . . Then the Navy took us to New York city and we stayed in the Plaza Hotel overlooking Central Park."

Everywhere they went, even with the occasional war protest, Randy was the center of attention. "You are told you are a wonderful big hero and eventually you believe it," said Sue. Nowhere was that truer than when the ace tour took him to his hometown of Shelbina. For Cunningham, this was even better than New York City. Here were three thousand people from town and the surrounding areas lining the streets for a parade that included an honor guard from the American Legion, Boy Scouts on bikes, and speeches praising the native son who had brought glory to the town. These were his friends and neighbors and family members and they were cheering for him. "My heart warmed at the recognition from people I had grown up with," he said. "It was a tonic and I enjoyed every minute."[5]

His life quickly settled into a routine: Sue would stay home with the kids while he gave speeches and interviews, spent time with his mistress, and flew whenever he could. When home, Cunningham made sure he stayed in the headlines. On August 14, he invited a photographer along when he attached his vanity license tags to his new Datsun 240Z sports car. The tags were not subtle—MIG ACE. Jerry Rife, the *San Diego Union* photographer who took that picture, said, "He was as happy as a pig in poop to have me there to photograph him." The photograph ran in more than fifty newspapers around the country.

Sue knew about her husband's most recent affair because she had been told by other Navy wives and because Randy could not explain a cigarette burn on the passenger side of their car. But he became even less discreet about his dalliances: He took his girlfriend, Pam, to Navy events, ignoring the dirty looks from his friends' wives. "It was pretty hard to hide that MIG ACE when he was parked in front of a bar," said Ron McKeown, who was Cunningham's first commanding officer at Miramar's Top Gun fighter school. "He was running around on her and she got tired of it and he got tired of her," he said. It was obvious, even to Sue, that Randy was not interested in saving the marriage. "He had even more of the attitude that he had worked hard, so he was going to play hard," Sue said.

The actual breakup did not happen until Pearl Harbor Day 1972, the night before Cunningham's thirty-first birthday. That was the night he told Sue he wanted out of the marriage; he had proposed to Pam. He seemed more nervous about this confrontation than he had been in the skies over Vietnam. "He told me he had almost flown into a mountain because he was so concerned about this and he couldn't concentrate the way he should," said Sue. She said he asked her to keep the kids over Christmas because he was "so upset or distraught or distracted by all that was going on with him with this affair . . . and that he had already asked Pam to marry him." Later, when Todd was inconsolable because Kristi had to go back to the adoption agency, Cunningham told him not to worry because Pam's kids would now be his "real" sisters.

But the affair never became a marriage; Cunningham was back on the bar scene after his divorce was finalized February 1973. For an ace, the hunt for available women really was a "turkey shoot," as aviators call a target-rich environment. That was particularly true at the Miramar Officers Club, especially on Wednesday nights, which routinely featured sex in the parking lots and sometimes in the bushes. Cunningham himself was no stranger to the police during these years. But these were different times, way before Mothers Against Drunk Driving and legislative crackdowns on drinking, long before the term "designated driver" existed. And not many cops, either on or off the base, were about to arrest a man they knew was the Navy's only ace. Far better to just make sure he got home safely without hurting himself or others.

It was at this time that the aviator met a pretty and smart kindergarten teacher at the bar of the Miramar Officers Club. Nancy Johnson, only twenty-one, said later that it was instant love. She was able to look beyond Cunningham's bluster to a softer, more vulnerable side that few others saw.[6] In her only interview after Cunningham's fall, this daughter of a sailor told the author Kitty Kelley that she was thrilled when he proposed. "Randy was what they called a 'brown shoe,'" she said. "For years, pilots wore brown shoes and people like my dad wore black shoes. There was always this pecking order—that pilots were superior to black shoes."[7]

Married on February 16, 1974, Nancy wasted little time injecting a little discipline into her new husband's life. No longer was he allowed to frequent his favorite bars. And no longer was he unchecked with his loud opinions. "When she was around, Duke wouldn't say boo," said Nick Criss, who had been Cunningham's commanding officer in Fighter Squadron 126. "Randy was a guy who talked first and thought second, and when he would do that, she would correct him and roll her eyes. She would manage him, or that's how it came across."[8]

She had a more difficult time with the other pilots and their wives, many of whom had been fond of Sue and now found Nancy considerably less than friendly. She never quite fit in, said Bob Clement, who was Cunningham's safety officer for several years. He said she dressed more fashionably, wore brighter lipstick and much more jewelry than the other wives. When she started wearing oversized replicas of her husband's medals, her nickname became "Mrs. T," Clement said, a mocking reference to the jewelry-bedecked ex-wrestler then starring in the popular television show *The A-Team*.[9]

But the temper and fury that had frightened his first wife resurfaced again in Cunningham's second marriage. Only two years into the marriage, in 1976, Nancy filed for divorce and a restraining order. Echoing what Sue had told friends, Nancy wrote in a court declaration that "he is a very aggressive, spontaneously assaultive person and I fear for my immediate physical safety and well being." They reconciled the next year and Nancy had parts of the divorce papers sealed from prying reporters when Cunningham entered politics. It was not until 2006 that the scariest parts of those papers were made public: "When we first married, he slept with a knife under his pillow," she disclosed to Kelley. "Well, the knife graduated to a loaded gun." Nancy attributed the temper, the nightmares, and the weapons under the pillow to Vietnam, stating that Cunningham was shell-shocked still.[10]

Still, she was in love with Cunningham, a man she said she "once idolized." And with reconciliation came two children—April in 1978; Carrie in 1982. Nancy's career also progressed. The kindergarten teacher became a principal in the Encinitas school district in 1989. Later, when she was promoted to administrator, she helped run the school district. Throughout it all, she remained troubled by her husband's extravagance, his seeming inability to wait until they were financially stable before acquiring the better things in life. Though they were strapped, they owned a motorcycle and three Datsuns. As he had done in his first marriage, he had insisted on spending much more than they could afford on wedding rings.

Duke was a hero now, after all. And he had now met people who lived the good life. He was a man who knew what he wanted and he didn't want to wait. But he was still in the Navy, a Navy that increasingly didn't quite know what to do with this hero who seemed ill-suited to the peacetime service and increasingly unwilling to follow the rules. He had been underperforming at everything but self-promotion.

At times, his fellow aviators and superior officers tried the "tough love" approach with Cunningham. Ron McKeown certainly used this strategy when Cunningham tried to boycott the ceremony giving him the Navy Cross. But no one could stay angry with the affable Duke. As infuriating as his growing sense of entitlement and endless boasting could be, this was, after all, their friend, and his bravery in Vietnam had earned their patience. They would usually try humor and kidding to keep him in line.

They made fun of his MIG ACE license plate. And they laughed openly at the drink he so ostentatiously kept ordering at the Officers Club. It was bad enough that he liked stingers, a combination of crème de menthe and cognac—not the drink of a dogfighter. But it was that added, showy touch that drove the other pilots crazy—Cunningham shunned the house cognac; only the more expensive Courvosier would do. "I told him that people were laughing behind his back and that you couldn't tell the difference in a stinger between Courvosier and regular cognac," said McKeown. "He said he could."

None of this diminished their respect for his abilities in a cockpit. Bob "Bunga" Clement said that when he first laid eyes on Cunningham, "it was something like seeing Charles Lindbergh or the Wright brothers." And Charles "Sneakers" Nesby, a black aviator who later benefited when Cunningham ignored a tradition of racial discrimination and pushed his career forward, said, "All the young pilots thought he was a god. What could be cooler, more macho, more like a gladiator than to strap on a jet and go up there in a duel with one adversary where the stakes are your lives."

But the officers above him and those under his command pretty quickly learned that Cunningham was much better at controlling an F-4 than he was at managing his ego. Most irritating was Cunningham's insistence on turning every conversation back to May 10, 1972.

"The essence of his life was the day he shot down those three MiGs," said McKeown. "After that everything else was sort of frozen in time. You could talk about anything, from quantum physics to football, and he would somehow twist it around to him and Willie Driscoll on that day." Jack Ensch, who became the executive officer at Top Gun after recovering from injuries he suffered as a POW—and who also received the Navy Cross—said, "Randy's fatal flaw was a combination of pride and greed."

Year after year, he fared poorly in the regular fitness reports from his commanding officers. Always, Cunningham reacted with indignation. The reports stoked a sense of grievance, a conviction that he had been targeted by men who envied the glory he had earned in combat. Finally, that anger boiled over in one of the most outrageous actions of his naval career.

Enraged by yet another poor fitness report, Cunningham broke into the office of McKeown's replacement, Jack Ready, and studied the reports for all the other officers. He then confronted Ready, finally admitting how he had gained his new knowledge. Reports of this incident have been heatedly denied by Cunningham, who calls them "outright lies." But since the story was first recounted by the author Gregory L. Vistica, it has been corroborated by most of the other officers involved. (Ready himself has tried to sidestep the controversy: "I have no knowledge of a break-in," he says in reply to questions about the incident.)[11]

"Ready ordered him out of his office and decided, hero or no hero, that Cunningham should be court-martialed," Vistica reported. "He met with the officers in Cunningham's chain of command, who all agreed the breaking and entering incident were grounds for serious discipline. But before they could go much farther, reality set in. The Navy was not about to kick out its only Vietnam Ace. That would be a public relations disaster."[12]

Jack Ensch agreed: "It was like the hierarchy of the Navy thought—this is our ace and we can't air out our dirty laundry. So Randy got by with stuff like that throughout his career." Ensch said Cunningham always had people "covering his six," a fighter pilot's term for protecting a comrade against an attack from directly behind—the six o'clock position. "So maybe it was the Navy that created this sense of entitlement he had in Congress," he said.[13]

That sense followed him on all his duty assignments before he retired from the Navy in March 1987. One assignment at that time helped shape his later politics and showed his limitations behind a desk. That was a staff job at the Pentagon, where he worked with a group that developed specifications for the purchase of aircraft and weapons systems. McKeown, who had a Pentagon tour that overlapped Cunningham's, said such analytical work was not a very comfortable fit for Cunningham. "I don't think it was part of his makeup or consistent with his education," he said.

McKeown said that Cunningham, who had enjoyed telling his stories to admiring young pilots at the Miramar Officers Club, found similar attention among Pentagon civilian employees and congressional staffers. Much to the annoyance of other aviators, Cunningham always made sure he left his audiences with something after his stories were told. In a habit still on display three decades later, Cunningham would reach into his briefcase and, with a great flourish, pull out autographed pictures of himself in his flight suit.

But the pictures failed to cloak his inadequacies as an officer. Denied any plum assignments atop a fighter squadron, he was heading to a dead-end job at an obscure communications post in the Philippines. Such an ignominious end to a glorious career was averted only at the intercession of McKeown, who worked the phones on his friend's behalf. "I said you've got to do something else with Duke because no matter what his record is, he's still the Navy's only ace," McKeown recalled. "So for us to give him a final tour in a communications station would just be a slap in the face. I lobbied long and hard."

The result was an assignment to Top Gun, this time as the executive officer of "the adversary squadron," which mimicked the flying techniques of MiGs to prepare naval aviators for combat. After a tour as executive officer, Cunningham became the adversary squadron's commander in mid-1985. "He was a really good pilot, but he wasn't a good leader," recalled Clement, who was Cunningham's safety officer. "A leader knows how to communicate, motivate, and create team spirit. Duke couldn't do those things. He also had trouble with the English language."

The squadron recorded its members' professional mistakes or social blunders in a book called the hit log. "It was a way to laugh at some silly things that people did, but it could also be a funny way to call attention to serious problems," said Clement. Offenders were called to account at occasional kangaroo courts that produced the fines that fed a party fund. But Cunningham was not amused when he was the target. After he made an entry marred by poor syntax and grammar, someone called it "a classic case of the rare disease, 'Dukelexia.'" Cunningham was furious, according to Clement and other members of the squadron. Mysteriously, the hit book disappeared. Cunningham displayed a similarly thin skin after practice dogfights with other pilots. When Cunningham won, he always showed up at the debriefing. "But if he lost, he had some other commitment."

Clement also witnessed firsthand Cunningham's growing desire to cash in on his May 10 heroics. He was no longer content to give his story away. In 1984, he and a co-author published a memoir: *Fox Two: The Story of America's First Ace in Vietnam*. Now he saw his many speeches as occasions to hawk the book. And it didn't matter whether the occasion was supposed to be about him: He never missed an opportunity to make a sales pitch. Once, he interrupted a speech by Clement at a Federal Aviation Administration conference in Long Beach. The speech was supposed to be about safety.

"It turned out that as far as Duke was concerned that safety wasn't what we were there for. It was just a pretext to sell his book. Next thing I know, Duke is up there giving his standard speech on his career and how he became an ace and his dogfight with Col. Tomb, and how he found the Lord and turned away from his carousing," recalled Clement, who said he was then pressed into service by Cunningham to help him sell the book. It turned out to be a pretty successful sales day and the two men headed back to San Diego with more than $1,000 cash in their pockets. But he was shocked when he was summoned to Cunningham's office the next morning.

"He said, 'Bunga, I'm $50 short,'" Clement recalled. Cunningham was so fixated on finding the missing cash that he ordered Clement to go home right then and there and conduct what turned out to be a futile search for the money. Clement was left anxious that the event would affect his own career and dejected about what had become of the fighter ace he had admired. "Duke is a nice enough guy, but there's a built-in greediness in his personality," he said. "With Duke, it was always about him. It was always about him getting his cut."

Never was Cunningham's penchant for making things all about himself more evident than in 1985 when Paramount Pictures and the producer Jerry Bruckheimer brought their crew to Miramar to shoot what turned out to be the next year's hit movie *Top Gun,* starring Tom Cruise. Pettigrew, then a retired vice admiral, was the principal technical adviser for the movie, and he even appeared in one scene as Kelly McGillis's date. The movie began filming soon after Cunningham took over as commanding officer of the adversary squadron. In the biography posted as late as 2005 on a congressional Web site, Cunningham boasted that his "real life experiences as a Navy aviator and fighter pilot instructor were depicted in the popular movie *Top Gun.*"

It simply wasn't true. In addition to Pettigrew's denials, the movie's prime script writer, Jack Epps, has laughed at Cunningham's self-serving assertions. "That is a myth," said Epps. "We didn't spend two minutes thinking about Randy Cunningham. . . . I never talked to Randy Cunningham—not once. And I never really paid attention to him or his story."

What's more, Epps said that as he interviewed pilots at Miramar, he learned about their disdain for Cunningham's self-glorification. "They basically came out and said it, that they don't like guys that make too much of themselves, that are so taken with themselves."

Cunningham claimed that he was the inspiration for one of the more memorable scenes in the movie—Maverick, flying upside down, canopy-to-canopy with a MiG pilot to whom he gives the finger. "Absolutely not," said Pettigrew. "An unqualified no."

He even claimed that he had wooed Nancy by singing the Righteous Brothers song "You've Lost That Loving Feeling" to her at the Miramar Officers Club and that it was the source of the scene in which Tom Cruise sings the song to Kelly McGillis. Again Pettigrew sets the record straight. Any connection, he said, would be "absolute serendipity." About the song, he added, "It certainly did not go into the movie because Randy sang that to Nancy. That's not where they got the idea."

But even if the movie was not based on his exploits, Cunningham at least managed to have a picture of himself taken with Tom Cruise, and that can't hurt if you're thinking of a career change or of going into politics. Cruise was not the only new friend Cunningham was making as the end of his military career approached. Being an ace opened a lot of doors and brought you into social circles previously closed to a boy from Shelbina, Missouri. One of those new friends— one who would prove crucial to Cunningham's religious and political maturation—was Dan McKinnon.

Once a Navy helicopter pilot, McKinnon was the son of a former Democratic congressman and Harry Truman ally. Before the twentieth century closed, McKinnon would build an impressive résumé— small newspaper publisher, pilot, owner of a country music radio station, president of the Country Music Association, ranch owner, and Reagan appointee as the final head of the Civil Aeronautics Board. He was a born-again Christian who helped organize Billy Graham's crusades and a staunchly conservative Republican. And when he met Cunningham in 1973, he was ready to reshape the Navy ace, ready to make him a different man.

When he met McKinnon in 1973, Cunningham was undergoing a crisis in faith. Raised a Baptist, now he didn't seem to know what religion he belonged to. In his book, Cunningham acknowledged he was not leading a wholesome life. "I failed my first promise to the Lord," he wrote; he added that he didn't think the Lord was "too pleased" with Cunningham. Nor was Cunningham himself, who wrote bluntly that he thought he had "hit rock-bottom" before he met McKinnon.[14]

"So I made up my mind to see if there was a God or not," Cunningham later told the University of Missouri alumni magazine. After rebuffing McKinnon's invitation to go to church, he accepted a dinner invitation from the San Diegan only to discover that his spirituality was the main course, with special guests Hal Lindsey and his wife Jan. Lindsey had just written the best-seller *The Late, Great Planet Earth,* and he sprinkled his preaching with virulent condemnations of liberals, warnings of the coming of the anti-Christ, and links between biblical prophecies and modern events. Now, at McKinnon's house, Lindsey "cast aside his busy schedule to bring one lost pilot to God." From then on, Cunningham officially listed his religion as "Christian" and described himself as "born again."

At the same time, Cunningham was reborn politically. Or perhaps it's more accurate to say that he took the final steps in a political rebirth that started with his dismay over President Lyndon Johnson's stewardship of the Vietnam War and gained steam when he served in the Pentagon during Jimmy Carter's presidency. "I sat in the Pentagon and watched Jimmy Carter nearly destroy this country," he said. "He could not have done more harm than if he had been wearing a red star on his hat." Now, the final element had been introduced—the tutelage of new friends Dan McKinnon, Duncan Hunter, and Robert Dornan. All three were firmly set in the conservative wing of the Republican Party, and all three ran for Congress; both Hunter and Dornan won their races. McKinnon had lost a close Republican primary in 1980 to City Councilman Bill Lowery of San Diego, a politician whose path soon would cross with Cunningham's.

After his own defeat, McKinnon tried to sand down some of Cunningham's rough edges and introduce the ex-aviator to a broad range of people. Some were politicians who could help Cunningham; some were people of wealth beyond anything Cunningham had ever seen. Because of McKinnon, he found himself riding dirt bikes with the race car drivers Parnelli Jones and Al Unser and talking music and redemption with Johnny Cash. Cash even introduced him to the world of antiques. Little known to the general public, Cash had a passion for antiques—and that passion was shared and surpassed by his wife, June Carter Cash, who ran an antiques store and made sure that they checked out the antiques on every stop of every concert tour.

With McKinnon's help, Cunningham became a constant speaker at church groups, military associations, and antidrug rallies at schools. He briefly served as a dean at National University in San Diego and, in 1988, he took a highly publicized 3,600-mile flight in a single-engine plane piloted by an eleven-year-old boy trying to duplicate Charles Lindbergh's famous solo flight. In 1987, he tallied up his appearances on radio and television shows and could count at least 230. But even with all this exposure and publicity, he was not wealthy—certainly not at the level enjoyed by his new friends. His financial report showed that he earned only $55,188 in 1989, $23,412 of that coming from his Navy retirement and $31,776 from Top Gun Enterprises, Inc., the company he had formed in 1988 to market his book and other souvenirs to take advantage of the craze triggered by the movie Top Gun.[15] But Nancy was pleased with the money coming in during the years prior to the campaign; she praised her husband's "great entrepreneurial skills" and noted that "everything he touched turned to gold." He was pulling in $10,000 for weekend speeches.[16]

When his first campaign began in 1990, his income fell because he could no longer charge for his speeches. But in politics he didn't need his own money; others would bankroll the campaign, letting him spend $300,000 in the general election.

He was ready for the big time, ready for his shot at Washington. It didn't take much to persuade him to run. But Hunter and Dornan didn't take any chances—they arranged for President Reagan to call Cunningham and urge him to make the race. McKinnon and Hunter had selected San Diego's 44th Congressional District, a district made for Democrats, held by a Democrat and kind to Democrats. Even Michael Dukakis had won the district. But, McKinnon and Hunter knew, the Democratic incumbent—Rep. Jim Bates—was damaged goods. Never considered a particularly effective congressman, he had not recovered from allegations that he had sexually harassed women on his own staff. And Hunter and Dornan devised a strategy to make sure he would never have the chance to recover. "I went after Jim Bates with a fury," recalled Dornan, calling it his mission to pummel the incumbent over and over again. With these almost daily reminders of Bates's shortcomings, it was easy for Cunningham to pose above the fray as a war hero nonpolitician pledging to be "a congressman you can be proud of."

With money raised by McKinnon and a strategy outlined by Hunter, Cunningham survived a tough primary battle that was not without its own controversy. Running against a former U.S. ambassador to Qatar, Joe Ghougassian, Cunningham tried to use his foe's Arab name to rouse fears of anti-Americanism, saying he was "bankrolled by Arab oil interests" and flashing a picture of Muammar

Gaddafi. Ghougassian called it "garbage" and "racism." But his campaign never recovered.

In the campaign against Bates, Cunningham donned a bomber jacket and used the kind of over-the-top language he was to become famous for. He called Bates a "MiG" to be "shot down" and labeled his opponent "a sexual pervert who's guilty as sin." He added, "Everybody knows what a jerk this guy is. He's a disgrace." This was coupled with a strategy outlined by Hunter to work the churches and capture a religious vote. In a letter sent to area pastors, Hunter wrote, "I'm sure you feel as I do that Duke is a solid reflection of the strong morals and values of your family, your ministry and your local community."

Cunningham was not without his own missteps. Although he successfully got Nancy's divorce petition sealed from public view, he got into trouble by—again—overplaying his link to the movie *Top Gun*. After including a picture of himself with Tom Cruise in his brochure, he received a stern letter from Cruise's agent demanding it be pulled and noting that the actor—who is pro-choice—did not support the anti-abortion Cunningham.

An even bigger problem was the embarrassing discovery that Cunningham had not registered to vote since he was twenty-five years old. From 1966 to 1988, he had not voted—a damning charge against a candidate asking for votes. He tried to explain it away as a function of his dismay at the way Washington prosecuted the war. Years later, his first wife, Sue, offered a different explanation. She reported that Cunningham had forbidden her to register to vote when they moved to California because he thought it would subject him to higher state taxes.

Despite this controversy, and despite the Democratic leanings of the district, the first-time candidate eked out a narrow victory that was not clear until the overseas and absentee ballots had been counted days after the election. The final margin was 1,659 votes— just 1 percent.

The election capped what was almost certainly the period that shaped the character of Randy Cunningham. Between May 10,

1972, and November 6, 1990, the man underwent a transformation. In those 6,754 days between becoming a hero and being elected to Congress he was coddled by his bosses, lionized by the public, taught how to market himself, shielded from the consequences of his mistakes, introduced to both Hollywood and politics and—perhaps most important—given a look at how the rich lived.

Now, with his narrow election win, he was a national political star. In the immediate flush of victory, Cunningham was close to tears: "Maybe I'm made of Mom and apple pie, but that's how I really am."

chapter five

MR. DUKE GOES TO WASHINGTON

RANDY CUNNINGHAM MARCHED TRIUMPHANTLY INTO WASHINGTON AS THE only ace in American history to be elected to Congress. He was a politician who would eventually be remembered for his outrageous comments, his brazenness, his greed, his corruption—and for his crying.

Certain members of Congress have been caught crying on special occasions. Senator Ed Muskie, for example, cried in New Hampshire during the primary campaign in 1972 when his wife was attacked. And Pat Schroeder famously cried when she dropped out of the 1988 presidential race. Both these members were criticized at the time. But both of them were amateurs. They could have learned a lot from Randy Cunningham.

Within days of his swearing in, he cried over a vote to authorize war in the Persian Gulf. During his career, he bawled when Newt Gingrich was to step down as Speaker of the House; he sobbed at the thought of flag burning; he wept when voting to impeach President Clinton; he wailed over funding for cancer research; he teared up at the death of President Reagan; he choked up when reading Peter,

Paul, and Mary lyrics in a debate; he sobbed when his son was convicted of drug dealing; he cried when talking about his mother; and he wept when the United States recognized Vietnam.

The subject of his own war service and the dogfight of May 10, 1972, gave him even more occasions to weep. Almost every time he talked about his own feats, he sobbed—as if on cue. He did so on the House floor; he did so when campaigning for other Republicans; he did so on television; most profitably, he did so when he appeared at events sponsored by lobbyists and benefactors and contractors.

"He was always weeping," said Robert Dornan, the conservative Southern California Republican who helped engineer Cunningham's first election and was a close ally in the House. Father Joe Carroll, the San Diego homeless advocate and a longtime friend of Cunningham's, said that sometimes when talking with Cunningham "you got halfway through the conversation and he was in tears." He added, "If it was an issue that got to him, boy, the tears flowed."[1]

Randy Cunningham was easily the Republicans' most visible freshman when he arrived in Washington. To Guy VanderJagt of Michigan, whose job was to elect more Republicans, he was their most bankable "commodity." He was just one of forty-four new members of the House, but none of the other freshmen found themselves on *The Today Show* or on CNN or being asked for autographs by staffers. Gary Koops, who worked for VanderJagt at the Republican campaign committee, said at the time that he had never seen anyone "get out of the starting blocks so fast." He added: "The Duke Man is dynamite!"[2]

Cunningham was tested immediately—only nine days after he took the oath of office and moved into his cramped basement offices, the new congressman was asked to vote to send the next generation of American warriors off to foreign battlefields. After publicly agonizing over it, Cunningham ended up giving President George H. W. Bush his vote for the Persian Gulf War. No one knew it at the time, but that January 12, 1991, vote may have been the high point of

Cunningham's congressional career. He was at his purest—poring over intelligence reports, seeking out opponents of the war to better understand their stands, worrying about the consequences for the families that would lose sons or daughters because of his vote.

He may even have given the best floor speech of his career, moving many in the audience when he said, "For those of us who have fought for life, and those that face death in Saudi Arabia, life has a special flavor that you, the protected, will never know." It was as close as Cunningham would ever come to eloquence. True, it did have the element seen in so many later Cunningham speeches of pointedly claiming a moral superiority over those who did not serve in the military. But it lacked the bluster and the bullying that would creep into those references.

It did not take long for the bluster to surface. Before his first year was over, he was mocking those who wanted to take assault weapons off the streets, claiming that he had killed eleven deer with one of the guns and that he should be trusted with whatever weapon he chose to use. "I have spent a lifetime with weapons. I flew over this capitol with an F-14. I could have disintegrated it in half a second," he boasted. And his effort to understand opponents of the Gulf War didn't last long. He was soon ripping them for having "turned their backs on the men and women" in the military. These, he said, were "the same people that supported the Sandinistas, that voted to burn the flag, that voted for Mapplethorpe and obscene art, to destroy the family unit, to not take drug tests, not to be tough on crime." His colleagues weren't quite sure when they had actually taken a formal vote to do some of those things. But Cunningham could not be challenged—after all, as he often reminded his colleagues, he had been an ace; they had not.

Cunningham's penchant for overstatements, outrageous comments, and ad hominen attacks has been well documented. By now, everybody has a top ten list of Duke's embarrassing episodes:

1. Inserting into the *Congressional Record* because it "raises some interesting questions" an article suggesting that Susan Smith's

murder of her children by drowning in South Carolina was "no different" from abortion.[3]

2. Joining Jim Moran and other congressional Vietnam vets in an emotional return trip to Vietnam on August 5, 1997, and—according to Moran—opening a formal dinner with Vietnamese officials by saying, "You gooks shot me down."[4]

3. Ripping liberals, in perhaps his most famous dust-up on the floor, on May 11, 1995, for wanting to "put homos in the military." He compounded the offense when Patricia Schroeder of Colorado stood up, commanding her to "sit down, you socialist."[5] When gay groups later condemned him, he apologized, contending that he did not know the word "homo" was offensive.

4. Calling Robert Reich, President Clinton's secretary of labor, "a communist supporter" because "he goes along with Karl Marx in many of his writings."

5. Saying that the "liberal leadership" of the Congress "ought to be lined up and shot"[6]—in the same week that he said presidential candidate Bill Clinton "would be tried as a traitor or even shot" in other countries.[7]

6. Lashing out at Rep. Patrick Kennedy on June 23, 2004, with an out-of-the-blue reference to his father's deadly 1969 car accident, in which a woman drowned. Cunningham was angry that Kennedy supported full disclosure in gun cases, muttering, "Maybe we should check into Chappaquiddick." Stunned, Kennedy called Cunningham "an idiot." Cunningham apologized when other Republicans urged him to do so, but said he did not regret the remark.[8]

7. Saying "Fuck you!" and giving the finger to an elderly cancer patient in his district on September 5, 1998, at an event for

cancer survivors in Escondido. Cunningham was angry because the seventy-four-year-old man had called for more cuts in the military budget. "When he started bad-mouthing the military, I had enough," explained Cunningham. "I didn't need that crap."[9]

8. Making a crude reference to homosexual sex at that same event for cancer survivors. Referring to his own prostate cancer, he called a rectal procedure he had undergone "just not natural, unless maybe you're Barney Frank." The Massachusetts Democrat, who is openly gay, responded that Cunningham "seem[ed] to be more interested in discussing homosexuality than most homosexuals."[10]

9. Challenging a fellow congressman to a fight on June 15, 1994, because he had dared to threaten Republican pork in appropriations bills. When David Obey of Wisconsin said he would eliminate GOP projects, Cunningham shouted: "I do not like to be threatened and if the individual wants to threaten, we can handle that real good. . . . If the gentleman wants to do something, he can just come right over here."[11]

10. Telling school kids in 2004 that he had flown over their city of Encinitas, California, "with a 20 mm Gatling gun" and that he could have "disintegrated this whole school in half a second." His point was that responsible, law-abiding people can be trusted with assault weapons.[12]

It is, without doubt, an impressive list. And it certainly provides insight into the mindset of Cunningham as a congressman. But too many analysts have started and stopped with this list when trying to assess Cunningham's political career. That is unfair and superficial because it misses both the good and the truly bad parts of his record. The fact is that he did strive to do some good and worthwhile things. He fought for a strong military and, thanks to the influence of his wife's work as an educator, he devoted much of his energy to improving the federal role in education. And he never complained about a committee assignment that most of his colleagues abhorred—dealing with the issues of the District of Columbia. Although it is true that his accomplishments in these areas were relatively minor, he deserves credit for them and for his willingness to work with both Democrats and Republicans to hammer out better legislation.

There is also no doubt that these good things were more than outweighed by the bad in his record. But Cunningham was not a bad congressman because he said outrageous things. He was bad—even before he began selling his services—because he never grew in office, never actually became more than the celebrity that Republicans lionized upon his arrival in Washington in 1991, never became more than an ace cashing in on his wartime fame.

Throughout his career, he often tried to explain things to "the people who have never been in the military," which he just as often suggested included all Democrats and, certainly, anyone who opposed Republican budgets for the Pentagon. Once in that first year, though, he misfired. It was November 22 and he was, as usual, belittling critics who wanted to cut defense. To one Democrat, he asked, patronizingly, "Could the gentleman tell me what a pop-up maneuver is?" Minutes later, he targeted Beverly Byron, a Democrat from Maryland. "Mrs. Byron has never strapped herself into it [the military jet]," he declared, and she lacks "the background she needs" to talk about the plane. This time, he had picked the wrong target—the other members knew that Byron, a member of a military family, was famous for test flying new equipment.

Minutes later, she addressed herself to her colleague "who questioned whether this lady had been strapped into a jet." She went on: "Let me assure him that I have, indeed, been strapped into a jet. . . . I need not say that I have eleven trap shots and eleven cattle shots from the USS *Kennedy* on A-6s and F-14s. I also happen to be the only female who has ever flown in an SR-71 over Mach 3.2." Democrats cheered her comeback; Cunningham was stunned. Later, he called that "one of the biggest mistakes" he had made: "She has not only flown in more aircraft than I have but knows more about military personnel," he conceded.[13] And she was a woman! And a Democrat!

Still, Cunningham never stopped trying to play his hero card in floor debates. In that regard, he was very much an oddity on Capitol Hill. Congress, over the years, has had more than its share of military heroes. Since his election, Cunningham had served alongside two senators who were recipients of the Medal of Honor—Daniel Inouye and Bob Kerrey—as well as several Vietnam POWs and countless veterans who had left limbs on foreign battlefields. Two of Cunningham's closest allies—former POW Sam Johnson of Texas and Vietnam veteran Duncan Hunter—fit this profile. Not one of them ever boasted or cited his own heroic tales.

But a complete reading of everything Cunningham ever said in floor debates yields at least two dozen instances of his bringing up his service in an effort to squelch debate. Often he was downright mean in the way he belittled his opponents. Never was he nastier than the last time he pulled his military card, only thirteen days before the first newspaper story about his corruption. It was May 26, 2005, and he became enraged at Jim McGovern, a Democrat from Massachusetts, for saying that Republicans were not doing enough to provide health care to veterans.

McGovern was only twelve years old when the Vietnam war ended, but Cunningham wanted to make sure that all knew he had not served, saying the Democrat's argument sickened him: "I am military retired." Then he said he had a question for McGovern: "Has he ever been in the Guard?" The Democrat replied, "No, Mr. Speaker. But I am in awe of those who serve this country." Cunningham then asked: "Has he ever been in the Reserves?" McGovern said he had not. But Cunningham was not finished: "Has he ever been in the active duty military?" Again, McGovern said he had not. Well, said a triumphant Cunningham, "I have." And as to McGovern's admission that he had not served, Cunningham added, "I thought not."[14]

McGovern had seen Cunningham treat other members like that in floor debates. But what stunned him was Cunningham's behavior when they got off the floor and away from the C–SPAN cameras. "He came up to me with a smirk and he pointed at me and he said, 'You're a Socialist,'" said McGovern. "When you got into an exchange with him, he always came off as a bully. He put himself above everybody else in terms of patriotism. . . . So far as he was concerned, you could never question his opinion."

Sometimes, this bullying so enraged his colleagues that verbal disputes escalated. For Cunningham, this happened when he took on another Irishman with a hot temper—Virginia Democrat Jim Moran—in a debate over President Bill Clinton's request to send troops to Bosnia to enforce the peace agreement. Cunningham was a staunch foe of the Bosnia involvement and of Clinton's presidency, so he aimed a personal barb at Moran, calling him "a guy who switched his vote and turned his back on Desert Storm." Moran, a former Golden Gloves champ, was furious and invited Cunningham to follow him off the floor. As the two men were walking off, Moran shoved Cunningham from behind, hurtling the San Diegan through the doors.

The closest congressman was Bob Dornan, who found himself in the unusual role of peacemaker: "Moran had Duke up against the wall and had him by the throat and was about to punch him," recalled Dornan. "I grabbed Moran around the neck from behind and pulled him off."[15] Both men apologized. "We agreed that we are both very emotional," Moran said that night. "He shared with me some personal experiences that I was not aware of."[16] Moran told the *Washington Post:* "I thought he had been bullying too many people for too long, and I told him so. He said he didn't mean to be so accusatory. . . . After that, he would bring me candy from California."[17]

It was, of course, not the only furor kicked up during Cunningham's congressional career by his penchant for personalizing disputes and questioning the patriotism of his foes. There were many, many of those. There were also many times that some of the former aviator's personal experiences affected his lawmaking. One thing his colleagues learned is that Cunningham tailored his views to things that he had seen, heard, tasted, or felt for himself. The military was only the most obvious.

It was a trait that led Father Joe Carroll to say Cunningham was "as close as you could get to a true compassionate conservative." He had seen sick children and, through his wife, he knew about the needs of education. He was willing to break with his party on those issues and to fight for more funding. And he was willing to talk with the other side. Before his wife insisted he meet with Peter Yarrow of Peter, Paul, and Mary, he had derided the singer as a "communist." But after meeting with him, he was reading his lyrics on the floor— and crying. And, as a champion of the pro-life cause, he had opposed Planned Parenthood—until he toured a family planning center.[18] "If you made the case, you could change his mind," said Father Carroll. "With a lot of conservatives, you can't even attempt to make the case. Duke would at least listen and if he bought your arguments, he could move."

The tendency to personalize policy was never more evident than in 1997, a very rough year for Cunningham. It started with the arrest of his son, Todd, on January 25, after he flew a plane containing more than four hundred pounds of marijuana into an airport in Lawrence, Massachusetts. Todd was charged with marijuana trafficking and conspiracy to violate drug laws. For a congressman who had railed against "soft" judges coddling drug dealers, it was a blow. "It has been devastating to our family having my son in the situation he is in," said Cunningham. But the get-tough talk had been politics and this was family, so he pleaded for leniency when his son faced the judge. He even cast his son's drug use in terms of the financial burden it put on the family. He recalled when Todd had entered drug rehabilitation: "On a lieutenant's pay, it was not easy to put him through that treatment."[19]

But this plea for sympathy from his colleagues was not the full truth. Yes, the rehab had been expensive—but Cunningham had not paid for it. Todd had been living with his mother, Sue, and he moved to San Diego for the rehab. And Sue said that Randy made sure that she actually signed Todd in. "He said he's not the one that signed the admittance papers so I was going to have to pay for it," Sue recalled. "He just thought that was real cool, that he had been that slick to not sign the papers so that I'd have to do it."[20]

That year was tough for Cunningham as well because in August a routine physical exam yielded the bad news that he had prostate cancer. His first reaction was, he admitted, denial. "No, it can't be me. You've got the wrong test. I'm invincible. It happens to the other person. I can't have cancer. I'm Duke Cunningham."[21] He agreed to surgery—though he spent a lot of time with the surgeon getting reassurance about the future of his sex life. "It is very, very difficult to go to your wife and say, 'Sweetheart, I may be impotent after the surgery. I may be incontinent and we may have to live with that.'" But he proudly made an announcement at a committee hearing almost two years later: "I'm happy to say I don't need Viagra."

Another revealing event was the contested 1996 election between Republican Bob Dornan and Democrat Loretta Sanchez. It was eye-opening because it provided a glimpse of Cunningham's sense of personal loyalty and his notion of how you ease hurt feelings when you betray a friend. Sanchez had upset Dornan, but by a razor-thin margin of 984 votes amid allegations that 748 ballots—maybe more—had been cast by illegal aliens. A long, bitter battle chewed up all of 1997: Dornan pressed his challenge to the official results and a special House committee was appointed to weigh his case. With the high number of political enemies Dornan had made during his tenure in the House, it soon became clear that the combative Orange County Republican was going to lose the challenge. Only his good friends and loyal allies were going to stand by him.

Certainly, he believed, Duke Cunningham would be on his side. This, after all, was the man he had helped elect in 1990 and whom he helped again in 1992 when he wanted a more Republican district. To win it, Dornan had helped Cunningham take on another incumbent, Bill Lowery, and forced him out of the race. But Dornan was wrong. Cunningham wanted to be on the winning side instead. Somewhat sheepishly, he approached Dornan and asked not to be held to his promise to vote to sustain the challenge. But Dornan would not consent, so Cunningham tried a different tack. "He said, 'Let me change my vote. I'll send you $1,000 from my campaign committee,'" said Dornan, who was highly offended that a friend would think his pain could be assuaged with a $1,000 check.

But by this point in his congressional career, that was how Cunningham viewed politics—money can solve anything. After all, it was what he saw when he looked at how his Republican Party was remaking the Congress after it became the majority in 1995. Hidden spending on personal projects, once relatively rare, was now the norm. And if you wanted to rise in the leadership—as the ambitious Cunningham did—you had better be raising money for other Republican House candidates. So, bringing his celebrity to bear whenever he could, Cunningham threw himself into GOP fund-raising.

Unfortunately, his rough edges were never really smoothed over. Cunningham often embarrassed himself—as he did when the party brought its national convention to San Diego in 1996. For Cunningham, this was a perfect opportunity to show off his fund-raising prowess. It also was a time to party for the fun-loving Duke. Cunningham became smitten with an attractive young woman who was staffing a hospitality suite for PacTel—one of the major sponsors of the convention—at a San Diego hotel. "He became so obsessed by one of the young women on the in-house government relations side that somebody had to call his chief of staff to say that Cunningham was really making her uncomfortable; she was not interested in him," said someone who witnessed this.[22] "Here was a married, older congressman chasing after a twenty-something . . . who's thinking, 'What the hell's going on here?'"

Cunningham also made some Republican candidates uncomfortable when he went to their districts. "It was always about him," said Anne Northrup, a Kentucky Republican who brought Cunningham into Louisville to help her with her campaign. His speech, she recalled, left her very uneasy. "It was all about him and his war heroics. It was the first time I heard it. But even then I cringed. He wanted everybody to know all about him and he actually cried about how much he loved this country. . . . It was sort of over the top. It was very maudlin."[23]

At that speech, Cunningham also pulled one of his standard tricks. He pulled out a coin and tearfully contended that it had been his good luck coin during the war; it had protected him and saved his life. Now, he said, he wanted Northrup to carry it for the rest of the campaign and return it to him when she came to Capitol Hill. Northrup lost the coin. "But I saw him give the 'same' coin to probably three other people. Always with the same tears and the same speech. It was too much for me. It always made me cringe. I thought it was like perpetrating a fraud."

Indeed, Cunningham repeated the coin gimmick hundreds of times over the years with school groups, church gatherings, and political rallies. But Cunningham believed those coins and those speeches would put him line for a leadership position. He admitted in 1997 that he had his eye set as high as the Speakership. "Like in the Navy, if I wanted to be a commanding officer, I had to do the right things to become a commanding officer," he said.[24]

So in 1997 he jumped into the race for the number six slot in the Republican hierarchy in the House—the post of conference secretary, which would put him at the table when legislative and political strategy was plotted. Like the others, he contributed to the campaigns of other Republicans, and he had high hopes. His own vote count showed him getting up to fifty-five votes.[25] What he actually got were forty-two votes, to finish a poor third. It was a defeat that angered him. "I'll never forget how disappointed he was when he didn't get in leadership," said Ray LaHood, an Illinois Republican who served with him on the Appropriations Committee. "And I remember the comment that he made to me that he'd never vote for a woman running for leader because none of the women in our conference said that they would support him."[26]

But Cunningham had much better luck getting on the committees that he wanted, thanks to his celebrity status. "Our leadership was impressed with him," said LaHood. "They gave him the very best committee assignments." LaHood's assessment was corroborated by other members and staffers. The Appropriations appointment was the work of Speaker Newt Gingrich. "I got a call one morning from the Speaker," said Jim Dyer, former staff director for the committee. "He said words to the effect of 'I'm going to put Duke Cunningham on the committee and you're going to put him on Defense Appropriations.' I said fine, I'll tell the chairman."[27] But the chairman—Bob

Livingston of Louisiana—was not pleased because Cunningham had gone over his head to Gingrich.[28] His initial response to Gingrich's demand, he said later, was "Hell, no!"

"I thought he was pulling rank and jumping over a lot of guys who had served on appropriations a number of years and were dying to get on the defense subcommittee," said Livingston. So when Gingrich would not back down, an angry Livingston summoned Cunningham to his chairman's office. "I said, 'I don't care what you've done elsewhere, you haven't earned the right to be on this committee. But I'm being told I've got to do it, and I just want you to know that if you step out of line, I'll come down on you like a ton of bricks.'" But Livingston was then taken aback by Cunningham's reaction. "Duke broke out in tears. He said, 'You won't regret it. You won't be sorry. I'll be your wing man. I'll be your wing man anytime you need me.'"

Also unhappy about the appointment was the future chairman, Jerry Lewis of California. "He was ticked off," recalled a former Capitol Hill insider. "He thought Duke was a meathead."[29] Other staffers and members were of a similar mind: "There was universal chagrin on the committee because Duke was regarded as a loose cannon and a poor fit on the committee, which is known as being one of the most collegial and cooperative on the Hill," said a staffer who asked not to be identified.

But Gingrich was impressed with Cunningham's military record and his willingness to raise money for other Republicans. Cunningham boasted that he had raised more than $1 million for the GOP and campaigned for more than sixty candidates during the 1996 campaign.[30] This was his payback. So the objections were ignored. The appointment to the Defense Appropriations subcommittee took effect on January 6, 1997. Then came the Select Committee on Intelligence on January 23, 2001.

One unspoken factor in the opposition of so many Republicans to the plum appointments for Cunningham was their doubt about his intellectual firepower. Dornan said it had never occurred to him to worry that Cunningham might be too corrupt to serve on the

Defense subcommittee. "I thought, 'Is he smart enough for the job?'" LaHood added, "I don't know that he was a really bright person."

Other members worried about Cunningham's maturity. In many ways, he was still the kid from Shelbina going through flight training and reveling in interservice rivalry. One manifestation of that came every time he encountered Heather Wilson of New Mexico. Wilson is one of the smartest members of the House—a graduate of the Air Force Academy, an expert on nonproliferation. But, almost without fail, when she interacted with Cunningham, he called her an "Air Force puke."

He couldn't even resist when the subject was his commander in chief, the president of the United States. This was the night that the president donned his own flight suit and flew out to the aircraft carrier *Abraham Lincoln* off the coast of San Diego, famously—or infamously—declaring "Mission Accomplished" in the Iraq War. During an interview on national television, Cunningham wanted to talk about the flying skills of the president, who had served in the Texas Air National Guard. When Pat Buchanan jokingly suggested that Cunningham "couldn't handle the plane" as well as the president had, Cunningham shot back, "I can fly a plane better than any Air Force weenie."[31]

None of this bothered the voters in California's 50th District, though. This was his new home; no longer was he running in a Democratic-leaning district. Redistricting had carved out a new, heavily Republican district in 1992 and Cunningham decided to jump into that one even though it meant taking on another incumbent Republican, the more senior Bill Lowery. Lowery had been weakened by his ties to the savings & loan scandal and had been embarrassed as one of the worst offenders in the check-bouncing debacle in which many members had written checks regardless of their balances because they knew the House Bank would never actually bounce their checks.

Suffering from these scandals, Lowery blinked and dropped out of the race, giving Cunningham an easy win and a district that would never make him sweat over any Democratic challenger. He won reelection with almost two-to-one margins. The voters knew that he was rough around the edges; they knew he could be insensitive; they knew he would embarrass them at times. But they respected his war record and—most of all—they really liked his ability to bring home the money for local projects and local business. This man had mastered what is now called the earmark at just the right time in history.

chapter six

THE EARMARK—
INVITATION TO CORRUPTION

RONALD REAGAN WAS HORRIFIED WHEN HE SAW THE HIGHWAY BILL CONgress passed in 1987, so horrified that he told the nation, "I got out my veto pen and used it fast." Reagan was steaming at the attempt by Congress to add 121 construction projects to the legislation drafted by his administration. Blasting the add-ons as pork barrel, he added, with typical Reaganesque humor, "I haven't seen so much lard since I handed out blue ribbons at the Iowa State Fair."

People laughed. But few knew at the time that with his welltimed joke Reagan was firing the first shot in a war against "earmarks," as the projects inserted into spending bills are called. It is a war still raging today, one that merited a call to arms in another president's State of the Union address in January 2007. But in between Reagan's warning and George W. Bush's lament, much ground was lost. The war against earmarks, clearly, was not being won.

Reagan had hoped that Republicans, their spines stiffened by years of rhetoric about runaway federal spending, would stand by his side. To seek support in his fight against the highway bill, he made a rare presidential trip to Capitol Hill and held what amounted to a pep rally with the Republican caucus.

Among those standing and applauding their leader that day were Bill Lowery and fellow California Republican Jerry Lewis of Redlands. Both men boasted that they were Reaganites; both spoke often of their love and admiration for the "Gipper." But on this occasion, applause was all they were willing to give. They sided with the Democrats—and one hundred other Republicans—in a lopsided 350–73 vote to override the highway veto. They loved pork more than they loved their president.

Reagan's veto was the first time a president had so dramatically called the nation's attention to earmarks. But it was not the last time that Lewis and Lowery would team up to protect spending unwanted by the executive branch. Two decades after that veto battle, the two Californians are still championing earmarks—so successfully that Reagan's lament almost seems quaint because the amounts he objected to would barely rate a mention in today's pork-saturated Washington.

Reagan, of course, never used the word "earmark" during that battle—the man had too good an ear for how ordinary Americans speak outside the Washington Beltway; he always shunned jargon and acronyms and government-speak. But that's what he was talking about. And perhaps the most dramatic way to grasp the impact of earmarks is to look at their explosive growth since that 1987 veto and how they have been used by those two skillful practitioners of the art, Lowery and Lewis.

Even though Reagan avoided the word, an earmark is not a hard-to-grasp concept. Quite simply, an earmark is a bit of spending that was not requested by the executive branch but is added to a spending bill out of public sight by a member of Congress who is permitted to remain anonymous. Although committees spend months poring over the major elements of appropriations legislation, there is usually no public debate—indeed, no discussion at all—of the earmarked spending. In recent years, the earmarks are often not even subjected to a vote because they are added in conference committees, long after both chambers have already voted on the spending.

"These special interest items are often slipped into bills at the last hour—when not even C-SPAN is watching," said Bush in his 2007 State of the Union address, lamenting that "over 90 percent of earmarks never make it to the floor of the House and Senate—they are dropped into committee reports that are not even part of the bill that arrives on my desk. You didn't vote them into law. I didn't sign them into law. Yet, they're treated as if they have the force of law."

The earmark growth over the last twenty years has been nothing short of phenomenal, particularly since the allegedly fiscally conservative party took over both houses of Congress in January 1995 and held that control—with only one brief break in the Senate—for the next dozen years. Republicans were not unaware of the dangers of such unchecked spending. But nonetheless earmarks pervaded the culture.

When Reagan took office in 1981, there were fewer than ten earmarks in the transportation bill, according to the Heritage Foundation. Seven years later, the president vetoed the bill because it had 121 earmarks in it. In 1991, that grew to 538 earmarks; then 1,850 by 1998; and by 2005 the total surpassed 6,373—costing a staggering $24.2 billion—according to Taxpayers for Common Sense.[1]

And the problem was not confined to the transportation bill. In a bitter irony for fiscal conservatives, the pork swelled in all spending bills after Republicans took over. Two years earlier, under Democrats, there had been 892 earmarks worth $2.6 billion. By 1998, there were about 2,000 earmarks worth $10.6 billion. By 2005, the number had jumped to nearly 14,000, at a cost of $27.3 billion.

The architect of the Republican takeover, Speaker Newt Gingrich, ordered appropriators to make sure that vulnerable Republican members got what they needed for local projects. Earmarking might have been terrible governance, but it was great politics. Earmarks were part of the Washington incumbent protection machine, especially for Republican leaders determined to protect their majority status.

Under the close watch of Gingrich and his top lieutenant, Tom DeLay of Texas, the Republicans took to assigning members from toss-up districts to Appropriations Committees. This paid immediate political dividends. It allowed newcomers, despite their lack of seniority, to deliver more pork projects to their district and it allowed them to raise more money because now they could hit up the companies that wanted the earmarks.

Not surprisingly, the ranks of Washington lobbyists swelled in tandem with earmarking. The selling of earmarks became a specialized industry because lobbying firms recruited former members of Congress and congressional staffers whose connections could grease the process. By one count in 2005, Washington had nearly thirty-five thousand registered lobbyists, more than twice as many as it had in 2000, and sixty-five for every member of Congress.

This list of projects from recent appropriations bills is typical:

- $223 million for a "bridge to nowhere" to get commuters from Ketchikan, Alaska (population eight thousand), to undeveloped Gravina Island (population less than fifty)

- $1.4 million for a dog kennel in Alaska

- $50 million for an indoor rain forest in Iowa

- $2 million for a study of "no flush" urinals

- $70,000 for the Paper Industry Hall of Fame

- $7 million for snowmobile trails in Vermont

Such projects inspire ridicule from late-night comedians and anger from those lonely crusaders inside Congress. Still, even Cunningham's sharpest critics acknowledge that there is nothing inherently wrong with a congressman's seeking a project. Some earmarks serve a legitimate public function, they admit. Duncan Hunter of

California defended them in defense appropriations by observing that "not all wisdom resides in the Pentagon." Speaker Gingrich was one of the biggest champions of earmarks, declaring even after the GOP defeat in the 2006 elections that earmarks are proper when they force policy changes upon a balky bureaucracy. "The legislative branch has every right to direct a policy action. . . . If there are policy earmarks they are exactly how the constitution is supposed to work, which is a head-on power struggle between 535 elected legislators and an elected chief executive."[2] One example he cited was when the Republican Congress forced a reluctant White House to spend millions on Radio Marti to beam news into Cuba.

But the Republicans let it get out of hand. What seemed like a good idea to the GOP in 1995 became too much—too much money, too much pork, and, sadly, too much corruption. The chance to sneak a project into a spending bill at the last moment proved to be too alluring an invitation to corruption for all congressmen and contractors to resist.

Incumbents of both parties grew increasingly addicted to the annual earmarks. The use of earmarks exploded during Republican control of the Congress between 1994 and 2006 partly because the GOP was trading them for campaign contributions to be used to keep control of Congress. Members of Congress routinely, though covertly, exchanged multimillion-dollar earmarks for tens of thousands of dollars in campaign checks contributed by earmark recipients and lobbyists. One of the most prolific Democratic earmarkers, Jack Murtha, would implicitly acknowledge the connection at fundraisers: "His basic pitch was: 'Thank you for helping me so I can continue to help you,'" according to a lobbyist who asked not to be identified.

This might strike many Americans as wrong, but that would not make it illegal.

"It's a fine line between a contribution and a bribe, but it's a line that keeps you out of jail," said Larry Noble, who was general counsel of the Federal Election Commission before he directed the campaign finance watchdogs at the Center for Responsive Politics. As long as there is no explicit quid pro quo, provable with documents or insider testimony, prosecutors say there is no way to make a case. That is why critics of the federal campaign finance system call it a system of legalized bribery. That is why advocates of public financing say that the current system makes the public pay for campaigns—through hidden earmarks and other favors.

As a Republican on the Defense Appropriations subcommittee, Cunningham controlled as much as $50 million a year in earmarks, although nobody can say for sure, except possibly Cunningham or Jerry Lewis, and they aren't talking. Because Cunningham also was a member of the Intelligence Committee, he was uniquely positioned to initiate and fund military intelligence programs that few of his colleagues even knew about.

Although many earmarks are handled secretively, others are announced publicly by the congressional sponsors. Far from being criticized, these earmarks tend to be celebrated by local opinion makers. "The problem with pork," said Jacques Gansler, an undersecretary of defense in the Clinton administration, "is that in the local press, it's always viewed as a plus. It's 'Congressman Jones just got us a $20 million project and isn't that wonderful'—even though the executive branch didn't ask for it and it's not necessarily in the nation's interest."

Winslow Wheeler, a Senate staffer for Democratic and Republican senators, is particularly outraged because the pork stuffed into defense bills diverts funds from important programs. "There is no oversight, no accountability. That's how the system operates. That's how it thrives," complained Wheeler, who now is with the Center for Defense Information. He lamented that the growth of earmarking is no accident.[3] It is the result of congressional policy as laid down every year in the bills that determine how public dollars are spent.

The Pentagon dares not resist the earmarking efforts of members of the Defense Appropriations subcommittee, said Wheeler. Otherwise, he said, the members make sure that "there would be hell to pay."

The kind of payback a spurned lawmaker can deal the military was amply illustrated by former Rep. Charlie Wilson, a Democrat from Texas, who used his position on the Defense Appropriations subcommittee during the 1980s to steer billions of defense dollars covertly to help Afghan fighters dislodge Soviet forces from Afghanistan.

"We would have never won the war if it hadn't been for earmarking because the [CIA] would have never spent the money the way we wanted it to," Wilson said in an interview. "There are three branches of the government and you have to explain that to the executive branch every once in a while and earmarking is the best way to do that."

Earmarks can be petty, too, such as one Wilson added during the 1980s to punish the Pentagon for keeping his girlfriend off a trip. An American spy plane was supposed to fly them from one end of Pakistan to the other. However, an Air Force colonel working for the Defense Intelligence Agency refused to transport the woman on the spy plane because it was against the rules. Wilson was miffed, but he got even with the Defense Intelligence Agency in the next appropriations bill.

"I just removed two planes from their inventory," he said. "The Louisiana National Guard was very glad to get them."

Norman Ornstein, a veteran Congress watcher at the conservative American Enterprise Institute, says earmarking has nourished a culture based on what he calls "the self-reinforcing loop" of legislators who grant earmarks, lobbyists who use their Capitol Hill connections to get them, and contractors who receive the cash.

"We now have a situation where billions of dollars of federal funds are allocated not on the basis of where it is most needed and can be spent most effectively, but according to who's sloshing the [campaign contribution] money around so they can get the earmarks," Ornstein said. "When you do that, then ultimately you are being very destructive to the society."

Washington's principal money sloshers are the lobbyists, whose influence is often measured by their ability to round up checks.

There is no better example of this ultimate insider game than the ties between Jerry Lewis and Bill Lowery. Their relationship has it all—campaign cash, cronyism, high-living, nepotism, arm-twisting, secrecy, and greed.

Elected to Congress in 1978, Jerry Lewis has long cut an impressive figure on Capitol Hill, where he is known for his megawatt smile, thick thatch of white hair, and a grandfatherly gentility that at times masks a hard-headed pragmatism. Thanks to a steady regimen of laps in the House pool, Lewis is nearly as fit and trim as he was as a high school swimming star at San Bernardino High.

Lewis knew from an early age that he wanted to be involved in politics. He earned a degree in government at UCLA in 1956. In 1964, while working as an insurance agent, Lewis won a seat on the San Bernardino school board; then he moved on to the California state assembly. Finally, he made it to Congress, representing a district that stretched from the eastern suburbs of Los Angeles to the arid immensity of the Mojave Desert. His campaign had featured a poster showing an Uncle Sam of Falstaffian proportions and the blunt admonition: "Uncle needs a diet."

In 1981 Lewis met Bill Lowery, who had ridden Ronald Reagan's coattails to a House seat representing San Diego. Blessed with a safe district, Lowery nonetheless barely survived his 1988 reelection campaign. He had been hounded by reports of his close friendship with Don Dixon, a Texas developer and one of the worst bandits in the savings & loan industry. Dixon had spoiled Lowery with a lavish fund-raiser and trips in his corporate jet. Common Cause listed Lowery, a member of the Banking Committee, as the House's number one recipient of cash from the entire S&L industry.

Lowery's twin embarrassments over House banking and the S&L scandal put him on the defensive as he approached a 1992 primary contest with Duke Cunningham. Cunningham had already weighed in with radio ads that questioned Lowery's character. His campaign slogan drove home the point. Cunningham declared himself "a Congressman we can be proud of." Lowery sized up his plummeting public opinion polls and dropped out of the race. After he finished his term, he became a lobbyist.

Like Lowery, Lewis had little discernible legislative agenda other than to ensure that his district and supporters got a decent chunk of the federal budget. Lewis's official biography is dominated by a list of the projects he funded in his district: repairing highways in the Mojave, building access roads at the regional airport, creating low-income housing for local residents, building a regional flood control project, creating a NASA research center at a local university.

To gain funding for such projects he needed friends on both sides of the aisle, and Lewis had a reputation of building friendships with what was then the Democratic majority in Congress. The members of the Appropriations Committee all had special projects they wanted to fund and they needed to work together to divvy up the budget. Lewis took pride in his ability to compromise. "Our job in the Congress is to govern," he said. "If we can't think through what the options are and come to a reasonable compromise, then we shouldn't be in the business in the first place."

Because of their shared pragmatism, Lewis and Lowery had worked well together on the Appropriations Committee, where Lowery had a seat for three terms. They became fast friends. By the mid-1990s, they were celebrating birthdays together, vacationing together, and dining together at restaurants near their Capitol Hill townhouses. In 1999, Lowery married for the second time, and Lewis was his best man. One year, when Lewis led a seven-member congressional delegation on a junket to the Paris Air Show, Lowery showed up with tickets to take everyone on a guided tour of the Louvre.

In Bill Lowery's world, no one was more important than Jerry Lewis. Lowery built his lobbying career around his membership in the clannish circle of Lewis's staff, which friends called "the Lewis family." He made sure that those ties went deep. When staffers worked late into the night, Lowery would send in food, including a $300 assortment of sandwiches from the Corner Bakery near his office. When staffers celebrated birthdays and retirements, Lowery was there bearing gifts; when one couple, Jeff Shockey and Alexandra Heslop, got married, Lowery was there with a present. And he was there again when they had their first child. He and Shockey even took a professionally guided fishing vacation together on New Mexico's San Juan River.

Lowery also lavished attention on Letitia White, Lewis's principal gatekeeper for earmarks requests. He knew she favored Veuve Cliquot champagne, and he made sure she had a ready supply. He also cultivated the staffs of other key appropriators—including that of Duke Cunningham. When Cunningham's staff held its 2001 Christmas party at the Oceanaire Seafood Room on F Street, Lowery picked up the $1,600 bill.

Lowery received a handsome return for his investments in good will. According to the Center for Public Integrity, a nonpartisan watchdog group, his firm's income more than tripled between 1998 and 2004, jumping from $1.58 million to $5.11 million. As the big rainmaker, Lowery pocketed about 40 percent of the take. It was more than enough to allow him to become a generous contributor to the campaigns of appropriators such as Lewis and Cunningham.

The famously disorganized Lowery sometimes wasn't able to get those contributions to their intended beneficiary. Lowery's staff knew well that papers were known to disappear in Lowery's briefcases, never to be seen again. That was how he once lost over $10,000 in checks he had bundled for Jack Murtha. By the time his staff realized what had happened, it was too late to give Murtha the checks. They were destroyed.

Lewis also was effective raising money to dole out to other Republicans. And when the party took over the House majority in 1995, Lewis became one of the Appropriations Committee's "cardinals," the subcommittee chairmen whose title reflects their power. For four years he oversaw spending for such agencies as Housing and Urban Development (HUD), the Environmental Protection Agency (EPA), and NASA. It was a turning point for Lewis, who began to evolve beyond his earlier belief in spending discipline. As Lewis settled into his role as a cardinal, he developed a taste for dispensing money with the same abandon that Pope Leo X must have shown in giving away indulgences before Martin Luther spoiled his ecclesiastical party. And like Leo X, Lewis made sure he got a lot in return for his favors.

How radically Lewis had changed became almost farcically clear several years later as he tucked into the spending bill for HUD—the very agency he had once insisted be cut—a $400,000 earmark to build a swimming pool in Apple Valley, a town in his district best known as the home of Roy Rogers and Dale Evans. Lewis declared: "It is important to help our growing communities in San Bernardino to improve the standard of living for our residents."

In 1999, Jeffrey Shockey, the Lewis staffer who had handled many of the earmarks for the home district, joined Lowery's firm. It was not long before he was seeking earmarks for clients across the district. The minutes of a Redlands City Council meeting illustrate why: "It is expected that [the cost] will be returned many times over in federal funds received," said council member Casey Hawes.

And so it was for all of Shockey's clients. He helped San Bernardino County get earmarks worth millions for projects that included a zoo, a museum, and a youth baseball complex. Twenty-Nine Palms got $200,000 for a visitor's center. For city and county governments, universities, hospitals, and water management agencies across Lewis's arid district, Shockey made the earmarks fall like manna from heaven.

When Shockey signed his alma mater, California State University at San Bernardino, to a contract, he was introduced to the school's administrative council as part of a firm whose "knowledge of funding opportunities that we may not be aware of could lead to increased federal funding." The minutes of that meeting noted that Shockey's former boss, Lewis, oversaw "one of the largest pools of money," and that "by having good strategies and ideas, CSUSB can be sure they will be placed on the table."

Before long, those ideas took the form of earmarks that found their way into the budgets of NASA, the EPA, the Pentagon, the Department of Education, and the Department of Transportation.

One funded a television station that promptly folded. Another bankrolled an institute to study water issues. Yet another paid to study "transportation issues." One of them combined the school with another Lowery client, San Diego State University, to establish a Center for the Commercialization of Advanced Technology, which tried to find nonmilitary markets for new technologies. Cal State Santa Barbara paid Lowery's firm more than half a million dollars between 1999 and 2005. During the same period, San Diego State paid the firm $1.4 million.

Shockey wasn't the only staffer-turned-lobbyist who made the Lewis and Lowery offices look like extensions of each other. Consider Letitia White, who had studied fashion design at the University of Richmond and worked at *Women's Wear Daily* before becoming a receptionist in Lewis's congressional office in 1981. She gradually climbed the job ladder, so that by the mid-1990s, she was Lewis's principal gatekeeper for the earmarks requests that poured in from contractors, lobbyists, and their congressional allies. White paid special attention to requests from Bill Lowery, often meeting with him and his clients in White's office.

In 2003, White joined Lowery's firm. Shortly before her departure from Capitol Hill, Lewis took an extraordinary step that allowed her to avoid a law that requires high-ranking congressional staffers who become lobbyists to wait a year before lobbying their former offices. He cut her salary from $125,000 to an annualized rate of $113,000, putting her $80 below the law's threshold. That allowed White to jump into lobbying with both feet: She racked up $850,000 in fees in her first year. As the *Washington Post* asked in an editorial about her, "Why endure a cooling-off period when your former boss makes you a hot commodity?"[4]

From 1999 to 2005, Lewis's perch atop the Defense Appropriations Subcommittee allowed him to supervise the enormous Pentagon budget that would grow to nearly $400 billion during his tenure. Word circulated throughout the defense contracting world that Lowery's firm owned an earmark pipeline. The firm discreetly fed the buzz from its Web site with a boast to potential clients: "When you need to negotiate the complexities of government policy and elicit the attention of pivotal representatives, an advocate with exceptional credentials and expertise can provide critical assistance."

In 2005, White pulled in more than $3.5 million in fees. She was so successful at winning earmarks for her client that Keith Ashdown of the watchdog group Taxpayers for Common Sense called her "the earmark queen." Meanwhile, her husband, a retired tobacco lobbyist, picked up a defense client who promptly cashed in by sharing earmarks with one of Letitia's clients. Those earmarks, funding a corporate research program in Washington State, were sponsored by Rep. George Nethercutt, who registered as a lobbyist for the recipients after losing his 2004 bid for the Senate.

The Whites showed their gratitude to Lewis by pumping $30,000 into his campaigns and PAC between 2003 and 2005. Their clients were also big donors, including Nicholas Karangelen of Trident Systems Inc., a software engineering company that rose from obscurity to fabulous wealth on the basis of defense earmarks. White joined Karangelen in starting the Small Business Tech Pac, whose Web site trumpeted their ambition "to establish a strong and clear voice for small technology businesses" dealing with Congress.

PACs usually spend their money in campaign donations. But the Small Biz Tech PAC had doled out only $15,600 to politicians when bloggers first revealed its existence in mid-2006. Far more—$42,000—went to the PAC's director, who happened to be Jerry Lewis's stepdaughter.

Influence flowed between Lewis and Lowery in a dizzying swirl. In 2005, Jeff Shockey returned to Lewis's staff to help manage earmarks for the appropriations chairman. This would mean a precipitous drop in his salary, which would be a relatively modest $160,000. To ease his pain, the lobbying firm gave him a check for $2 million. Lowery also pitched in, hiring Shockey's wife. That meant that she was lobbying appropriations staffers who worked for her husband—and was doing it on behalf of her husband's former partners.

Initially, the cozy relationship between committee staffers and Lowery was going on out of public view—until Copley's Jerry Kammer first wrote about it in late 2005. Despite the questions, a lawyer for the Shockeys said their professional arrangements met ethical guidelines established by the House. But Larry Noble of the Center for Responsive Politics said: "If what they are doing is appropriate, I think it reflects an ethics culture in the House that is blind to what most people would say are conflicts of interest."

Jerry Lewis saw no conflicts, no problems, no skirting of ethical rules by the Shockeys, the Whites, or Lowery. "I'm very proud of the fact that these people basically are motivated by . . . public service," Lewis told Kammer. "They came to Washington because they actually wanted to serve."

The tight circle that formed around Lewis certainly served him well as he set his sights on the chairmanship of the Appropriations Committee. He knew the rules that Speaker Newt Gingrich had set—if you wanted a big chairmanship, the size of the contributions you funneled to other Republicans would count for more than the number of years you had served. Cash now outranked seniority.

Lewis liked having the ability to leap ahead of more senior Republicans, but he hated the thought of having to raise money. He called fund-raising "the last thing I want to do with my time." But as he looked around at other Republican leaders, he saw how they established political action committees to raise money to be distributed to cash-strapped candidates in competitive races. The very names of the PACs told the story—Tom DeLay's "Americans for a Republican Majority PAC"; Speaker Dennis Hastert's "Keep Our Majority PAC"; Virginia Rep. Eric Cantor's "Every Republican Is Crucial PAC."

So Lewis dutifully established the "Future Leaders PAC." And Lowery, White, and Shockey set out to stuff it with cash—hundreds of thousands of dollars they raised from clients in private industry and from fellow lobbyists. The money allowed Lewis to impress his party elders in 2004 when he flashed a check for $600,000 at a GOP gathering in 2004. It blew away his top rival, Ralph Regula of Ohio. In the old days, the chairmanship would have been Regula's, who had greater seniority on the committee. But Regula was no fund-raising match for Lewis. When Congress convened in 2005, Republicans picked Lewis to chair the Appropriations Committee.

Once he was chairman, Lewis was able to lavish even more attention on what had become his favorite cause—Loma Linda University, a Seventh Day Adventist institution about four miles up Timoteo Creek from his hilltop home in affluent Redlands. A 2001 study found that Loma Linda had received $150.6 million in earmarks since 1988, placing the tiny school—enrollment about three thousand—among the top ten recipients in the country. No elitist here—Lewis made sure Loma Linda was taken care of better than most of the schools in the Ivy League.

Earmark defenders insist that this freedom gives smaller schools a chance to get money that otherwise would go to top research institutions. But they have a hard time justifying why those smaller schools almost always are in the home districts of the appropriators. Or at least that was the finding of the *Chronicle of Higher Education,* which reported in 2003 that eight of the top ten pork-receiving institutions were in states represented by appropriators. Regardless, the explosion in academic earmarks duplicated the increase seen in the transportation bill. The *Chronicle* in 2003 tallied just over $2 billion in academic earmarks, more than six times the $296 million Congress inserted in 1996. Not so coincidentally, it also tracked a huge jump in the money universities were dishing out to lobbyists as they joined the Capitol Hill treasure hunt.

But it certainly was a great way to protect incumbents. In mid-2006, Lewis enjoyed a ritual that had become familiar to him as he basked in the glory of one of his earmarks for his home base. He was honored at the dedication of the Jerry Lewis San Bernardino Regional Training Center for firefighters. A discordant note lingered in the background, however. On that same day, San Bernardino County confirmed that federal prosecutors, who had launched a criminal investigation of the Lewis-Lowery relationship, had subpoenaed the records of its dealings with Lowery's firm. The firm, meanwhile, split in two, with Lowery and White going their own way.

The Lewis-Lowery connection helped highlight the attitude championed by Tom DeLay. When Republicans took over the House after forty years in the political wilderness, DeLay looked at the people who filled the lobbyists' offices on K Street in Washington and saw Democrat dominance. He wanted Republicans in those offices, he wanted them there quickly, and he was willing to flex his muscles to get what he wanted. The result was "The K Street Project," an aggressive, not-at-all subtle effort to force lobbying firms to hire Republicans if they wanted doors to open for them on Capitol Hill.

"They hire staff and farm them out to lobby shops so that the staffs can sell their access to their former bosses and generate campaign contributions from people who want government contracts," said Nathan Facey, a disillusioned former congressional staffer who said many of his former colleagues saw their public service as a finishing school for K Street.

A dissenter who often felt very lonely as a soldier in the battle begun by Ronald Reagan was Rep. Jeff Flake of Arizona. Repeatedly, he tried to call his Republican colleagues back to their fiscally conservative roots. Just as repeatedly, he lost in vote after vote. And when exit polls that tracked voters in the 2006 elections reported deep discontent with congressional earmarking, Flake said his party deserved the drubbing that took both houses of Congress out of Republican control.

The lesson Flake drew for his party applies to the country as well: "We need a major course correction." In this, he was saying nothing that President Bush didn't say to a standing ovation at his State of the Union address. In that speech, Bush cited the earmark system as a major flaw in the current operation of the federal government and demanded that Congress "expose every earmark to the light of day and to a vote in Congress and cut the number and cost of earmarks at least in half by the end of this session."

But just as applause for Reagan did not mean true support back in 1987, applause for Bush in 2007 did not signal an embrace of his message. And now there was a lesson for Flake, one that taught him reform would not be easy: When Republicans met in 2007 to divvy up their committee assignments, they pointedly and unceremoniously dumped Flake from his post on the Judiciary Committee. The message was clear—we will not tolerate criticism of our earmarks.

chapter seven

SEEDS OF A SCANDAL

I N OCTOBER 1992, AS RANDY CUNNINGHAM ENTERED THE FINAL STRETCH IN his race for a second term in Congress, Brent Wilkes sat nervously in his suite at the Hyatt Regency Hotel in Washington, D.C., with a briefcase full of at least $30,000 in campaign contributions sealed in envelopes. Some were marked with the names of half a dozen key figures in Congress; some were for the Republican National Committee.

In just a few weeks, Congress would pass the fiscal 1993 budget and Wilkes—who was working as a political consultant—hoped the donations would help ensure that his client's voice would be heard. So there he was, making his pitch and handing out envelopes as, one by one, lawmakers trudged up to his suite in the Hyatt. Duke Cunningham was not one of the politicians taking the donations. But, in many ways, this pass-off of campaign checks dramatically showcased the money-for-influence atmosphere that was growing in Washington and soon would envelop the still-new congressman from San Diego.

Federal authorities would later determine that about half the donations in Wilkes's suitcase violated campaign-spending laws since one of Wilkes's clients—Barry Nelsen, the CEO of Evergreen Information Technologies—had paid for some of his associates to make the contributions. But the feds never accused Wilkes or the congressmen of knowing about the illegalities after Nelsen said he could not remember whether he had told Wilkes what he had done to collect the money.

By 1992, Washington was familiar turf for Wilkes. Washington, after all, had been his base of operations during the Contra days of the mid-1980s. But his mysterious business trips to Central America had ended about 1987, when Congress was intensifying its probe of President Reagan's covert funding of the Contras. Wilkes abruptly shut down his company, World Finance Group Ltd., and went back to live in his mother's home in Chula Vista. He left a sizable chunk of debt in his wake, including more than $10,000 in unpaid federal taxes and $10,000 he owed to First Interstate Bank, World Finance's primary lender.

The IRS slapped a lien on him to collect the taxes. But First Interstate had to send a police officer to his mother's home to tell him to repay the loan, plus 18 percent interest. By the time he made his first payment, after a protracted legal dispute, Wilkes owed the bank more than $25,000.

To rebuild his finances, Wilkes tried his hand at municipal bond arrangements at the San Diego offices of Kidder Peabody and Smith Barney, where he met his stockbroker wife, Regina Waller, the mother of two adolescent sons from her first marriage. One month after their Las Vegas wedding, Regina gave birth to the couple's first daughter: Alexandra. With his instant family, there were even more debts; the situation pushed Wilkes to seek a job where he could make more money.

In April 1991, Wilkes went to work as a political consultant for a small investment firm called Aimco Securities Co. Wilkes's chief duty was to invite politicians to talk to Aimco clients, brokers, and prospects. Visitors included Willie Brown, the flashy Speaker of the

California State Assembly; conservative gadfly Alan Keyes, who was running a quixotic campaign in Maryland for the U.S. Senate; Rep. Bill Lowery, who hadn't yet lost his House seat to Cunningham; and a string of B-list state and local politicians. The politicians would typically tour Aimco's offices, give a talk in the office's conference room or patio, collect $10,000 or so in political donations or speakers' fees, and then head back to Washington, Sacramento, City Hall, or wherever else they came from.

At the same time that Wilkes's political guests were drawing people into Aimco, the firm's founder, Marvin I. Friedman, was getting into trouble with federal securities laws. In 1991, Friedman—who had previously been admonished twice by regulators—misappropriated more than $800,000 from one of his clients. When the National Association of Securities Dealers found out, it fined Friedman, ordered him to repay the client, and virtually forced him out of the securities industry.[1] But before that happened, Wilkes was hired as a consultant by an ebullient entrepreneur named Tom Casey.

Casey was a muscle-bound, barrel-chested wrestler's son with curly blond hair that fell to his shoulders. In his youth he flirted with the idea of becoming a professional wrestler, and in his spare time he still liked to wrestle with Ultimate Fighters, who mix in jiu-jitsu, judo, karate, kickboxing, and fisticuffs. Casey approached business with the same take-no-prisoners, no-holds-barred attitude.

While making his rounds as a traveling salesman fresh out of college, Casey chanced upon a technology designed to scan maps or drawings and turn them into a digital format that could be revised or edited on a computer. The technology was still in its early stages of development, but Casey felt it had great potential. Power companies could digitize schematics of gas pipelines or electricity wires. Manufacturers could computerize their blueprints. Police dispatchers could chart the quickest route to an emergency.

In 1983, at the age of twenty-six, Casey launched a company called Audre Inc., an acronym for Automated Digitizing and Recognition. Using $20 million raised by two Wall Street stock promoters, Casey hired thirty-five engineers and salesmen, rented office space near San Diego, and set about collecting clients. He envisioned the worldwide civilian market for Audre to be worth at least $1.5 billion. And that was just the civilian market. Work for the government could be worth much more.

But Audre was not alone in the market. At least half a dozen rivals were pioneering document-scanning technologies, and the list of competitors was growing. Each system had flaws, including Casey's. Audre took up so much computer memory that customers had to buy an entire computer workstation loaded with a Unix operating system to use it. Even then, it sometimes overloaded the system. "The program was full of bugs," said Dirk Holland, an Audre engineer. "It was crashing all the time."

Nevertheless, Casey managed to build a small list of big clients, including Chevron, Kodak, United Airlines, and Pacific Bell. Most of the contracts were small—typically between $100,000 and $300,000—and they did not cover Audre's growing expenses. But the government sector showed more promise. The California Department of Transportation—Caltrans—bought $740,000 worth of Audre's systems in 1989 to computerize the state's highway maps and engineering blueprints. Two U.S. military clients bought even more. With a few more government contracts, Audre could soar. But how could Casey get them?

In the spring of 1992, Casey went to several of Wilkes's political seminars at Aimco. Although Casey wasn't particularly impressed with the speakers, he hired Wilkes as a consultant, hoping that his connections in Sacramento and Washington could help Audre get more government contracts.

Wilkes's first task was to convince Caltrans to buy more Audre systems. After equipping its San Francisco and Los Angeles offices with Audre software in 1989, the agency did not feel the need to make further purchases.

Wilkes figured out an end-run around the agency. California State Assemblyman Steve Peace, a Democrat who sat on the assembly's Transportation Committee, was the son of Wilkes's former high school English teacher. In the summer of 1992, Wilkes and Casey told Peace that Caltrans needed more money for digitization. One of Peace's aides suggested turning to the feds. Congress had just passed an important bill to modernize the nation's highways. Why not use that money? Within the next seven months, Peace pushed a bill through the assembly that required—not "authorized," not "allowed," but "required"—Caltrans to apply for federal funds to convert its data from paper to computer-readable format.[2]

Peace even suggested to his fellow legislators that they should try to get federal funds for document scanning in other departments as well. "A window of opportunity exists to secure funding to enhance not only our roads and highways but virtually every state information function," he wrote.[3]

For Wilkes, this would set the pattern for his dealings with the government. If a government agency doesn't want to buy something you're selling, find a friendly legislator who can order it to make the purchase. Now that Wilkes had shown his skill at getting favors from lawmakers, a colleague of Casey's, Barry Nelsen, asked him for help.

Nelsen, a defense contractor in his mid-forties, had been involved in military information systems for the past twenty years. His current company, Evergreen Information Technologies, focused on transferring military specifications, or milspecs, onto the Internet. Milspecs are a vital source of information for federal contractors, setting forth the Pentagon's specific requirements for supplies. On paper, milspecs take up more than seventy-five thousand pages—too many for a busy contractor to plow through. Nelsen's idea was to post that information online. Because he needed to convert the milspecs into computer-readable format, Nelsen built strong ties with Audre, going so far as to invite Casey to be chairman of the board.

Nelsen's main hurdle was that the military—especially the Navy—was slow in giving him milspecs. He figured he needed some "political heat," meaning pressure from Congress, to prod the Navy along. After hearing of Wilkes's success with Caltrans, Nelsen asked him to get the heat roaring.

At this time, the person that Brent Wilkes was closest to in Congress—Rep. Bill Lowery—had just abandoned his bid for reelection in the face of Randy Cunningham's onslaught.

Wilkes and Lowery had crossed paths repeatedly over the past decade. Wilkes had faithfully supported Lowery's campaigns for city council and Congress. During Lowery's most recent appearance at Aimco, Brent and Regina Wilkes had given him $2,000 in campaign contributions—the legal maximum—and helped arrange for several thousand dollars more in contributions by inviting their friends to donate. That kind of money stood out, especially since it came at a time when many of his financial backers were abandoning him because of the House bank and the savings & loan scandals.

In the summer of 1992, Wilkes took Nelsen to Lowery's congressional office. As a congressman, there was little Lowery could directly do for them. He was the lamest of lame ducks. His chief congressional duty during the next six months would be to pack up and leave. But he was open with his advice. It would be good practice for his reentry into the private sector because he was already toying with the idea of becoming a lobbyist.

According to Wilkes, Lowery stressed that gaining funding from Capitol Hill was a two-step process: first came political contributions, then came the funding. "Transactional lobbying" was how Wilkes later described it, although a political contribution given as a quid pro quo to gain a government contract technically constitutes a bribe.[4] Lowery denies he ever told Wilkes there was a quid pro quo for contributions.

But Nelsen, too, says that Lowery stressed the importance of political contributions. At the time, individuals were permitted to give only $2,000 to a congressional candidate each election: $1,000 during the primary and $1,000 during the general election. But Lowery told Nelsen that contributors could magnify the impact of their donations by collecting checks from business partners, friends, relatives, and employees and then bundling them into a group contribution.

"Wilkes and Lowery were both telling me, 'Let's get a bunch of checks together. But they can't be over $1,000 each,'" Nelsen says.

In September 1992, Nelsen asked his friends, relatives, and employees to write $1,000 checks to politicians they had never heard of. At least seven of his associates were reluctant to part with such heady sums, so Nelsen offered them a deal: Sign the check and I'll pay you back. That would be a violation of federal election laws, but Nelsen denied knowing that. "If I had known it was illegal, obviously I wouldn't have done it," Nelsen says. The Securities and Exchange Commission (SEC), which regulated Evergreen, later fined Nelsen $65,000 for the campaign violations and banned him from heading a publicly traded company.

As Nelsen and Casey gathered the checks, Lowery helped arrange appointments between Wilkes and half a dozen key congressmen, most of whom served on the defense subcommittee of the House Appropriations Committee, which oversees the Pentagon budget. Nelsen set aside a desk in Evergreen's offices in McLean, Virginia, for Lowery and Wilkes to use for phone calls.[5]

Although Lowery and Wilkes were both Republicans, most of the lawmakers that Lowery arranged meetings with were Democrats because Congress was controlled by Democrats at the time.

In late September 1992, Wilkes established his base in the Hyatt. He sorted the checks into envelopes: $7,000 for John Murtha of Pennsylvania, who chaired the defense subcommittee of Appropriations; $6,000 for Steny Hoyer of Maryland, an Appropriations member who also headed the House Democratic Caucus; $5,000 each for Vic Fazio of California, an Appropriations member who headed the Democratic Congressional Campaign Committee; and Charlie Rose of North Carolina, chairman of the House Administration Committee. All were Democrats.

But there were also contributions for two Republicans: $4,000 for Joseph McDade of Pennsylvania, the leading Republican on Appropriations, who was then under indictment for bribery (he would later be acquitted), and $3,000 for McDade's lieutenant Jerry Lewis, who was destined to take over the defense subcommittee in 1999 and the entire Appropriations Committee in 2005.

Wilkes soon learned they were not interested in the technical details about Evergreen's project and got bored if he droned on too long about it. As bored as they might have been by milspecs, none of them had a problem taking Wilkes's contributions. "I was the king of the ten-minute meeting," he liked to say.

But the meetings achieved their intended effect. On October 23, 1992—which was coincidentally the date of one of the six checks that Wilkes passed to Murtha—Congress passed the Defense Authorization Act for fiscal year 1993. Barry Nelson says the budget that year included $500,000 for a pilot project to test Evergreen's brand of technology. Bill Lowery's vote to pass the budget was one of his final major votes as a congressman.[6]

Two months later, Lowery and Wilkes donned scuba gear, clambered off the deck of a rented boat, and dived into a dark abyss known as the Blue Hole, sixty miles off the coast of Belize. The water in the Blue Hole is a dark blue because the undersea cavern is too deep for sunlight to pierce. Angelfish and butterfly fish glide through gardens of coral at the rim of the cavern. Hammerheads, tiger sharks, and bull sharks prowl the murky depths below.

The trip to Belize was the perfect coda to Lowery's twelve years in Congress. In recent weeks, he had removed the pictures from the walls of his congressional office and packed his files for shipment to his home in McLean, Virginia. His life as a legislator was behind him. "Free in '93" was the bumper sticker on his car. But there would be nothing "free" about the new Bill Lowery. After more than a decade of envying the lifestyles of lobbyists, he was about to become one— joining Democrats Jim Copeland and Fred Hatfield in a firm specializing in California clients. One of his first clients at the newly named Copeland, Hatfield & Lowery would be Wilkes, who would pay the firm $340,000 over the next decade.

The junket illuminated Lowery's view of the proper role of lobbyists. Thoroughly relaxed by the swim, Lowery couldn't help but boast to U.S. Ambassador Eugene Scassa about the glories of having a friend like Brent Wilkes, who was footing most of the expenses of this trip. The conversation started because Lowery was so impressed by Scassa's official residence, a two-story mansion with a thirty-six-seat dining hall in one of Belize City's finer neighborhoods.

"How much does it cost to be an ambassador?" Lowery asked, wondering how many campaign donations Scassa made to get the job.

But Scassa had not gotten the job through political connections. He was a careerist who had worked his way up. Nevertheless, after thirty years as a diplomat, he was prepared for the question.

"This job has cost me some money—mostly out-of-pocket expenses for entertaining visitors," he said with a smile. "We don't get enough funding from Washington to cover all those costs, so I have to pay for some of them on my own."

Lowery's response was immediate: "What you need is a chuck wagon."

Scassa didn't understand. The only place he had heard the term before was in Roy Rogers movies.

"*He* is a chuck wagon," Lowery said, pointing to Wilkes. "You know, back in the days of the Old West, a chuck wagon followed the cattle herds with supplies for the cowboys. When a cowboy needs food, he goes to the chuck wagon. When a cowboy needs boots, he goes to the chuck wagon. A chuck wagon is someone like Mr. Wilkes, who pays your expenses. If you need boots, he pays. If you need to go to lunch, he pays."

Around six weeks later, Lowery and Wilkes returned to Belize, this time accompanied by Jerry Lewis. Officially out of Congress, Lowery was ready to take on the role of chuck wagon to Lewis. And Lewis wanted help raising money, funds that could be passed on to other Republicans to build up IOUs that could be cashed in the battle to rebuild his damaged stature in Congress.

The days after that 1992 election were tough for Lewis. In a political coup in December, he was ousted from his slot as the third-highest Republican leader in the House by the militantly combative Texas Rep. Dick Armey, who was seen as less likely than the amiable Lewis to be friendly with Democrats. After being booted from his high-profile position, Lewis was ready for a break when a lobbyist for the sports equipment giant Rawlings Corp. mentioned that the company was donating basketball gear to the government of Belize for a youth sports program engineered by Ambassador Scassa. Lowery was invited along for the ride on the Rawlings corporate jet. And Wilkes tagged along, too.

Lowery was barred from directly lobbying his former congressional colleagues for one year. But that didn't keep him from using the trip to build Wilkes's relationship with a key member of the Appropriations Committee. Wilkes had met Lewis several months before, and their relationship grew stronger during the visit to Belize. After a brief ceremony handing the basketball equipment to Belize's president, the delegation headed out to the Blue Hole for scuba diving and deep-sea fishing.

It was at this time that Lowery began to tell Wilkes what a useful contact Lewis would be in Congress. Just make the campaign contributions, Wilkes recalls him as saying, and Lewis would steer a bill through Appropriations.

"Jerry will make the request. Jerry will carry the vote. Jerry will have plenty of time for this," Wilkes quotes Lowery as saying. "But if you don't want to make the contributions or chair the fund-raising event, you will get left behind."[7]

Over the next couple years, Jerry Lewis would be Wilkes's most important contact in Congress. When Wilkes and Casey flew into Washington from San Diego, the first place they would head was Lewis's office in the Rayburn Building, one of the congressional office complexes across the street from the Capitol. Lewis would rise from his desk, greet Wilkes with a bear hug, and point to a corner of the room where he could park his luggage and hanging bags. Occasionally, he let Wilkes use his phone or fax machine as he made appointments to see other congressmen or Pentagon officials.

Since Lewis was going in and out of the office to cast votes on the floor, there were long periods when he didn't need to use his office, which gave Wilkes and Casey some privacy. "These were in the days before everybody had a cell phone, so we needed a place to call from," Casey says. "If you were on one floor of Rayburn, and you needed to make an appointment with someone on another floor, it was very convenient to use his office."

On September 11, 1993, Wilkes, Casey, and other Audre employees and investors donated $11,000 to Lewis's campaign—representing nearly a third of the major individual contributions he received during that nonelection year.

At roughly the same time, Lewis inserted an amendment into the Pentagon's budget to provide $20 million to test automated document conversion systems, known as ADCS, which was exactly the type of system that Audre produced. As is typical practice, Lewis did not write the earmark himself. Instead, he dispatched Letitia White to come up with the wording.

"Letitia was the Queen Bee and she went around buzzing," says Tom Casey. "She would tell Jerry, 'Okay, boss, I'll do what you want.' And zip, zip, zip, it would get done."

Brent Wilkes began courting her shortly after they met: taking her out to lunch, providing her with gifts. But this was not a romance; White was a happily married woman. She often brought her husband Dick, a tobacco lobbyist, to her meetings with Wilkes—including an evening cruise down the Potomac with Bill Lowery, Casey, and Jerry and Arlene Lewis. But it was a courtship nevertheless. And it paid off.

When it came time to draft the congressional appropriation for automated documents, White invited Casey to accompany her down into the subterranean depths of the congressional offices. They descended through the basement of the thirty-eight-year-old Rayburn Building to the narrow corridors of the subbasement. The ceilings were lined with pipes bringing heat, water, and air-conditioning to the upper levels of the building. To Casey, it looked like a scene out of Terry Gilliam's futuristic movie *Brazil,* in which the world is connected by metal ducts that lead to the sinister Ministry of Information.

White led Casey into a small room, full of computers, where half a dozen congressional aides were drafting legislation. The aides did not seem surprised to see visitors from the outside. One of them yawned as Casey entered. Another stood up to get a cup of coffee. None of them said anything to the visitors. After offering a perfunctory greeting, White grabbed an unoccupied desk and sat down to type while Casey looked on over her shoulders.

The ADCS earmark would not mention Audre by name. That would be a no-no. At least two dozen companies provided document conversion systems, and if there were any outright favoritism they would raise a stink, especially since some systems were faster, cheaper, and easier to use than Audre's. On the other hand, there were some things that Audre excelled at. It could read symbols better, for instance. And geometric shapes. And foreign alphabets. With some competing systems, if the computer scanner came across an unfamiliar symbol or shape, it would transform it into a piece of digital gobbledygook that a human computer programmer would have to spend hours revising.

It was a tradeoff between lower price and faster speed on the one hand and a higher degree of accuracy on the other. But Casey gave his company an advantage. Taking a seat at White's computer, he added a sentence to the earmark, specifying that to qualify for the Pentagon test, an ADCS program had to "recognize and distinguish between printed alpha numerics, geometric representations (including arcs, circles, splines and ellipses), symbols and foreign font sets"— precisely the qualities that Audre excelled at.

"Under that wording, this was still open to competitors," Casey says. "All I was doing was saying: 'If you can do these things, you can show up. If you can't do these things, don't show up.' But there was never any exclusion about who could or could not show up."

In September, the House of Representatives passed a budget that included Lewis's proposed $20 million appropriation for automated document recognition. In negotiations with the Senate, the figure was whittled down to $14 million. On November 10, Congress passed the bill.

Among Audre's backers was Randy Cunningham, who had just received nearly $2,750 in contributions from Casey and his chief investor, Donald Lundell. Cunningham's aide, Lindsay Lloyd, later explained that Wilkes had asked for Cunningham's help. "They needed some funding and some language to allow tests to go forward," Lloyd told *Federal Computer Week*.[8] Wilkes had known Cunningham since the late 1980s—before he ran for office—but this was the first known time that Wilkes asked Cunningham for help.

Coincidentally, only one week before Congress passed the bill, Letitia White bought a large amount of stock in Audre.[9] The day the bill was passed, Audre's stock price shot up from $1.94 to $2.56—a healthy 31 percent jump in value for White's shares. In the world outside Washington, White's actions might have constituted insider trading. But members of Congress and their staffs are exempt from insider trading laws.

"That kind of stuff happened all the time," said Casey. During one spike in his company's stock, on the eve of a major Pentagon contract, he checked to see where the investors were based. All the trading came from D.C. and its suburbs in Virginia and Maryland. "There's a reason Congress exempts itself from those laws," he said.

The influx of cash from the government breathed new life into Audre—and into Brent Wilkes's lobbying efforts. The more work that Audre did for the Pentagon, the more time Wilkes spent in Washington. Instead of camping out in Jerry Lewis's office, he was soon renting a three-bedroom suite at the Watergate Hotel as his base of operations.

Wilkes's suite, looking across the Potomac River to Arlington National Cemetery, was well situated. In good traffic, Wilkes could make it to the Pentagon or the Rayburn Building in just fifteen minutes. Congressmen came to the hotel in chauffeur-driven limousines to hear his ten-minute pitches and receive their check-stuffed envelopes. But the suite was best known for Wilkes's late-night poker games.

Every so often, a small cadre of CIA agents would drop by the Watergate for a few rounds of poker. Wilkes's best friend Dusty Foggo showed up whenever he was in town. So did their friend Brant Bassett, a CIA operative better known by the nickname of

Nine Fingers because he had lost one of his digits in a motorcycle mishap in his youth. Randy Cunningham and Charlie Wilson, an influential Texas Democrat who served with Lewis overseeing military spending at the Appropriations Committee, were among the people who showed up at the parties. "It was absolutely fun and games," Wilson recalls. "I think Brent liked to hang out with CIA guys."

Wilson—a boisterous figure who had recently gotten into political hot water for taking a dip in a hot tub with a pair of naked cocaine-sniffing Las Vegas showgirls—also had an affinity for cloak-and-dagger types. One poker night, he showed up at the Watergate with a sack of "party favors"—mostly guns from China and Eastern Europe, including a collection of .32-caliber weapons that the KGB had disguised to look like Mont Blanc pens. Wilson cheerfully distributed the weapons among the poker players; to Foggo he handed a Chinese .45 automatic.

Wilkes's suite was clouded with smoke from Dominican cigars. The smoke was too thick for Wilson, who left halfway through the evening with his friend Joe Murray of the *Atlanta Journal-Constitution*. Murray later wrote about how eagerly one of the CIA officers accepted a Cuban cigar from him.

"You know, of course, this is considered contraband," the CIA officer told Murray. "But you've done the right thing as a good citizen. You've turned it in to the proper government agency. Be assured that very shortly it will be destroyed by fire."[10]

Wilson had met Foggo during a congressional trip to Austria a couple years before. Foggo, who was stationed in Vienna at the time, had shown the lawmakers around town; later, he let it be known that he had introduced some local women to the notoriously libidinous Wilson. "Did Dusty introduce me to some women?" Wilson asks. "I don't remember. But you've got to understand that I was single back then."

In the meantime, problems were developing on the Pentagon's testing of Audre. Pentagon officials grumbled that they did not need a new system for document conversion because they already had their own systems, known as JCALS and JEDMICS. Other Pentagon officials felt that the congressionally mandated tests—which put more emphasis on alphanumeric reading capabilities than price or speed—would give the military no idea of how much manpower or funding the ADCS systems would require or how much saving would result. On Capitol Hill, Senator Wendell Ford, a Democrat from Kentucky, started raising questions over whether political influence had played a role in the ADCS funding process.

To smooth things over, Jerry Lewis wrote letters praising the ADCS program to Vice Admiral Edward Straw, head of the Defense Logistics Agency, and James R. Klugh, deputy undersecretary of defense for logistics. Three other congressmen joined Lewis in signing the Klugh letter—Wilkes's poker-playing buddy Charlie Wilson as well as his two hometown congressmen: Duncan Hunter, who held an influential position on the Armed Services Committee, and Randy Cunningham, who was gaining in seniority on the same committee.

"We believe this technology to be a critical link," read the letter.

The Klugh letter was written on September 7, 1994. Over the next several weeks, each of the letter's signers received a cluster of contributions from Audre's investors: $9,000 to Lewis, $6,000 to Wilson, and $4,000 each to Hunter and Cunningham. And on September 29, Congress passed a defense budget setting aside $20 million more for the ADCS program. Of course, the politicians say the contributions had no effect on their support of Audre.

"Brent Wilkes and Tom Casey were aggressive and enthusiastic promoters of a breakthrough technology," Hunter says. "They always made their case on the argument that they had the best system."

But there were more red flags going up. On September 30, a day after the budget passed, the General Accounting Office—a federal watchdog now known as the Government Accountability Office (GAO)—issued a report finding that the tests being ordered by Congress had little value to the Pentagon. "Defense officials responsible for reviewing the ADCS test plan say it will not confirm the efficiency or the effectiveness of the system," the GAO report said.

Two months later, something happened that drowned out the GAO's warnings. Republicans seized control of the House of Representatives for the first time in four decades, radically changing the makeup and leadership of congressional committees. Jerry Lewis moved up to become second-in-command at the Appropriations Committee. Duncan Hunter was appointed chairman of the House Armed Services Committee's subcommittee on military procurement. And Randy Cunningham gained new clout on the committee. Suddenly, all the Republican relationships that Brent Wilkes had been nurturing for the past two years were ready to pay off. With Republicans in control of Congress, Wilkes thought Audre had a good shot of getting even more money through appropriations. And he wanted to bill Tom Casey accordingly.

On December 7, 1994, executives from Audre met for a strategy dinner at a restaurant in Long Beach, where they had been demonstrating their products at a trade show. To Brent Wilkes, this was a prime opportunity to lay out his strategy for how to deal with the Republican Revolution.

To Wilkes, Newt Gingrich's takeover of the House meant that the company could drop its support of most Democrats. But it would have to spend $40,000 more per year on lobbying and political contributions to build relationships with the newly installed Republican leadership.

Casey balked. He felt that Audre, which had not turned a profit in eight years, was already spending too much money on Capitol Hill. In the past two years, under Wilkes's guidance, the company and its investors had spent about $70,000 in political contributions and he did not understand why more was needed.

After a heated argument, Wilkes stalked out of the restaurant. And within six months, he started a company to compete with Casey's: Automated Document Conversion Systems Inc., or ADCS, with its initials taken from the congressionally mandated program that he and Casey had lobbied to create.

It was time to test the loyalties of those congressmen.

chapter eight

DUNCAN VS. DUKE

B Y THE MID-1990S, IT WAS CLEAR TO BOTH AUDRE INC. AND BRENT WILKES that the way to get contracts from the Pentagon was to find congressmen who had the best ability to strong-arm the Defense Department into doing their bidding.

"At what point in time is the decision made as to which of these contractors is going to get the money for their particular contract?" Audre's corporate attorney, Ian Kessler, once asked Richard Gehling, who headed the company's federal sales after Wilkes left.[1]

"Normally, it boiled down to . . . who [their] House or Senate member was and how much pressure they put on the undersecretary [of defense] about getting the funding for their constituents," Gehling answered in a sworn deposition.

"So it's fair to say that that, in turn, depends upon how much political muscle, how much influence [a company has] with a particular congressperson?" Kessler asked.

"The majority of the time, it's [which company] has the most clout," Gehling said.

"When you say the most clout, you mean the most political clout?"

"Who has paid more."

"I'm sorry," Kessler said, not sure that he had heard Gehling correctly. "Who has what?"

"Who has paid more."

"Paid more in terms of political contributions?"

"Fund-raisers. Sponsoring."

Kessler, who apparently held the reasonable but naïve belief that Pentagon contracts were controlled by the Pentagon, came back to the topic a little while later.

"But the ultimate decision rested with the Department of Defense as to where to put the money, correct?" he asked.

"Not really," Gehling replied. "It could always come down to some House or Senate member putting enough pressure to actually change the direction where the money went."

According to Gehling, the politician who applied the most pressure on behalf of Audre Inc. was Duncan Hunter, a beefy former U.S. Army Ranger who represented a congressional district bordering Duke Cunningham's.

Hunter had first gone to bat for Tom Casey and Brent Wilkes in September 1993, when Lewis and Lowery were collecting signatures for their letter extolling Audre's scanning program. Hunter had no great love for either Lewis or Lowery. But he was always happy to help out a San Diego company, which is one reason why San Diego defense contractors pumped hundreds of thousands of dollars into his campaigns over the years. And he liked Tom Casey and Brent Wilkes. Unlike some of his colleagues, Hunter actually listened to their explanations of the value of Audre's document conversion system.

"If people in the Defense Department came up with reasons why they did not want to use the product, they always had a counterargument," he says.

After Wilkes and Casey fell out in December 1994, Hunter continued to support Audre. And now he had a lot more clout than the average hometown congressman. Thanks to the power shift of Newt

Gingrich's Republican Revolution, Hunter was appointed chairman of the military procurement subcommittee at the House Armed Services Committee, making him an invaluable contact for contractors who were peddling goods to the Pentagon.

Already, some voices within the Pentagon were raising doubts about Audre's software: "The current system does not produce documents that are acceptable to the majority of customers," read a report by the Defense Information Systems Agency (DISA), which was leaked to *Federal Computer Week* in January 1995.[2] Computers loaded with Audre's software crashed as much as twice a day, the report found. Only one out of three Audre users felt the system was easy to use.

The leak of the agency's report infuriated Tom Casey. He was convinced that the final version of his software, which was still in the testing phase, would be much better than the report implied. But the leak was not his only concern. The Pentagon had been dragging its heels on buying all the software that Congress had authorized it to buy. Casey went to Hunter and demanded a meeting with General James R. Klugh, deputy defense undersecretary for logistics. And Hunter easily complied. "Our job as San Diego congressmen is to do our best to make sure our guys get a fair shot and are fairly evaluated."

In late March, Klugh went to see Hunter and Casey, accompanied by John Karpovich, who evaluated technology at the Navy's printing service, and Roy Willis, the Defense Department's liaison with Congress. To enhance the effect of Hunter's newfound power, the meeting was not held in Hunter's office. Instead, it took place in the office of Texas Rep. Dick Armey, who had just taken the role of House Majority Leader, the second-highest position in the House.

Casey didn't think much of the men who came to the meeting. His pet nickname for General Klugh was "General Clueless." (Klugh, who has since gone into private industry, now says he cannot remember Casey.) And he despised Karpovich, whom he dubbed "Johnny the Karp." As one of the military's chief experts on document-conversion technology, Karpovich was a key contact for companies hoping to sell their goods to the Pentagon. The chances for selling technology to the military rose or fell with his recommendation. And for the past two years, he had been recommending against Audre.

Karpovich felt that although Audre's system was useful—and was definitely faster than manually inputting data—other systems on the market were faster and cheaper. He thought the Pentagon should not have to pay $30,000 per unit for a document-conversion system, which was Audre's price tag, at a time when some software packages cost $7,000 or less. And there was still the problem of the military's having to buy Unix-based workstations. Audre's competitors were selling software that could be used on a standard PC.

Casey felt Audre's system provided higher quality than the competitors'. And it was close to developing a PC product. The amateur wrestler went into the meeting as if it were a smackdown staged by World Wrestling Entertainment. "I tore them to pieces," Casey says of the meeting. "Duncan was like a referee at a WWE match, with me jumping off the top ropes to pile-drive Karpovich into the carpet. Klugh got so mad at my 'insubordination and lack of respect' I thought he was going to have a stroke, which would not necessarily have been a bad thing."

Karpovich tried to hold his own against the onslaught. "The software is too expensive," he said. "There's a warehouse full of software that nobody is using." But Hunter took Casey's side. Karpovich says that when he tried to point out alternatives to Audre, Hunter turned to Klugh and said, "Apparently your boy doesn't know how to play the game." Karpovich interpreted the remark as meaning that Congress sometimes prefers expensive technologies.

After the meeting, Hunter took a more active role in promoting Audre to the Pentagon. On April 11, a couple of weeks after the meeting with Klugh, Tom Casey donated $1,000 to Hunter's campaign. At roughly the same time, Hunter agreed to let Casey use his office as a showroom where he could demonstrate his newest product—Automatic Choice Release 2.2—to potential buyers from the Pentagon.

On May 8, Audre sales rep Richard Gehling and an assistant showed up at Hunter's office to hold a two-week round of demonstrations. Audre's marketing team had already developed a specially drafted set of talking points that Hunter could use during the demonstrations.[3]

In effect, Audre was turning Hunter into its Pentagon lobbyist. What Hunter did not know was how worried Audre's own engineers were about the system's flaws. In an internal memo dated March 31—just five weeks before the demonstrations in Hunter's office—the marketing team wrote "we promise not to report any bugs" when it obtained a copy of Release 2.2 to use in demonstrations. A memo dated May 12 notes that after months of work, Audre engineers still had no idea how much memory or storage space Release 2.2 would require.[4]

"Duncan Hunter was pushing a product that was not very effective, without adequate testing to see if it met the Defense Department's needs," says Robert Lear, a former Audre salesman. "It's not that it didn't work. It's just that it didn't work well enough."

But with Hunter's office giving a tacit stamp of approval to Release 2.2, Audre had little problem selling the system to the military. On June 1, less than two weeks after the demos were concluded, the Defense Department placed a $1.2 million order for fifty Audre systems at five defense sites around the United States. "When you're in a position like Hunter was, you have a lot of clout, and we're not supposed to rock the boat," says a former Pentagon procurement official who declined to be named.

Three months later, Audre filed for bankruptcy protection. The cause had nothing to do with the firm's business operations. For the past decade, Casey had been locked in a fractious divorce battle with his estranged wife, Catherine. In September 1995, the divorce judge ruled that Catherine was entitled to half of Audre's market value. Casey responded by taking Audre into bankruptcy court, arguing that it was financially incapable of complying with the decision. Audre's stock price, which had been in the tank for months, sank even deeper after the bankruptcy filing and never recovered.

But even without the problems caused by the divorce, the company was in bad shape. The Pentagon wasn't buying enough software to keep it afloat. Shortly after the bankruptcy filing, Casey drove to

Hunter's house in the rural hill country of eastern San Diego County and pleaded with the congressman to put more pressure on the military. Casey was practically in tears, saying that his company could well disappear unless it got more Pentagon funding.

At Casey's urging, Hunter asked the Pentagon's inspector general to launch a probe into why Audre wasn't getting more contracts. But when Assistant Inspector General Robert Lieberman concluded his investigation in June 1996, it was of little comfort to either Hunter or Casey. Lieberman wrote that "little demand exists" for automated document conversion systems. Apart from Port Hueneme, a Navy base on the California coast that was quite pleased with Audre, no military installation said it needed the systems. Most of the software packages that Congress had ordered the military to buy were being kept in storage.[5]

Lieberman's findings did not sway Hunter. In late 1996, Congress added $38.8 million to the Pentagon budget for document conversion systems, again without receiving a request from the military. The National Security Committee—temporarily the name of the Armed Services Committee on which Hunter sat—said it was "disappointed" that the Pentagon had not asked for funds.

By that time, Audre had a new worry—its one-time political consultant, Brent Wilkes.

Until Tom Casey fired him, Brent Wilkes had spent all his time in Washington promoting other peoples' interests. Now he decided it was time to grab a piece of the pie for himself. He had no experience running a computer company. But he was a fast learner. And he was skilled at piggybacking off other people's ideas.

During his days at Audre, Wilkes had heard of a document-scanning system called VPMaxNet, developed by Softelec, a software firm in Munich, Germany. In early 1995, Wilkes bought licensing rights for VPMax and then hired a team of U.S. engineers—including some from Audre—to customize it for the military market. For financial backing, he turned to Dennis Wise, a fellow graduate of San Diego State University who invested in real estate and technology ventures with his then-wife, Joanne. Wise loaned Wilkes $1 million with the understanding that he would be rewarded handsomely once the company got off the ground.

In May, Wilkes founded ADCS Inc., after the generic term that he and Tom Casey had pushed to insert into the military budget. In Pentagon and congressional documents, many of the references to automated document conversion systems were already being abbreviated as ADCS. Over the next few years, Wilkes would point to that line item and say, "I created that program. That's my money."

ADCS Inc. was a family affair. Most of the company's top executives were related to Wilkes or his wife, Regina, who variously referred to herself as the company's co-owner, vice president, and manager. Brother Jeffery Wilkes was director of facilities. Brother Robert Wilkes was an ADCS department leader. Sister-in-law Marilyn Wilkes was put in charge of shipping and receiving. Nephew Joel Combs headed the firm's lobbying efforts. Other members of Wilkes's extended family were pulled in to help on political fundraisers and to write checks to friendly politicians.

Wilkes had chosen his technology well. In early 1996, a Defense Department evaluation of half a dozen document-conversion systems ranked VPMax as one of the best in the business. It was faster and easier to use than Audre. And it was a lot cheaper. ADCS's VP-Max system cost $6,035 per unit, roughly half as much as Audre's $11,479 system built for personal computers, and a fifth of the cost of Audre's $29,950 Unix-based system, which was by far the most expensive of the technologies tested.[6]

VPMax beat, matched or came close to matching Audre on eleven out of the fourteen categories. The only categories in which Audre sharply bested VPMax—and every other competitor—were its ability to read symbols and to read or clean up nonhorizontal text.[7] But the evaluation noted that those qualities had to be weighed against Audre's slow processing speed. "Audre won in categories I would equate with glove box and tire sizes," Wilkes boasted. "But in terms of cost, ease and speed, we killed them."[8]

Even so, Hunter backed Audre. A firm believer that the military should buy U.S.-made products only, Hunter could not bring himself to support ADCS's German-born software. "I did oppose having a German firm get the business," he explained, although Softelec was getting little more than licensing fees for the ADCS project. Brent Wilkes had ensured that a large chunk of the profits would stay within the United States.

Tom Casey skillfully played on Hunter's nationalistic sentiments. When speaking to Hunter, Casey never mentioned ADCS by name. Instead, he referred to it as "the German software," "the German technology," or "a third-rate foreign supplier."

With Hunter squarely behind Audre, Wilkes needed a new champion on Capitol Hill. He turned to Randy Cunningham. Wilkes had known Cunningham for more than a decade, meeting him well before he first ran for Congress. Wilkes and financial backer Dennis Wise started donating money to Cunningham in October 1995, five months after launching their firm. Three months later, Cunningham was named to the National Security Committee. Cunningham's position on the committee made him more valuable to military contractors, including Wilkes. Over the next eight years, Wilkes, his family, and his associates would donate more than $80,000 to Cunningham's campaign and his aptly named American Prosperity political action committee.

But Wilkes's gifts went beyond campaign contributions. Starting as early as 1996, Wilkes began taking Cunningham to fancy eateries near Washington, ranging from the techno-pop disco Ozio's to the Serbian Crown, a four-star restaurant in northern Virginia featuring strolling gypsy violinists, crystal chandeliers, rococo decor, and meals of emu, antelope, lion, and wild boar.[9] In 1997, Wilkes bought a 14.5-foot jet boat for $11,255 for Cunningham's personal use. And he hinted at more gifts to come.

It did not take long for Cunningham to start promoting ADCS's technology. In September 1996, Cunningham began pushing the Pentagon to provide more funding for document conversion efforts.[10] By early 1997, Cunningham allowed Wilkes to print his endorsement of ADCS in the company's promotional materials.

"The success achieved by ADCS Inc. is an asset to the San Diego business and technological communities," said a Cunningham quote reprinted on ADCS pamphlets and press releases. "VPMaxNet's time-saving functions and overall performance have proven to be an asset to the DoD, ultimately leading to savings for taxpayers and contributing to a stronger, more efficient national defense."[11] Wilkes built stronger relations with other legislators as well. When the Republican National Convention was held in San Diego in 1996, Wilkes and Dennis Wise rented a hospitality suite across the street from the convention, where congressmen and their staffers could meet local businessmen. When the businessmen donated money to the congressmen, it not only gave them better access to Congress but also enhanced Wilkes's standing as a fund-raising rainmaker.

Among those dropping by the suite was Wilkes's favorite legislator, Jerry Lewis. With the support of Lewis and Cunningham, ADCS quickly outpaced bankruptcy-tainted Audre. By April 1997, Wilkes was able to boast that VPMax was "the most widely used software conversion product by the federal government."[12] The funding for the ADCS purchases, of course, came out of the set-asides of the House Appropriations Committee, where both Lewis and Cunningham now sat.

At Audre, meanwhile, angry shareholders—facing declining revenues and a long slog through bankruptcy court—ousted Tom Casey from the company and replaced him with two of the company's top investors: Don Lundell and James Fiebiger. The corporate coup did not change Hunter's opinion about the company. Lundell's relatives and friends had been contributing money to his campaign ever since Audre began seeking contracts on Capitol Hill, even though they lived in Arizona, several hundred miles away from Hunter's district. Hunter continued to back their crusade against the "German software."

In February 1997, Hunter met repeatedly with Audre sales rep Gehling, eating with him twice at the Members Dining Room in the Capitol and grabbing a cup of coffee at a congressional cafeteria.

Audre was just coming out with a new product, and Gehling was trying to line up a $2.5 million contract with the Pentagon.[13]

Gehling had his own doubts about Audre's new product: "There were still problems with the software," he said later. "It's always been flaky. It's still flaky." But during his meeting with Hunter, he kept such thoughts to himself. "I just want to make sure we still have your support," he told Hunter. "I'll have Vickie look into things," Hunter replied. "She can look into the status of the program and let General Phillips know where I want the funding to go."[14]

Hunter soon dispatched Vickie Middleton, his defense department liaison, to contact Maj. Gen. John Phillips, the deputy undersecretary for logistics at the Defense Department. This wasn't the first time she had been assigned such duties. In the past, Middleton had called Pentagon officials as well as other members of the House and Senate to solicit support for Audre. Hunter also wrote a letter to Phillips about the document conversion program. "Whenever possible, use products that are made in the United States by American taxpayers," he wrote.

But Audre did not get the $2.5 million contract. In August 1997—shortly after Brent Wilkes and his nephew Joel Combs donated $2,000 to his campaign—Cunningham stepped in to divert the Pentagon contract to ADCS. But by now, the value of the contract had somehow risen to $3.2 million.

It is unclear exactly how Cunningham persuaded the Pentagon to change its mind or how he prevailed over the more senior Hunter. But almost immediately after the shift was made, Gehling began hearing from Pentagon insiders that Cunningham had "dictated" that the money go to ADCS. "He had pretty well twisted them, because the various groups [in the Pentagon] know that if they don't keep the House and Senate members happy, they may not get their other projects' funding," Gehling said.[15]

Donald Lundell, Gehling's boss at the time, speculated that Cunningham had been swayed by Wilkes's political contributions. "I know that Mr. Wilkes has been very active in campaign financing activities," he said. Cunningham later admitted to reporters that he had talked up ADCS to Pentagon officials. But he rejected any criticism of his actions. "I'm on the side of the angels here," he said, and he added that anyone who questioned his motives "can just go to hell."[16]

Even so, the document-conversion program was continuing to draw criticism from Capitol Hill. In June 1997—just weeks before Cunningham shifted contracts to ADCS—Republican Senator John McCain of Arizona included the document conversion program on a list of more than $5.5 billion of "objectionable defense adds" that Congress had tacked onto the military budget without the Defense Department's blessing, "virtually ignoring the request of the Pentagon and impeding the military's ability to channel resources where they are most needed."[17]

McCain blamed the add-ons on the Armed Services Committees in the Senate and in the House, which included both Hunter and Cunningham.

"With military training exercises continuing to be cut, backlogs in aircraft and ship maintenance, flying hour shortfalls, military health care underfunded by $600 million, and 11,787 service members reportedly on food stamps," McCain said, Congress should not be funding "a plethora of programs not requested by the Defense Department."

But McCain was largely ignored. Three months later, Congress passed a budget that included a $20 million allocation for document-conversion systems for the 1998 fiscal year. The funding increased to $25 million in fiscal 1999 and $32 million in fiscal 2000. For both ADCS and Audre, the biggest contracts were yet to come—thanks to continued backing from Jerry Lewis, Duncan Hunter, and Duke Cunningham.

chapter nine

OUR MAN IN PANAMA

O N MARCH 20, 1997, DUNCAN HUNTER AND DUKE CUNNINGHAM CALLED reporters to the House Radio/TV Gallery at the Capitol to make a dramatic announcement: the People's Republic of China was vying to gain control of the Panama Canal. And once it did, the communist government could strangle shipping throughout the Western Hemisphere.

What the two Congressmen were referring to was a bid by the Hong Kong–based shipping company Hutchison Whampoa to operate the entrances to both sides of the Panama Canal. Hutchison-Whampoa is a venerable firm founded in the days of Queen Victoria. But to Hunter and Cunningham, it was an arm of the People's Liberation Army. The congressmen warned that once the United States ceded control of the canal to Panama on December 31, 1999, the Chinese could take over.

"This is a strategic influence. They aren't going to Bismarck, South Dakota. They're going . . . to both ends of the Panama Canal!" Hunter warned the small cluster of reporters.

Hunter, of course, had misplaced the capital of North Dakota. Undeterred, he proceeded to explain that if the Chinese sank just one ship in the middle of the Panama Canal, they could block most sea traffic from the Atlantic to the Pacific. "Right now we have a Chinese fleet coming up the coast. It's been stopping at Central and South American locations. It's coming, I believe, shortly to San Diego," he said, referring to a goodwill tour of two Chinese destroyers and a supply ship. "We think that, taken as a whole, this raises very serious national security issues."

"Let me just interject one thing," Cunningham told the reporters. "Let me tell you what my experience is and what I base a lot of this on. I was an executive officer of a fleet coordinating group that coordinated all exercises in Southeast Asia. That was in the context of Team Spirit, Tangent Flash, Yama Sakura, Cobra Gold [war games off the coasts of Japan, South Korea, and the Philippines]. . . . We know how these companies operate."

Cunningham rattled off a few more non-sequiturs and then hurried out of the room, leaving the reporters wondering how his experience with naval war games gave him insights into the operations of a Hong Kong cargo firm.

But where Hunter and Cunningham saw a threat, Brent Wilkes found an opportunity. Since the United States took over the Panama Canal in 1904, the government of the Canal Zone had accumulated 1.2 million documents, squirreled away in musty storehouses throughout Panama. If lawmakers like Cunningham and Hunter really felt that Panama was about to fall into Chinese hands, something would have to be done to preserve those documents. And Wilkes believed he was just the guy to do it.

Wilkes was tapped for the Panama project in mid-1997, just a few months after the Hunter-Cunningham press conference. The project was the brainchild of Mark Adams, an assistant undersecretary of defense overseeing document-conversion programs, and his chief deputy, Ann Barnes.

In 1997, Adams was putting together a proposal to use ADCS-style technology to computerize military maps and engineering drawings at the military facilities in Alabama, New Jersey, Maine, and San Diego. Barnes, who was born in the Panama Canal Zone, noted that more than a million government documents were stored at military bases and government offices around the canal. The Panama Canal treaty specified that copies of these documents had to be handed over to the Panamanian government.

Many of those documents had no practical value to the military. There were hand-drawn sketches of Panama from the 1870s; photos of World War I steamships plying through the canal; diplomatic cables from Teddy Roosevelt's White House; floor plans of government buildings that had long since been torn down. There was no reason these documents had to be digitized. But some of the documents, including blueprints of military facilities around the canal, could be valuable if the United States were ever drawn into a conflict in Panama. Adams gave a green light to the Panama project and then steered the work to Wilkes.

In recent years, Adams had developed a close working relationship with Wilkes. And that relationship was about to become much closer. Within a year, Wilkes would hire Adams away from the Pentagon, paying him a much higher salary than the government could afford. And he would hire Adams's secretary, Francis Regina DiPilla, at an equally dramatic jump in pay. Within a year or two of grooming her, Wilkes even cosigned for the house that DiPilla and her parents bought in suburban Virginia.

Wilkes faced a major hurdle in landing the contract because ADCS had not been qualified to work as a prime contractor for the government. Its previous work had been as a subcontractor or supplier. To get the job, Wilkes would have to find a prime contractor. After a quick search, he settled on Maryland businessman Rollie Kimbrough.

Kimbrough, in his early sixties, was short and stocky with a closely cropped head of graying hair and a wisp of a white beard. He was a religious man, very active within the Metropolitan African Methodist Episcopal Church in Washington, D.C. But Kimbrough had no illusions about how to play the government procurement system.

For years, Kimbrough had a history of donating money to politicians in Maryland and Washington while seeking government contracts for his computer consulting firm, MCSI Technologies. Recently, he had qualified as a prime contractor for the Department of Housing and Urban Development (HUD) and the Department of Veterans Affairs (VA).

"I've had an extremely good relationship with the VA," Kimbrough told Wilkes at their first meeting, at a high-tech trade fair in the Washington Convention Center in December 1997. "I've had terrific relationships with many different agencies, both at the federal and state level."[1] Together, Wilkes and Kimbrough came up with a plan that would allow MCSI to serve as a prime contractor for the Panama project, receive a cut of the profits, and do none of the work. Wilkes would handle the bulk of the workload—and the profits.

Even with Kimbrough on board, there was a stumbling block. Kimbrough was not qualified to be a prime contractor for the Pentagon, which was in charge of the Panama project. But that was a minor hurdle for Wilkes. Jerry Lewis headed the VA subcommittee at Appropriations. With Lewis's help, Wilkes and Kimbrough could get the project rolling under the VA's auspices.

On January 13, 1998, Wilkes flew Jerry Lewis to San Diego for a day-long series of meetings at ADCS's headquarters. Kimbrough was present as well, and there is little doubt that the talk focused on Panama. The Panama project had nothing to do with veterans' affairs, of course. But under an "interagency agreement," one agency, such as the VA, could agree to be a funding conduit for another agency, such as the Pentagon. A little nudge from Congress could help.

So Wilkes and Kimbrough kicked some cash into Lewis's campaign. Wilkes, his wife, Regina, his nephew and lobbyist, Joel Combs, his lobbyist, Richard Bliss, and Rollie Kimbrough each gave $2,000—$1,000 for his primary and $1,000 for his general election—for a total of $10,000 in one day.

It was a bit unusual for Kimbrough, a life-long Democrat, to donate to a Republican congressman. In the previous four years, Kimbrough and his wife had given more than $80,000 to the Democratic

Party and Democratic congressional candidates. Even more money had gone to Democrats in state and local campaigns. But Kimbrough was a pragmatist.

"Contracting with the government is very political," Kimbrough says. "If you can't go to people on the Hill, it's very difficult to remain viable. So if the party in power doesn't happen to be your party, what are you supposed to do? Stop doing business until the other party comes into power? My experience has been that you should always have friends on both sides of the aisle. You have to talk to people."

Shortly after Wilkes's meeting with Lewis, Mark Adams and Ann Barnes got the ball rolling on the Panama project. By mid-May, they were contacting Gail Cotten, a specialist in high-tech contracts at the Department of Veterans Affairs, with suggestions about how the money should be allocated. At the age of forty-five, Cotten had spent half her life working as a contracting specialist for Veterans Affairs. She had worked her way through four separate locations before settling down in the department's technology purchasing center in Austin, Texas. For the past year, she had been dealing with Rollie Kimbrough because he had set up an MCSI field office in Austin as part of his VA contract.

Under the interagency agreement, Cotten would be the official contracting officer on the Panama project, overseeing funding, but Barnes would oversee the technical details. Although the project was supposed to be open to other bidders, Barnes left no doubt that the money was intended to go to Kimbrough (and through him to Wilkes). In her e-mails, she referred to the project as the "MCSI task."

"This program is under congressional oversight and will be scrutinized at every point," Barnes warned Cotten. "We're used to highly politicized programs," Cotten replied. "I'll take every precaution to make sure that the project will not be criticized."[2]

Since the government could not show out-and-out favoritism to Wilkes and Kimbrough, it was important to make it look as if they had won the contract competitively. On June 4, Cotten wrote to half a dozen companies, including Andersen Consulting and Price

Waterhouse, asking them to bid on the contract. The companies were given twelve days to submit a proposal—not much time for a multimillion-dollar project that was spread throughout the United States and Panama. Not surprisingly, MCSI was the only company that submitted a bid.

By this time, Randy Cunningham was becoming one of the main congressional point men on the project. In May, Cunningham sent a letter to C. W. Bill Young, the chairman of the Appropriations subcommittee on defense, asking for $64 million to be added to the budget for document conversion programs. In June, Wilkes, Kimbrough, Combs, and Bliss donated $8,000 to Cunningham's campaign. Another $8,000 went to Republican Rep. Ken Calvert of California, an influential member of the House Science Committee. And in July, as the bill was going through the Appropriations Committee, Kimbrough joined Brent and Regina Wilkes to kick in $15,000 to a political action committee run by Appropriations Chairman Bob Livingston, a Republican from Louisiana. (Political action committees can receive $5,000 from individual donors.)

Already, though, problems were developing on the project.

Not surprisingly, several of the military bases that were supposed to take part in the project didn't want ADCS-style document conversion. The Redstone Arsenal in Alabama preferred the military's own document-conversion program, JEDMICS. Officials at the Navy Engineering Station in Lakehurst, New Jersey, felt ADCS's goals were too "ambiguous."

It soon became apparent that Panama would be the main site where the work would take place. Making matters worse, Gail Cotten was becoming increasingly skeptical of the bills she was getting for the project. Since early July, she had been asking for paperwork detailing the project's costs. Wilkes's failure to provide documentation was beginning to bother even Kimbrough.

"I've never seen a project that is so helter-skelter," he told Wilkes at a meeting on August 14. "We can't let this project go awry."

Wilkes tried to allay his fears, noting that "Congress is in the audience for approval of the project." As long as Congress was happy,

Kimbrough didn't need to worry about some mid-level VA bureaucrat. "Let's play politics," Wilkes suggested. "Let's let Gail know who's involved."

"With political pressure, we can play Federal Acquisition Requirements and the bureaucracy," Kimbrough agreed, according to the handwritten minutes of the meeting. "We can be bastards. Let's let them know that this is a project with a lot of oversight."[3]

The political pressure came into play not long afterwards.

On September 9, 1998, MCSI handed Cotten a series of invoices for $3.5 million, covering goods that ADCS had allegedly purchased or services it provided. Cotten went through the invoices line by line, checking out the prices that Wilkes was listing versus the guidelines that the General Services Administration (GSA) recommended for governmental purchases. Two-thirds of the prices were above the GSA guidelines. In fact, Wilkes was often billing the government more than twice as much as the GSA suggested. For example, under the GSA guidelines, a set of six mini-tables that Wilkes billed at $3,498 should have cost only $1,644. A CD server that Wilkes invoiced at $18,452 was valued by the GSA at $8,772. Cotten calculated that the overages on Wilkes's invoice totaled $1 million. What's more, ADCS did not provide the government with documentation to show why the equipment was so pricey—or whether the prices being quoted were the actual prices that ADCS was paying.[4]

In addition, MCSI submitted bills for work that ADCS had allegedly performed at Redstone, Lakehurst, and other domestic U.S. sites. Cotten knew that no work had been performed in Redstone and Lakehurst, and there was no evidence that ADCS had done any work in Alabama or Maine either. She notified Kimbrough and Wilkes that she could not pay those bills.

Unhappy with his reception from Cotten, Cunningham started placing calls to other officials involved in the project. Paul Behrens, who had recently taken Ann Barnes's post as the Pentagon overseer of the Panama project, got one call at his office in the Redstone Arsenal, near Huntsville, and another during a visit to the Canal Zone.[5]

"Veterans Affairs is refusing to sign invoices on this project," Cunningham fumed. "It's up to the Defense Department to keep this moving forward."

In Washington, Wilkes invited Behrens to the ADCS suite at the Watergate Hotel. When Behrens showed up, Wilkes had a cell phone in his hand. "I'm going to be getting a call from Congressman Cunningham soon, and he's going to want to talk to you," Wilkes said. Sure enough, the phone rang. It was Cunningham, calling to repeat his message: Pay the invoice.

At roughly the same time, Wilkes handed Pentagon logistics official Gary Jones half a dozen invoices totaling as much as $750,000 for scanning work that had supposedly been completed in Panama and San Diego. But Jones determined that Wilkes had not performed the work. He thought the bills were fraudulent. When he told Wilkes what he thought, Wilkes withdrew the invoices. Soon afterward, Jones got a phone call from Cunningham.[6]

"I've heard from Brent Wilkes that there was some problem with the paying of bills," the congressman said. Jones came back with a snappy reply: "I think we've uncovered about $750,000 in fraudulent invoices to the government."

Cunningham's voice turned icy after Jones mentioned the word "fraud." Without bothering to ask for details, Cunningham blurted out an awkward goodbye; he added: "Tell me if you ever need anything." He then called Jones's supervisor, Lou Kratz, an assistant undersecretary of defense for logistics architecture, to berate him over how Wilkes was being treated. Kratz would later say that he had never experienced anything close to the "meddling" and "arrogance" that he encountered from Cunningham and Wilkes as they fought to get funding for the project. Gail Cotten was being pummeled so badly that Marion Porter, MCSI's vice president of operations, wrote to apologize.

"Brent has been complaining about what he feels is our apparent inability to effectively manage this project—I translate this to mean 'rollover' to his political cronies," Porter wrote. "I assured him that you were doing your job as we were trying to do ours. At any rate, I don't know what Wilkes may be trying to accomplish, but do not put anything past him. I am so sorry that this thing has turned into such a mess and wish I had never been asked to facilitate the whole thing, much less bring it to you."

"Marion, you'll never be as sorry as I am," Cotten replied. "If this goes bad, my entire career is on the line. I didn't deserve this."

During this first go-round, Cotten and Behrens stuck by their guns. Cotten took Wilkes's $2.9 million invoice for equipment and whittled it down to $1.9 million. But this was only the first battle in what would prove to be a long-running war over Wilkes's billing.

Meanwhile in Panama, ADCS workers were combing through military warehouses in search of documents to digitize. Wilkes and a handful of associates coordinated the operation, but much of the actual work was done by military wives, who preferred to make from $10 to $15 an hour preparing and scanning documents than to sit at home waiting for their husbands to return.

Wilkes and his crew went to painstaking lengths to convert century-old drawings and photographs into electronic format. "We've scanned images such as the first craft to sail through the Panama Canal and hand drawings from Ferdinand de Lesseps, the original designer of the Panama Canal and builder of the Suez Canal," Wilkes boasted. "These objects are tangible pieces of history and ADCS is honored to be the ones to preserve them for generations to come."

However valuable the documents might have been for the National Archives, which is where the scanned images were going, they had no military value. A simple computer scan could have preserved them for posterity, much more cheaply than the state-of-the-art technology of ADCS. Instead, Wilkes used his most expensive piece of equipment—a "ruggedized" scanner developed for the battlefield. His processing fee rose from $3 per page, which the government initially intended to spend, to $4.07 per page. And that didn't include the fees that Wilkes was charging for document preservation.

"They would bring down a document from an attic where pigeons were shitting on it and before they scanned it, they would take the same kind of steps that the Smithsonian would do to clean, preserve, or protect it," recalls one military official who worked on the project. "They could charge $500 to protect a document until it was photographed and then it would go back up to the attic where the pigeons would shit on it."

Pentagon officials stress that ADCS was processing plenty of valuable documents: blueprints of power stations, canal mechanisms, military fortifications, government buildings. But people close to the project say that Wilkes was also processing tens of thousands—or perhaps hundreds of thousands—of pages that did not need to be digitized. And at $4.07 per page, that came out to a hefty sum.

Flush with cash from the Panama project, Wilkes lived large whenever he visited the Canal Zone, occupying a plush suite in an upscale hotel downtown. At the local casinos, where low-ranking U.S. military officers and government employees played blackjack for a couple bucks a hand, Wilkes, armed with hundreds of dollars, would make a grand entrance; when he sat down at the table and flashed his wads of cash, the stakes at blackjack would rise to $200 or $300 per hand. And then, after a short appearance, he would disappear, heading, it was believed, to the nearest strip joint.

Still, Wilkes continually complained that ADCS was not making enough money on the Panama project. He said Rollie Kimbrough owed ADCS at least $970,000 for the work that it had done. Kimbrough, in turn, accused Wilkes of failing to give him enough information to determine how much money ADCS was owed.

The issue came to a head in December 1998, when ADCS and MCSI executives met with government officials in Panama. During a raucous encounter, Wilkes suggested that the government should remove MCSI as the prime contractor if it didn't give him the money he was owed. But Kimbrough claimed Wilkes was merely looking for an excuse to squeeze him out of the contract so that ADCS could be the main contractor and pocket all the profit.

"You don't know shit about government contracting," Kimbrough railed.

Over the next two months, Wilkes and his lieutenant, Michael Williams, repeatedly asked Gail Cotten to remove MCSI from the job and let ADCS take over as prime contractor. A bureaucratic mechanism known as a "termination of convenience" could let the government break the contract without incurring legal liability. But Cotten said she could not terminate the contract without MCSI's consent.

Wilkes joked that there were other ways of taking care of the contract dispute. "People disappear all the time in Panama and never make it back home," he told one of the government officials working on the case.[7] But things never got that far. Instead, Wilkes's congressional contacts came into play. On February 17, 1999, Cunningham told his staffers to call Paul Behrens to press for more support for ADCS. And on February 24, Wilkes and Bill Lowery went to Capitol Hill to meet Jeff Shockey. After eight years working on Capitol Hill, Shockey was in his final months at Jerry Lewis's office. He soon would join Bill Lowery's lobbying firm for earnings that would rise to $1.5 million per year—roughly ten times his paycheck on Capitol Hill. Not surprisingly, he was quite interested in everything that a potential employer and his client had to say. Wilkes told Shockey that MCSI and the government owed him a total of $1.3 million. He singled out Gail Cotten and Gary Jones for not doing more to help him obtain the money.

"The entire project is in jeopardy of failure due to the imminent shutdown that will occur if this situation is not remedied," he complained. "I respectfully ask that your office request that the Veterans Administration issue a termination of convenience, without cost, to MCSI Inc."

Wilkes gave Gail Cotten's phone number to Shockey so that he could call her directly. Instead, Shockey contacted Paul Behrens, who then asked Cotten to "request immediate action" to terminate MCSI's contract. By March 5, MCSI was out of the picture; by June 18, ADCS was officially named prime contractor. Now that Wilkes was a prime contractor, he wanted to vie for work directly from the Pentagon.

Thanks to deft appropriations work by Randy Cunningham and Duncan Hunter, among others, the military had $40 million to fund document-conversion programs in fiscal 1999. The Pentagon had just conducted an exhaustive review of the best ways of using its funding of document conversion. After a year's worth of visits to military bases around the country, the Pentagon had come up with a list of top priority sites, formulating a proposal to digitize engineering plans and blueprints at the Army Aviation and Missile Command, the Oklahoma City Air Logistics Center, and the Pacific Air Forces Base Command.[8]

But Wilkes had other ideas for the money. Using the equipment and technology he had acquired in the Panama project, Wilkes pushed for the creation of a National Ground Intelligence Center, in which he and Mitchell Wade would provide much of the technology. Although Wilkes would continue to work in Panama, even after the Canal Zone was turned over, the bulk of the work would be done in the Washington, D.C., area.

In his office at the Pentagon, Lou Kratz resisted the idea, arguing there were more pressing needs elsewhere. But Randy Cunningham quickly swung into action, egged on by Wilkes. On July 6, 1999, Wilkes sent Cunningham a list of "talking points" for how to deal with Kratz.

"Lou . . . we need $10 million immediately," read the script that Wilkes gave Cunningham. "If necessary, take money out of [another program]. . . . This is very important, and if you can't help others will be calling elsewhere, i.e., Duncan Hunter and Jerry Lewis."

Cunningham called Kratz on July 19, stressing that he wanted more money for ADCS. Four days later, Wilkes asked one of his employees to buy another Sea-Doo Speedster jet boat costing $14,497 for Cunningham's personal use. On September 9, Cunningham and his legislative director met personally with Kratz, asking him to divert $4.7 million in funds to ADCS. Four days later, Wilkes bought an inflatable jet dock for Cunningham's use for $7,101.

Hunter was already putting pressure on Kratz because he wanted $4 million in funding for Tom Casey's bankrupt Audre Inc. In the meantime, Cunningham urged Behrens to pay all of Wilkes's invoices, even though Cotton had not verified that the work had been performed.[9] (Casey got the money, but it wasn't enough. Audre shut down in 2003.)

Faced with strong political pressure from key members of the Appropriations Committee and the Armed Services Committee, Kratz felt he had no choice but to accede to their wishes, delaying the Air Force and Missile Command projects.

"All is not well in the world of automated document conversion services," Kratz's deputy, Gary Jones, wrote to Gail Cotten on September 28, 1999. "We had Congressman Cunningham come down very heavy on the program and force us to withdraw money from one of my projects and send it to ADCS Inc., indirectly of course."

"My 'gut instinct' still says that this whole affair is bad news," Cotten responded. "I'm sorry you had to 'give' them more money. It's that kind of congressional interference that really turns my stomach."

John Karpovich, who helped run the document conversion program at the Defense Department, said Wilkes infuriated Pentagon staff by claiming that the document conversion money belonged to him. "Brent came in and said, 'That's our money,'" Karpovich recalled. "He said, 'The congressmen put the money in there for us.'"

Upset about the congressional interference in his duties, Kratz asked the inspector general of the Defense Department to launch an investigation. Cunningham was irate. On March 23, 2000, he told the secretary of the Army that Kratz should be fired, since the Defense Department was not releasing funds that had been authorized to one of his constituents, that is, ADCS. (Kratz was not the only Pentagon official whose job was threatened for standing up to Cunningham's support of Wilkes. A year later, Cunningham called for the firing of Cheryl Roby, a deputy assistant secretary of defense, when she balked at providing funds for ADCS.)

But Kratz was vindicated in June 2000, when the Pentagon's inspector general reported that several important projects had lost funding because "two congressmen" (apparently Cunningham and Lewis) had pressured defense officials to shift the money to Panama, and "one congressman," Hunter, had pushed for funding for projects for Audre. The shift in funding was causing some military officers to "lose confidence in the fairness of the selection process," the inspector general reported.

By that time, the influx of money from Panama, which was by far ADCS's biggest project, had helped fund a heady lifestyle for Wilkes and his associates.

The Department of Defense opened an investigation of the ADCS contracts in 2000 and even told federal prosecutors in San Diego of their concerns. But the investigation was quickly called off, since the allegedly fraudulent invoices had either been withdrawn by Wilkes or trimmed of their excess by Cotten and her colleagues. "Essentially, it appeared to be a case of 'no harm, no foul,'" said one source close to the prosecutors. On the other hand, there is no guarantee that there was "no harm." The Veterans Affairs Department pulled back on its intense scrutiny of the Panama contract in early 2000, giving Wilkes a freer rein in order to ensure the continuity of the project after MCSI was removed as a prime contractor.

chapter ten

LIVING LARGE

IN THE MOUNTAINOUS WILDERNESS OF WESTERN IDAHO IN AUGUST 2002, a safari of four-wheeled all-terrain vehicles rumbled through a dense forest of pines, chewing up a narrow dirt trail that led between rocks and trees. Brent Wilkes was near the lead. Somewhere behind him was Duke Cunningham, doing his best to keep his four-wheeler under control.

The former fighter pilot was having a tough time managing his ATV, which looked like a squat four-wheel motorcycle. Of course, at the age of sixty-one, he was not in the same shape that he had been as a pilot. With his weight now pushing 265 pounds, keeping up with the younger, leaner men surrounding Wilkes was a chore.

Over the past several years, Wilkes had become a regular at the Coeur d'Alene Resort, a posh hotel in the foothills of the Rockies where politicians, business executives, and movie stars often retreat for a quiet getaway. Wilkes shelled out $2,500 a night to stay at the resort's premier penthouse suite, which was equipped with an indoor swimming pool and a Jacuzzi on the balcony overlooking Lake Coeur d'Alene.

At least once a year, typically in summer or fall, Wilkes would show up at the resort with an entourage of about a dozen family members and ADCS executives—there was quite a bit of overlap between the two groups. They would dine at the resort's priciest restaurant, Beverley's, where a meal for the group and wine from the well-stocked cellar could easily hit several thousand dollars. After dinner, the men would adjourn to the smoking parlor down the hall, a rustic wood-paneled chamber decorated with the stuffed heads of woodland creatures, where they would puff on cigars.

During the day, Wilkes might play a round on the resort's exclusive golf course, famed for having the world's only moveable "floating hole"—a manmade floating island that golfers boat to in a special "Putter Boat Shuttle" in order to complete the 175-yard, par three, 14th hole. But Wilkes preferred more macho pursuits, such as jet-skiing, hunting, fly-fishing, and tooling through the woods on ATVs.

Wilkes flew Cunningham to Idaho at least twice. In August 2001, Wilkes paid several thousand dollars for Cunningham's food and lodging at the Coeur d'Alene resort as well as paying for golf equipment rentals and a session on the firing range with a fully automatic machine gun. In 2002, he spent at least $34,000 bringing Cunningham and several ADCS employees to Coeur d'Alene on a three-day excursion.[1] Cunningham's expense records do not show that he paid a dime during the trip. Wilkes's chuck wagon was at it again, doling out favors to one of his best friends in Congress. Like a good cowboy, Cunningham was enjoying the ride—until the ATV jaunt, that is.

As the four-wheelers twisted and turned along the winding path, Cunningham had a tough time keeping up. And then, suddenly, on one sharp curve, he lost control. The ATV skidded down an embankment, crashed through a thicket, and pinned the congressman against a tree. "I almost died," he later said.

As it turned out, Cunningham survived with some serious scrapes and bruises. Because of his injuries, he missed a golf game that he was supposed to play that afternoon with Senator Larry Craig—another beneficiary of Wilkes's copious donations—but he was well enough to attend a fund-raising dinner for Craig that evening.

Of course, Cunningham had done some serious damage to the ATV, but Wilkes took it in stride. Flush with cash from federal contracts, he didn't mind incurring a few expenses if it meant keeping his congressman happy.

That wouldn't have been the case, though, before Wilkes landed the Panama contract. Before then, he had nowhere near enough money to take care of damaged ATVs and wounded congressmen, much less enjoy a penthouse lifestyle. But the influx of money from Panama had an immediate impact on Wilkes's lifestyle. In June 1999, the month Wilkes became its prime contractor, he moved his family out of the house they had been renting and bought a $1.4 million mansion in a gated community in Poway, an affluent inland suburb of San Diego. Wilkes's home had once been owned by former San Diego Chargers quarterback Stan Humphries. He also maintained a three-bedroom hospitality suite at the Westin Grand, so that he could entertain congressmen and senators.

The most fabulous of all Wilkes's properties, about ten minutes' drive from Wilkes's home in Poway, was ADCS's new headquarters, an $11 million, ninety-four-thousand-square-foot monument of polished limestone, blue-tinted glass, and stainless steel. At its height, the company had around a hundred employees in the building, although there was room for many more. Visitors entered through a spacious two-story lobby that featured a gleaming black granite floor. Receptionists—usually young women in their twenties—sat behind a custom-built desk of cherry wood; the wall behind them was made of large smoked-glass panels.

To the right of the lobby stood the W Pavilion ("W" as in Wilkes), a glass-enclosed meeting hall wide enough to seat 450 people at banquet tables and tall enough to host the aerial acrobatics of Cirque du Soleil, which once performed for Regina Wilkes's birthday. A ten-foot-tall, twenty-foot-wide panel of twelve video projection screens, flanked by state-of-the-art speakers, dominated one wall of the room. Overlooking the pavilion stood a karaoke balcony supported by limestone columns. Adjoining the pavilion was a two-thousand-square-foot fully stocked commercial kitchen—bigger than the typical four-bedroom house—as well as a cafeteria, a lounge, and a game room. And there was a theater equipped with a hundred plush seats, a surround-sound speaker system, and a bar.

Steel-railed stairs led from the lobby to the second floor, where Wilkes's executive team worked. The centerpiece of the second floor was a huge sandbox lined with customized surfboards. The executive conference room was walled by floor-to-ceiling windows that could cloud over at the push of a button to ensure complete privacy. And then there was Wilkes's office itself, which featured a private kitchen, a restroom, an elevator, a pool table, and a fireplace. Employees referred to the opulent building as "the palace."

When politicians visited Wilkes's palace, as they often did, Wilkes would line up attractive female employees to greet them. "When he used to line us up, we would joke that it was the pimp and all his girls," recalls one former worker. This is not to say that the women were doling out sexual favors. They were typically very hard workers, although some former employees concede that they were probably hired more for their looks than for their skills.

"He would always invite us to parties," one worker recalls. "I had my own private life and didn't always want to go. One time, I thought it would be the perfect excuse to tell him I didn't have anything to wear. Instead, he said, 'We'll go shopping and write it off on the company credit card.' He'd dress us up in gowns and jewelry."

To Wilkes, the women were another symbol of his growing wealth and influence, just like his fancy home, palatial headquarters, and fleet of jet-black cars, which included a Hummer, a Range Rover, and a Jaguar, as well as a BMW for his wife. To members of his coterie, Wilkes left no mystery about the source of his wealth. "I'm not in the business of converting documents. I'm in the business of printing money. All of this is about printing money," a former associate quotes Wilkes as saying. Wilkes denies that he made such a statement. But there is no denying the message of the vanity license plate on his jet-black Hummer: "MIPR ME." MIPR stands for "military interdepartmental purchase requests," the forms the Pentagon uses to pay for contracts. None of the other cars in Wilkes's brand-new fleet bore such naked homage to the power of taxpayers' dollars, but the message was there nonetheless.

Wilkes, who liked to break into Broadway show tunes when he was happy, was almost giddy with the amount of government cash flowing into his company. "The Lord loves a workin' man!" he would shout—quoting Steve Martin in *The Jerk*—when he got a bit of good news on a government contract. Or he would smile, punch the air, and yell, "Boom-shaka-laka," the chorus from the 1960s rock anthem "I Wanna Take You Higher." Another favorite was Austin Powers's "Yeah, baby," which he'd deliver with a faux mod accent.

Wilkes made sure that Randy Cunningham shared some of the benefits of his largesse. Between 1995 and 2005, Wilkes and his family and associates donated $115,000 to Cunningham's campaign and political action committee. On October 5, 2002, shortly before the trip to Idaho, Wilkes spent $36,000 on a lavish banquet—"A Tribute to Heroes"—honoring Cunningham and several veterans in the Aerospace Museum in San Diego's Balboa Park. Wilkes and Cunningham wore matching tuxedos and cummerbunds to the event; as they wandered through the museum, in the shadow of fighter jets like the ones that Cunningham had flown in Vietnam, they looked almost like brothers.

Wilkes went to great lengths to keep Cunningham happy, showering him with gifts such as a personal computer, a computer desk, tickets to a Jimmy Buffett concert, skybox tickets to the 2003 Super Bowl, and a GPS navigational system for his yacht. Some of the most lavish gifts were the vacations that Cunningham took using Wilkes's corporate jets.

ADCS's government contracts had brought in enough money for Wilkes to lease a tiny fleet of Lear jets and Gulfstreams. He didn't own the jets outright. Instead, he participated in time-sharing arrangements with other owners. But that was enough to conduct his business as well as ferry around friendly legislators. Meals on the jets included fine wines, platters of seafood, and filet mignon. Besides Cunningham, the passengers included House Speaker Dennis Hastert and Majority Leader Tom DeLay and other influential congressmen.

Cunningham was the most frequent flyer. Wilkes flew Cunningham to a boat show in Las Vegas; a round of golf in Palm Springs; a scuba-diving jaunt in Key West; and the trips to Coeur d'Alene.

Wilkes also took Cunningham on at least two trips to Hawaii, a favorite haunt to which he took his ADCS entourage at least once a year. They would stay at spots like the King Kamehamea Suite at the Royal Hawaiian Hotel at Waikiki or the seven-bedroom beachfront mansion of the late hair-styling mogul Paul Mitchell, which rents at close to $50,000 per week. Cunningham's trips included high-priced prostitutes.[2]

In mid-August 2003, Wilkes treated Cunningham to a three-day stay at the Hapuna Suite in the Hapuna Beach Prince Hotel on the big island of Hawaii. The Hapuna Suite, which rents for $6,600 per night, is an eight-thousand-square-foot villa with four bedrooms, each with a private bath and lanai. A staff of round-the-clock personal attendants caters to the occupants' every need.

On the evening of August 15, Wilkes dispatched one of his employees to find two prostitutes for the evening. As they waited for the prostitutes, Wilkes, Cunningham, and several friends had a catered dinner on the suite's private lawn, featuring gyozas stuffed with Kona lobster, shrimp, scallops, seared Hawaiian snapper, and Manoa lettuce leaves.[3]

At 11:00 P.M., a driver showed up with two prostitutes. By that time, Wilkes and Cunningham were nearly alone. Wilkes told his employee to pay the driver $600 for two hours' worth of the prostitutes' services. After a short conversation, Wilkes and Cunningham escorted the women to separate bedrooms upstairs. At about midnight, Wilkes tipped his prostitute $500 for her services, even though they'd spent only forty-five minutes of the two hours he'd paid for. There's no word about whether Cunningham gave a tip. But he apparently was not very happy with his service. According to prosecutors, Cunningham asked Wilkes to find a different prostitute for him the next night. Wilkes obliged.

"It was a frat party with taxpayer money," said Kenneth J. Hines, head of the Internal Revenue Service's criminal investigation arm in San Diego.[4]

Sources close to the corruption case allege that Wilkes arranged for rendezvous between Cunningham and a particular prostitute in Washington at his suite in the Watergate Hotel, with transportation provided by Shirlington Limousine and Transportation Inc., which had been providing services for Wilkes since the mid-1990s. Cunningham unquestionably developed an affinity for the limousine service. In 2004, he helped Shirlington win a $21 million contract with the Department of Homeland Security, noting that the president of the company, Christopher Baker, "has been completely dedicated to his work and has been of service to me and other members of Congress over the years."

Wilkes denies any allegations regarding prostitutes in the Watergate. But a former business associate of Wilkes says that he was present in the Watergate suite twice when Baker brought prostitutes there, although Cunningham wasn't present either time. Shirlington's lawyer, Bobby S. Stafford, confirms that Baker "provided limousine services for Mr. Wilkes for whatever entertainment he had in the Watergate." But Stafford stresses that Baker was "never in attendance in any party . . . where any women were being used for prostitution purposes."

Later, rumors floated in Washington that up to six current or former congressmen—four Republicans and two Democrats—may have had liaisons with hookers in the Watergate. But there has never been any substantiation of the rumors, and at least two of the legislators have privately denied the rumors.

Regardless of whether the rumors were true, the fact is that Wilkes went out of his way to befriend legislators. Between 1995 and 2003, Wilkes and his family and associates contributed more than $630,000 to congressional campaigns, largely targeting the House Armed Services Committee and the defense subcommittee of the House Appropriations Committee. He invited congressmen and young women to parties on board boats that would cruise the Potomac. He shelled out copious amounts of cash just to play golf with legislators, including a three-day, multi-city tournament with Tom DeLay that hopped from Torrey Pines Golf Club in San Diego to the

Bighorn Country Club near Palm Springs to the Riviera Country Club in Pacific Palisades.

Using money that came from his defense contracts, Wilkes spent up to thirty weeks a year in Washington wooing the legislators and procurement officers responsible for getting him those contracts. The more clout a legislator wielded over the budget at the Pentagon, the more donations he got. Wilkes's efforts paid off. Senator Larry Craig of Idaho helped Wilkes get an earmark for $3 million, two days after taking in $43,500 in contributions from Wilkes and his crew at the fund-raiser that Cunningham attended. Rep. George Nethercutt of Washington—another member of the House Appropriations Committee—helped Wilkes get a $1 million earmark for a naval communications system after Wilkes paid $80,000 for lobbying activities by Nethercutt's former chief of staff.

Rep. John Doolittle of Sacramento helped Wilkes get an earmark for a military sound wave technology after taking contributions from Wilkes and a handful of select associates through a fund-raiser at ADCS's headquarters. After dining on Applewood smoked bacon-wrapped filet and truffle mashed potatoes prepared in the building's expansive kitchen, the group settled down to watch a screening of *Terminator 3,* Arnold Schwarzenegger's most recent movie. Doolittle's wife—and campaign manager—claimed 15 percent of the donations as her commission, sending more than $14,000 of the $118,000 that Wilkes and his associates contributed to the Doolittle campaign over the years directly into the Doolittles' personal coffers.

Wilkes's political ties extended beyond the halls of Congress. In California, Wilkes was also a heavy contributor; he made hefty contributions to municipal, county, and state officials—especially Governor Arnold Schwarzenegger. Wilkes and his wife gave Schwarzenegger $42,200 during his 2003 campaign to recall and replace Governor Gray Davis. Once he was elected, a grateful Schwarzenegger appointed Wilkes to a board overseeing the state's racetracks.

"He was just on a power trip," said Steve Caira, the former chief executive of TomaHawk II, a document conversion company that both competed and cooperated with ADCS. "You would be at a party, and he would come out and say he paid this guy so-and-so, if you throw enough money at him you will get your share back."[5] Wilkes denied making those comments.

One of Wilkes's most valuable contacts was his old friend Dusty Foggo, who had risen up the ranks of the CIA. In the early 2000s, Foggo was based at the CIA station in Frankfurt, where he oversaw the agency's expenditures in Europe and the Middle East—including Iraq. But in the aftermath of the terrorist attacks of September 11, 2001, Foggo was repeatedly called for consultation in the Washington area, which gave him a chance to spend quality time with Wilkes.

At night, Foggo and Wilkes dined at the Capital Grille, journeyed to the Camelot strip club, or played poker at the Watergate with such people as Duke Cunningham and Brant "Nine Fingers" Bassett, who was then working as a staffer on the House Intelligence Committee. By day, Foggo and Bassett made inroads into the committee, on which Cunningham sat. The two provided government trinkets to committee members and staffers, such as a carpet emblazoned with the words "War on Terror," as they pushed for initiatives related to the management of the CIA. Foggo became particularly friendly with Rep. Porter Goss of Florida, a former CIA operative who chaired the committee. That friendship would serve him well when Goss was appointed to head the CIA.

When the Iraq War began in the spring of 2003, Wilkes was ecstatic. "He and some of his top executives were really gung-ho about the war," one former employee recalls. "Brent said this would create new opportunities for the company. He was really excited about doing business in the Middle East." And Foggo was the person who could help him get the business.

"I am now, have been in the past and will continue to as long as I breath[e] be your partner," Foggo wrote Wilkes during his tenure in Frankfurt. "So what do you want me to do?"[6]

In August 2003, Wilkes took Foggo and his family on an all-expenses-paid vacation to Scotland, including $12,000 in jet flights, $4,000 for a helicopter ride to a round of golf, and $44,000 for a stay in the Pitcastle estate in Scotland.[7] Wilkes and Foggo went trout fish-ing and skeet shooting together, puffed on fine cigars, and talked about CIA operations in Iraq, including the fact that money could be made by supplying bottled water and other provisions to CIA opera-tives stationed in the war zone. At the time, CIA operatives in Iraq were relying on contractors in Kuwait and other friendly countries to supply them with water. But Foggo had found a cheaper supplier. If Wilkes could act as a middleman between that supplier and the CIA, he could jack up the price and make a healthy profit.

Shortly after their return, Foggo sent Wilkes an e-mail message titled "Scotland and Cigars." In the e-mail, Foggo assured Wilkes: "I'll work this water thing. . . . Group W [Wilkes's holding company] is in this deal."[8] In his Poway headquarters, Wilkes placed an array of wa-ter bottles on his desk and boasted to visitors: "It looks like we're in the water business now."

By this time, a number of people within the CIA knew of Wilkes and Foggo's friendship. So Wilkes set up a separate company, which would eventually be called Archer Logistics, headed by his nephew and lobbyist Joel Combs. Foggo coached Combs on how to deal with CIA contracting officers.

"I would like the 'President' or 'CEO' of ['Archer'] to come visit," Foggo wrote Combs in January 2004. "Brent told me that was you (smile), so let's get to it. I'll need to brief you a bit on how you need to play this, but that needs to be face-to-face, before you meet my people."[9]

Foggo told Combs not to tell any CIA officials about his familial relationship with Wilkes. If anyone asked, Combs was supposed to say that he and Foggo had met in a cigar bar in Washington.[10] In Sep-tember 2004—after going through bureaucratic hoops—Combs landed a $1.7 million contract from the CIA. Some CIA operatives in Iraq balked at having to pay Group W for supplies. At least one operative in Baghdad complained to higher-ups, noting that the sup-plies could easily be purchased off the shelf.[11] CIA operatives in northern Iraq had been buying drinking water from a bottling plant there even when Saddam Hussein was in power. Wilkes's water had a 60 percent markup over his purchase price.[12]

By October, the most powerful higher-up that the Iraqi operatives could complain to was Foggo himself, since he had been appointed executive director, the agency's third-highest position slot, by Porter Goss.

Foggo did not intend to oversee the CIA's activities for long. Shortly after his appointment, he wrote to a banker that he expected to retire within three years, since he had "a big offer from a company in California." Wilkes had set aside an office for Foggo in his Poway headquarters and he began introducing Foggo as a future ADCS executive. According to one well-placed source, Wilkes offered Foggo the chance of heading the operations of the entire company.

In the meantime, Wilkes's most important relationship continued to be with Cunningham. Foggo, after all, had gotten him only a single contract worth a couple million dollars. Cunningham oversaw contracts worth tens of millions of dollars.

chapter eleven

THOUGHTS BY A LAVA LAMP

LIKE ALMOST EVERYBODY ELSE WHO WORKED ON CAPITOL HILL, THE TWO women thought they knew Randy Cunningham pretty well when they bumped into him at the restaurant on a chilly November night in 1997. His reputation after six years in office was captured by his "Duke" nickname. Even after all these years, he was a man people still thought of in uniform, not surprising for a politician who gave strangers and well-wishers glossy photographs of himself much younger and clad in his aviator's flight suit with its antigravity leggings, steel-toed flight boots, oxygen mask, and harness.

But especially after an evening at the restaurant hearing some of these war stories, the women were ill-prepared for what they saw when they accepted the congressman's invitation to drive over to his river yacht for a nightcap.

There, standing before them when they boarded the boat, was a fifty-five-year-old man with thinning and graying hair and a substantial paunch that made it almost impossible to recall the strapping Top Gun pilot of three decades earlier. There he stood, on an ivory shag carpet, wearing plaid pajama bottoms and a red turtleneck. The women couldn't help noticing that the only illumination inside the boat came from candles and lava lamps.

One of the women later confessed that it was all she could do to restrain her laughter at the sight of the aging congressman. The scene was unquestionably surreal as the women settled in to help Cunningham polish off the chilled champagne.

For those who lived near the *Kelly C,* this was just one more party hosted by the fun-loving and gregarious Duke. To them, Cunningham had what seemed to be a never-ending party aboard the sixty-five-foot flat-bottom riverboat moored along the seawall in Slip B-24 of the Gangplank Marina on the Potomac River.

Cunningham, of course, was not alone in preferring life on a boat when in Washington. In fact, he was part of the congressional sea caucus, a loosely knit, bipartisan group of congressmen who made the D.C. waterfront their home while in Washington. It is a group that at various times included Ohio Reps. James Traficant Jr. and Robert Ney—both of whom, like Cunningham, were eventually forced to make the transition from Congress to prison. Others in the caucus were Gene Taylor of Mississippi, Sonny Callahan of Alabama, and Gary Ackerman of New York.

To some, it was a cheaper alternative than paying rent in the high-priced Washington market. To Cunningham, it was vastly superior to what he saw some of his colleagues do for housing when away from their families. Some congressmen get roommates and share small apartments; some take semipermanent hotel suites; some even sleep on cots in their offices. Most do not uproot their families from schools and jobs if only to avoid a pummeling in the local press for not really living in their districts. But the result is a lonely existence that some members fill with nonstop work and others fill with heavy drinking, constant parties, and plenty of mischief.

Cunningham spent the long, lonely hours away from his family making mischief in restaurants such as the nearby Capital Grille and then aboard his river yacht with its view of the Washington Monument and the Jefferson Memorial.

Located at Sixth and Pennsylvania Avenue, the Capital Grille was blessed with perfect timing and an opportune location beneath the nighttime glow of the Capitol building. The owners had gambled $3 million that Washington was ready for a throwback to the restaurants and bars that thrived in the 1950s, the kind whose large martinis, thick steaks, and unadulterated cholesterol were once a magnet for politicians and lobbyists. Then they lucked out—opening their doors (with $100,000 of free food and drinks for invited members of Congress) only one week after the Republicans in 1994 swept back into power by reclaiming both the House and the Senate and making Newt Gingrich suddenly the most important Republican in town. Gingrich wasted no time signaling to one and all that his new favorite restaurant was the Capital Grille. It was a message that Duke Cunningham took to heart.

Now, three years later, they knew Cunningham well at the Grille. He was a congressman; he was a war hero; he was a Republican; and he was a frequent diner. Not, of course, on his own dime. That, after all, is what lobbyists were for. In years to come, he would become such a fixture at the Capital Grille that he had his own private wine locker, though it was never clear whether he stocked it himself or benefited from the generosity of others. Wilkes and Foggo also shared a wine locker, even when Foggo was the number three official of the CIA and Wilkes was making his money from intelligence contracts.

On this November night, Harold "Hal" Ezell walked into the happy club with its long, curved bar and brass fixtures. He was soon joined by two young women active in immigration battles. Ezell was an old pal of Cunningham, a Republican soul mate and ally in past conservative battles. Like Cunningham, he had often been accused of getting himself into trouble with inflammatory rhetoric. A former western regional commissioner for the Immigration and Naturalization Service, he was now a hero to conservatives and to those unhappy with the flood of illegal immigrants into the United States. In 1994, he was one of the two key authors of Proposition 187, the still-controversial California ballot measure that excluded illegal immigrants from public education, nonemergency health care, and such social programs as welfare. The proposition passed with an overwhelming 60 percent of the vote, though the courts promptly struck it down as unconstitutional. A decade earlier, Ezell had said that illegals should be "caught, skinned, and fried."

So Ezell was Duke Cunningham's kind of guy. And when Ezell was named to the U.S. Commission on Immigration Reform, Cunningham arranged for a special meeting of the House Committee on Economic and Educational Opportunities. The meeting, in February 1996, was held three thousand miles away from Washington, in San Diego. Ezell was the star witness.

Now, less than two years later, Ezell was promptly waved over to Cunningham's table at the Grille. The only drawback for Cunningham was that Ezell, an old friend, had already heard all his stock war-hero stories. But the two women—who asked not to be named because they still work with other members of Congress—had not. They were fresh ears, more than ready to provide Cunningham the forum he craved.

By all accounts, the congressman from San Diego was delighted to have two attractive, right-minded Republican women as a ready audience for his war stories. As always, he was the star of his tales, the hero, the all-American boy triumphing over the communist enemy. And this night, he included the suggestion that he was the model for Tom Cruise's "Maverick" in *Top Gun*.

When Cunningham had finished his dinner and the women their drinks, Cunningham announced, with great enthusiasm and obvious pride, that it was just a short ride to the Gangplank, a 310-slip marina in Southwest Washington, where the *Kelly C* was moored. Ezell begged off because it was late. But the two women agreed to follow the congressman's directions to the boat. Of course, neither of the two young women was quite prepared for the reception Cunningham had waiting for them when they arrived about twenty minutes after the Duke had boarded his boat.

This was the Cunningham persona later scathingly referred to by his estranged wife as "Mr. Fun Ball."[1] The sight of Cunningham alongside the lava lamps was pathetic, but very funny to the women. But what the women remembered most sharply were the odd comments by the congressman who seemed to be struggling with some moral decisions. He confessed to them that he very much craved a more expensive yacht in the marina. It was something that he certainly could not afford on his $133,600 a year salary as a member of the House.

But he really wanted it, a desire he had shared with a defense contractor he did not name but who is believed to be Brent Wilkes. Duke had demurred when Wilkes had offered to buy him the yacht—reluctantly, he admitted, because it "might look bad." Faced with such a stout ethical stand, Cunningham said, the contractor had made a proposition—he would buy the yacht and then let Cunningham "rent" it at a minimal rate. Clearly, it was an idea with appeal to Cunningham. But, again, he said that it might not look good. So the idea was shelved.

Or so the women thought.

Almost a decade later, when Cunningham's corruption was revealed, they could not help but remember the spirited conversation that November night and the dark temptations Cunningham was struggling to resist. It was clear that the seeds of corruption had already been planted in Cunningham's mind. His resistance, so weakly stated that night, eventually would fade. In fact, the cracks in his stand had already appeared. What Cunningham hadn't mentioned over the champagne was that less than two months earlier he had helped insert $20 million into an appropriations bill to enrich none other than Wilkes and the company he had founded, ADCS Inc.

Seven years later, another lobbyist would buy that yacht for Cunningham, rename it the *Duke-Stir,* and allow him to live on it rent free.

All the neighbors knew he was a congressman and they couldn't help but know about his frequent parties. Sometimes, when he was alone, Cunningham would try to persuade other boat owners to join him. One morning, a resident of the Gangplank's B Dock watched with amusement as Cunningham, who apparently had been drinking, jumped into a dinghy and maneuvered the small boat to the stern of a neighboring houseboat. Then, while a steady rain soaked him, he loudly implored one of the residents—who just happened to be a very attractive but very married woman—to come out and join him for a little cruise.

Many of his neighbors were themselves pretty unconventional free spirits. But even they worried that Cunningham's failure to hide his antics might get him into trouble and thus bring unwanted attention to the marina. Their concern peaked in January 1999 when *Hustler* magazine publisher Larry Flynt, infuriated by the ongoing impeachment trial of President Bill Clinton, made a public offer of $1 million for information about sexual indiscretions by members of Congress. At the time, Cunningham was one of the more vocal Republicans demanding Clinton's conviction by the Senate. To shield Cunningham's partying from public view, a marina employee even recommended that Cunningham move farther out on the B Dock, away from the public seawall. But Cunningham demurred. He moved out to the end of a dock only when he got a slip a few hundred yards away at the Capital Yacht Club, which was somewhat more exclusive and had its own full-service bar.

The *Kelly C*—and eventually its replacement, the *Duke-Stir*—served as something of a riverfront club house for Cunningham and his lobbyist friends. One defense contractor, who didn't want to be identified because he is still in the contracting business, recalled what he described as Friday night fund-raisers aboard the *Kelly C*. Wilkes, he said, sometimes would round up a group of fellow contractors and lobbyists. He would hire attractive young hostesses for the occasion to serve shrimp and turn the heads of the older, male crowd. Sometimes Wilkes even provided the cash for the political donations made that night, although in the names of the partygoers, said the defense contractor, at the time the CEO of a company feasting on earmarks provided by Cunningham.

Wilkes even opened what he called "the *Kelly C* operating account" and directed one assistant to write checks on the account to keep Cunningham's boat fully stocked with hundred-dollar bottles of his favorite White Oaks wines. A second Wilkes assistant helped out, making sure that anything Cunningham wanted on the boat—

including a laptop computer—was there for him. The catering for some of the parties was handled by Blue Danube Corporate Support, a company operated by Brigitte Foggo, wife of the CIA staffer.

But even Wilkes drew a line on what he would do for the congressman. For one thing, Wilkes was totally disgusted by the hot tub Cunningham put on the boat's deck during the autumn and winter. What repelled Wilkes—and others invited to the parties—was both the water Cunningham put in the hot tub and the congressman's penchant for using it while naked, even if everybody else at the party was clothed. Cunningham used water siphoned directly from the polluted Potomac River and never changed it out during the season. "Wilkes thought it was unbelievably dirty and joked if you got in there that it would leave a dark water line on your chest," said one person familiar with the parties. "The water was so gross that very few people were willing to get into the hot tub other than Duke and his paramour." That was a reference to Cunningham most frequently seen girlfriend, a flight attendant who lived in Maryland.

One of these parties started at the Capital Grille with Cunningham ordering his usual filet mignon—very well done—with iceberg lettuce salad and White Oak. Wilkes used the dinner to update Cunningham on the appropriations he wanted. Cunningham then took the whole group back to the boat where they drank more wine, sitting on white leather sofas while Cunningham told more war stories. Cunningham then took his clothes off and invited all to join him in the polluted hot tub that was hidden from the neighbors by a white tarp. There were no takers.

Cunningham's only complaint about his life on the two boats was that the government of the District of Columbia did not do a great job of maintaining and improving the marinas. Too often, Cunningham compared the D.C. marinas with what he knew back home in San Diego. And he seethed.

But, as a member of the committee overseeing the District, Cunningham had an outlet for that anger. Once he'd gotten the hang of earmarking, he could—and did—use his congressional clout to force improvements in his "neighborhood." In October 1998, Cunningham used his position on the Appropriations subcommittee that oversees federal funding for Washington to earmark $3 million to clean up the docks and a floating fish market by the marina. He did it, he said, because he wanted to spruce up the nation's capital and make it a safer place; he said his effort had the imprimatur of the then-powerful Newt Gingrich.

"The Speaker said he wants to make D.C. a shining city, and so I said, 'OK . . . I want to clean up the waterfront' . . . not for Duke Cunningham. I haven't got a nickel invested," he said. "I walked down there and almost fell [off] the dock. It's dangerous. I looked and there was an electric wire that was bare, that was hanging very close to the water."[2]

Tenants of the marina and fish market wanted long-term leases from the city, which owns the waterfront. Cunningham pushed their cause in a speech on the floor of the House on September 25, 2001, during a debate over the 2002 appropriations bill for the District of Columbia. He blasted city officials for resisting the pleas from the tenants for long-term leases. Then—incredibly and out of the blue— he added a pretty serious accusation, stating, "The city council at that time was taking money under the table to support the leases." Neither Cunningham's staff nor researchers at the *Washington Post* could find any evidence to back up the claim.[3]

And Cunningham was not bashful about using his influence over D.C.'s purse strings to help out his family. At a 2003 D.C. Appropriations subcommittee hearing, Cunningham suggested to a witness making a funding pitch to the panel that he consider hiring the congressman's brother: "My brother was the president of the Chamber of Commerce in St. Peters, Missouri, right outside of St. Louis. He's looking for a job here in D.C., so if you've got an opening in the chamber, I'll give his résumé." The flustered witness replied: "It would be great, Mr. Chairman [sic]. We'd be glad to advance that."

chapter twelve

MEET MR. WADE

RON MCKEOWN HAD NEVER MET MITCHELL JOHN WADE. BUT, AS IT TURNS out, he could very well have been thinking about Wade when he tried to give some friendly advice to his old flying buddy Randy Cunningham. McKeown, who had long since forgiven Cunningham for his Navy Cross blunders, welcomed his friend to Washington when both spent part of the late 1970s at Pentagon posts. "I told him that in Washington you can't take friendship personally," said McKeown. "Some people act like they're your friend but only because they want something from you."

It is hard not to think of McKeown's warning when you read the anguish and shock in a 2006 letter Cunningham sent from prison to Marcus Stern, the reporter who brought him down. Looking back on the path that led him to prison, Cunningham—with his usual mangled spelling and syntax—said that "90% of what has happed [*sic*] is Wade. He showers you with gifts, he pretended to be my best friend for 16 years. Taking me to his wife's parents home many times. Taking Nancy & I to Sunday brunches with his wife, hunting together at his father in laws Eastern Shore place. Me taking him to a place where I hunt. When I was in town we were together."

Cunningham had known Wade only about six years when he wrote the letter—not sixteen. And his rage at Wade might have stemmed largely from Wade's decision to roll over on him with prosecutors. But Cunningham had committed a mortal sin in Washington—he had taken this "friendship" personally. He had refused to see where that friendship was leading him. He had failed to see what a toxic combination it had been when his own grand sense of entitlement met Mitch Wade's enormous greed.

Little is known about Wade's childhood. His parents are deceased and neither he nor his brother, Gregory, living in San Diego, has ever agreed to be interviewed by any of the reporters who swarmed all over the case after it broke in 2005. His sisters, Diane and Valerie, similarly have stayed out of public view. And those who were willing to talk about him confess they know little despite their close ties to him. Former MZM employees—even some who worked closely with him—have had to admit that they really didn't know this man who never—ever—talked about his past.

All that is known are the basics—his birth in the nation's capital on June 6, 1963; his graduation from Robert E. Lee High School in Springfield, Virginia, and the financial modesty of his early life. He grew up outside the great economic and social divide that separates nondescript middle-class suburbs like Springfield from the tonier Washington addresses Wade would inhabit in later years—Georgetown, DuPont Circle, and Kalorama Circle. He particularly favored Kalorama, one of Washington's most prestigious addresses with its historic Embassy Row mansions on the fringe of downtown Washington. Wade's stepping stone to the heart of the nation's capital was George Washington University, an urban campus near the State Department in Foggy Bottom. It was there that he received his degree in 1985.

After graduating, he went through a series of civilian jobs at the Pentagon: special agent, intelligence specialist, program analyst, then a program manager in the Office of Assistant Secretary Defense, Command, Control, Communications, Intelligence—known in military shorthand as ASD/C3I.

Richard Peze, who would later serve as executive vice president in Wade's firm, first met Wade when Peze joined ASD/C3I in 1993. Both he and Wade were among the dozen program managers. Each oversaw the development and deployment of a particular piece of hardware used in intelligence activities, a pretty straightforward job. "There would be money appropriated in the defense budget to buy [a piece of hardware]. And the fact of the matter was, you don't buy them off the shelf. They were something that had to be developed," said Peze, and he added, "The project manager would be given a budget, a schedule, and a set of requirements. And it was his responsibility to work with a contracting officer to put a contract in place and get a contractor."

Several months after Peze began working at ASD/C3I, Wade left to start his own intelligence consultancy. The consulting firm was named after the initials of Wade's three children. For eight years, he ran MZM from his home on N Street in Georgetown without a prime contract from the government.

In 1998, when the Panama project revved up, Pentagon officials told Brent Wilkes that he should add Wade to his team. Wilkes's strategy was for contracts to be given to MZM with ADCS getting much of the benefit as a subcontractor.

As a former intelligence officer, Wade had something that Wilkes desperately needed: a high-level security clearance. ADCS needed to process a large amount of classified documents in Panama, but neither Wilkes nor the military wives he had hired had the proper clearances. Wade proved to be a valuable asset to Wilkes, putting together a team of professionals with proper clearances. He was well organized and knew how to keep the intelligence people in line. He was also attracted to Wilkes's flashy displays of wealth.

It was during this time that Wade became close with Wilkes's most valuable friend, Randy Cunningham. By 2002, Wade was plotting to usurp that friendship and get Cunningham to shift his attention to help Wade establish his own little empire in Washington.

That same year, ASD/C3I spawned a separate intelligence branch that would play an expanded role in the post–9/11 era: It was the super-secret Counterintelligence Field Activity (CIFA). Almost unknown to the general public, CIFA easily got lost amid the mind-numbing array of Pentagon acronyms. But in the war against terror it had a crucial mission—protect U.S. defense facilities, programs, and personnel from attack or infiltration. And with its mission came hefty funding from a Republican Congress that rarely said no to the Pentagon.

Soon after September 11, Cunningham was helping Wade take full advantage of the gusher of federal spending. This would transform the company overnight into a military-intelligence prime-contracting juggernaut. The first prime contract came in 2002, a $140,000 deal to provide "office furniture" for the executive office of the president, according to the Federal Procurement Data System, a public database. But the contract actually was to screen the president's mail, according to a person familiar with the contract. The contract raises questions for the first time about possible links between Wade and officials at the White House because such a sensitive contract is unusual without personal links. Wade often boasted of ties to Vice President Dick Cheney. The contract is classified, making it all but impossible to know how it came to be awarded to MZM. But with contracts like this, Wade himself would undergo a transformation.

The first milestone in the transformation came that July when he bought a $2.3 million townhouse to serve as the company's headquarters. The stately five-story brick row house sits on a tree-lined street near DuPont Circle, long favored for its restaurants, book stores, and art galleries. The building, which Wade purchased from the University of California, would be MZM's home as the company exploded from obscurity into one of the nation's top one hundred defense contractors, amassing $163 million in contracts along the way, almost all of them sole source and classified.

The number of employees grew from a small handful to about four hundred. And their workplace grew in opulence. Expensive antiques, curios, and artwork suddenly were everywhere. Each office got an oversized antique desk bought from Wade's favorite dealer, Onslow Square, situated in a warehouse in the West Howard section of Kensington, Maryland, just outside the District. Antique carpets were scattered throughout the headquarters to give the offices an air of old money. "It was very important to [Wade] that every single office had an antique desk in it," said one former executive. "They were nonfunctional. They were the dumbest things you've ever worked with. Drawers didn't open. Nothing worked on them. But for the look, every office—every office!—had an antique desk."

Visitors approached MZM from the street by stepping down and entering an English basement from beneath a hunter green canopy. The formal reception area featured a baby grand piano and busy gallery of photos of Wade with political luminaries—including Congressman Cunningham. Wade's office was up the stairs and toward the back of the second floor, which also housed other offices, a small kitchen, and a bathroom. Wade had the option of using an elevator to get to his office on the second floor. But everyone else used the stairs. Entering his oval office, visitors viewed him across the expanse of his desk, which was usually obscured under a clutter of files, documents, books, and a laptop. More clutter was stacked alongside the desk. The room had a fireplace and a bookcase filled with "vanity books" he'd purchased—including Cunningham's 1984 *Fox Two*. Wade liked to buy such books, primarily to curry favor with the authors, and he was generous in handing them out to guests.

Most of Wade's employees considered him affable and chatty during agreeable moments. But those moments too often were surrounded by far less agreeable stretches. Former employees describe him as intense, arrogant, secretive, and controlling. With a slack, six-foot-four frame, he could be intimidating when angry. He rigidly maintained a circle of trust. Once you were outside, you stayed outside. If you ever crossed him, it would cost you. He could befriend you and then destroy you. He was a man to fear.

Haig Melkessetian, an MZM interpreter and later vice president for Middle Eastern operations, learned firsthand the consequences of crossing the boss. When Melkessetian tried to break away from

MZM in the spring of 2004, his career was devastated. He was not only without a job but also without a security clearance, which was mysteriously lifted. Nobody could tell him why; nobody could help him get it reinstated. He was, in essence, blackballed from working as a contract interpreter in military intelligence and the diplomatic community. He was suddenly cut off from his livelihood. Although he didn't know the particulars and didn't produce any evidence, Melkessetian had no doubt who was behind his ruin. This was a reprisal for challenging Mitch Wade, Melkessetian said.

Wade didn't like being challenged by his employees, and to encourage loyalty he greatly overpaid them. By giving them salaries that might be up to three times what they had been receiving before joining MZM, he slapped golden handcuffs on their wrists when they walked through the door. For many, little was expected except a résumé, a security clearance, and loyalty. It was the kind of arrangement that made it easy for a puzzled employee to keep from asking unwanted questions. It took the sting out of Wade's sometimes off-color comments and profane tirades. And it helped them accept the code of extreme secrecy and compartmentalization he imposed upon his workers. Programs, projects, and information were carefully walled off so that nobody but Wade had an overall sense of what MZM was doing at any given minute. He disclosed almost nothing about his personal life—very few of his employees even knew what the initials MZM stood for.

Like many manipulators, Wade was a master at mixing acceptance and rejection. He could be warm and chatty one minute, icy and silent the next. He gave out hams and Tiffany knick-knacks at Christmas, but he also pressured his workers to donate to his favorite charities. "He seemed like a Dr. Jekyll and Mr. Hyde type. You know, one minute he's nice, and the next minute he's just an arrogant ass," said a former employee. Added yet another: "He was a recruiter, just like with any cult. Find those who are weak and bring them onto the team."

The reason for Wade's secretive approach no doubt was rooted in his personality. But it also was rooted in the nefarious way in which he drummed up business for MZM. He was one of a new breed of boutique defense entrepreneurs who made their money by going after smaller contracts worth a few million dollars a year that were of less interest to the big companies.

Wade's formula was elegant in its simplicity: Set up shop in the district of a congressman on a key committee. Give thousands—sometimes tens of thousands—of dollars in bundled campaign contributions to that congressman. Then propose plausible-sounding multimillion dollar programs to be housed within the lawmaker's district. The lawmaker then makes the MZM project a top priority on his or her annual earmark list submitted to the Appropriations Committee. Wade would end up with a lucrative contract without having to suffer through hearings or submit to scrutiny. And the congressman would be able to brag about bringing federal contracting jobs into the district.

The only loser was the Pentagon or the intelligence agency that ended up having to divert millions of dollars into a new program that it had never asked for and probably didn't need.

And what about the public, or even other members of Congress? They almost never know anything about it. In the arena Mitch Wade played in, the programs are classified. Few members of Congress knew anything about those contracts. There was virtually no scrutiny. It was a win-win-win game—except for those concerned about spending discipline.

Having worked as a program manager at the Pentagon, Wade knew there were ways to circumvent oversight and transparency. He also knew the beauty of something called a Blanket Purchase Agreement, or BPA. He knew that this could be another shortcut to profits, another way to dodge scrutiny and oversight—particularly from a Republican Congress that had shown almost no appetite for oversight of anything involving the military or intelligence. A year after MZM moved into its headquarters, the Pentagon awarded MZM a five-year BPA worth up to $225 million. The purchase agreements are a streamlined but controversial tool that privileged contractors can use to conduct high-volume business with the government. In recent years, they have come into broader use, drawing praise in some circles for simplifying and speeding the procurement process but criticism in others for reducing accountability, competition, and transparency.

Originally, agencies used the procedure to simplify the routine ordering and reordering of inexpensive, everyday supplies such as paperclips. The process makes it quick and simple for agencies and contractors to do business by lifting many of the usual competitive and performance safeguards—including the competitive bidding process. But the federal government now allows agencies to use the agreements to buy far more sophisticated wares from technology companies. The deals can be worth hundreds of millions of dollars over several years.

How MZM obtained its Blanket Purchase Agreement remains shrouded in secrecy and the subject of an ongoing investigation by the Pentagon's Office of Inspector General. In late 2001, Congress enacted a bill increasing the required number of bidders from two to three for a prime contract, but the law would not take effect until October 2002.

In 2002, before the new requirements took effect, the Defense Information Systems Agency (DISA) sought proposals from two companies for a Blanket Purchase Agreement worth up to $225 million. They solicited the requests from MZM and Turtle Mountain Communications in Tennessee. But Turtle Mountain Communications never submitted a bid, leaving MZM as the sole bidder. Under rules at the time, the award was considered competitive "because we had sought more than one proposal," according to a statement issued later by a DISA spokesman.

The award was made to MZM in September, a month before the new regulations requiring three bidders on contracts took effect. The general counsel of DISA's parent agency, the Defense Information Technology Contracting Organization (DITCO), reviewed MZM's agreement in light of the new requirement. It ruled that the provision should *not* be applied retroactively and that the award should remain in place even though MZM was in reality the sole bidder.

MZM would take full advantage of the ruling. When Wade pled guilty later, Kenneth L. Wainstein, the U.S. attorney for the District, called the Blanket Purchase Agreement "a $225 million blank check drawn on taxpayer funds."

Wade, as his coworkers were astonished to discover, wasn't big on security. Even with classified documents, security wasn't even an afterthought for the MZM boss. It never seemed to enter his mind at all—and he got angry and abusive with staffers who dared to raise the issue. He was concerned not at all that the MZM offices lacked even routine security features. For instance, the lobbyists for the University of California who occupied the building before MZM bought it had run Ethernet through the walls and above the ceilings. With Ethernet running out of sight, there was no way to be sure that the security of the local area network had not been breached by covert splicing. Only after being prompted by the Defense Security Service, which oversees security at contracting sites where classified material is handled, did MZM place the cables in full view so that they could be monitored for tampering.

Classified documents themselves were subject to sloppy handling, sometimes being left lying out on desktops or just slid under doors. The Defense Security Service threatened to revoke the company's security clearance, but it never did. Wade also played tricks with his applications for security clearances by saying that new employees were being assigned to projects that would expedite their clearance even when they weren't being assigned to those projects.

Getting contracts depended on being able to showcase an impressive roster of people with security clearances. So Wade would pay top dollar to people from the government who already had them. And he would cut corners and bend the truth to get them for new employees who didn't.

But, to Wade, the important thing he wanted you to know was that he was a patriot helping his country win the war against terrorism. It was only the true insiders who knew the greater truth—that Wade didn't really care that much who won this global war. What he cared about was the profits to be won during the war.

chapter thirteen

PATRIOT GAMES

W HEN MITCH WADE THREW A PARTY, THE MOST IMPORTANT PROPS— always—were American flags. And if he could sprinkle a few wounded veterans around the room, even better for the image he worked so hard to create of himself as a true American patriot working to give our troops the tools they need to win.

It was an image that Haig Melkessetian bought into at first. But it didn't take long for disenchantment to set in. When Melkessetian came on board, first as an MZM interpreter and then as vice president for Middle Eastern operations, he made one big mistake. Melkessetian—naïvely—thought Wade wanted MZM to help the United States win the war against terror. He didn't know that Wade's patriotic blather was a marketing tool.

Melkessetian had cut his teeth in the military world as a young fighter in a Christian-Lebanese militia commando unit during the bloody civil war that destroyed Beirut in the 1980s. Later, he moved to the United States and became a U.S. citizen. He worked as a contract interpreter for the State Department and other U.S. agencies. Wade hired him as an interpreter in 2003 and sent him to Iraq.

There, Melkessetian served with coalition intelligence units. He interpreted for the hastily established Office for Reconstruction and Humanitarian Assistance and, later, its successor, the Coalition Provisional Authority. He served the directors—first Jay Garner and then Paul Bremer. In one news photograph, Melkessetian can be seen brandishing a Heckler & Koch MP5 submachine gun as he escorted Bremer down a street in Baghdad.

When Melkessetian returned stateside after six months, he complained bitterly to Wade about what he described as serious flaws in the way coalition forces were handling the early months of the Iraq occupation and reconstruction. He warned that critical mistakes were being made, such as bringing in thousands of unskilled workers from Southeast Asia and the Indian subcontinent to do jobs that could have been done by unemployed Iraqis. Coalition authority leaders did not understand the Arab culture and were alienating the very sheiks whose hearts and minds they needed to win over if the nascent democracy had any hope of surviving, Melkessetian argued.

But Wade wasn't interested:

> He said, "Close the door" [Melkessetian recalled]. "Haig, I'm not sending you there to fix the problem. I'm sending you there to make money. That's what we're here for." I was shocked because I saw all these car bombings in front of my eyes, flashbacks, and all these people dying, and this guy is sitting here telling me, basically, "I don't give a flying fuck what happens there, we're there for the bucks." I was depressed all afternoon. It was like, how are we going to win this war? We can right these things.

The final break between Wade and Melkessetian would be triggered by an opportunity Wade saw for making money off the Saudis. By then, Melkessetian was MZM's vice president for Middle Eastern operations. He recalled that Wade entered his office one morning in 2004 and said he'd had dinner the night before with a congressman, who, Melkessetian believed without knowing for sure, was Cunningham. Nonetheless, the congressman had told Wade there was money to be made by helping the Saudis restore their good name in the United States. Saudi Arabia's image in America had suffered after the 9/11 attacks. Osama bin Laden, the mastermind, is a Saudi. And fifteen of the nineteen hijackers had been Saudis.

Wade saw dollar signs and wanted Melkessetian to spearhead what he expected to be a lucrative covert charm offensive on behalf of the Saudis. But the former Lebanese Christian militiaman balked. Surreptitiously waging what he saw as a propaganda campaign in America on behalf of the Saudis seemed in conflict with MZM's primary mission of protecting the country from future terror attacks. Wade chastised him for being "ideological" rather than practical. Melkessetian thought Wade's attitude bordered on treason. "He's claiming to be a patriot," Melkessetian said of Wade. "But in reality, I don't think he really cared if we win or lose, as long as he gets the money in his pocket."

That mercenary view was consistent with the account of another former executive of MZM, who spoke on the condition that she not be identified because of her ongoing work with the military. Wade told her in early 2005 that he planned to sell MZM to its employees in January 2006 and walk away with $100 million in his pocket. "He wrapped himself in the flag, but he was really all about the money," she said.

Former Executive Vice President Richard Peze said that Wade did everything he could to showcase his love of country. "All of his efforts were cloaked in patriotism," said Peze. For instance, Wade made a large contribution to the Pentagon Memorial Fund, a drive to raise money for a two-acre monument to the fifty-nine passengers on board American Airlines Flight 77 and the 125 military and civilian personnel who were killed on 9/11 when the doomed aircraft slammed into the Pentagon.

Wade's 2003 Christmas party provided a perfect opportunity for him to display his patriotism. On December 10, 2003, there was plenty to celebrate. A war was on, which meant lucrative contracts would continue to flow his way. In the ballroom of the Four Seasons Hotel in Georgetown, a dinner chime quieted a student jazz quartet, marking the end of cocktails and hors d'oeuvres. MZM's employees, dressed in tuxedoes and evening gowns, began finding their seats for a Christmas banquet Wade promised would be special.

Inside, a nineteen-piece orchestra serenaded them through dinner. The formal opening number was the national anthem. But for this pro-defense crowd, with its high concentration of retired military officers, the real musical highlight would come when the orchestra played the military service anthems: "Off We Go, into the Wild Blue Yonder," "Anchors Aweigh," the "Marines' Hymn," and "The Army Goes Rolling Along."

Then Wade himself welcomed a handful of soldiers recovering from war injuries at Walter Reed Army Medical Center, just five miles away. Thanks to Wade, the soldiers were enjoying an evening of music, finery, and elegant dining, a respite from their daily drudgery in the rehab rooms of Walter Reed, where so many of them were being fitted for prostheses and learning to cope without limbs. After dinner, some of the wounded soldiers won expensive prizes raffled as part of the holiday celebration.

It was an emotional evening both for the wounded soldiers and for the commerce hawks in the room. But there were more than emotional links between the Iraq veterans and Wade's company. Overall, 2003 had been a year of explosive growth for MZM, thanks in large part to the invasion of Iraq. The growth had been fueled by a profusion of those sole-source, classified contracts awarded under tight secrecy as part of the rapid, post–9/11 military-intelligence build-up for the war on terrorism. Most of the funds came from earmarks inserted into the "black" portions of the annual defense-spending bill. No one really knows how much money is spent in the Pentagon's "black budget"; some estimate it reaches $40 billion. It is inarguable, though, that very few knew about those earmarks beyond Wade, Randy Cunningham, and a small group of mid-level congressional and defense staffers.

Thanks to Cunningham, profit margins on some of the earmarked contracts ran as high as 850 percent. Examples include Cunningham's $6 million earmarks in 2002 and 2003 to buy storage devices for the Counterintelligence Field Activity. The spy agency had not requested the devices and had no real need for them. Nonetheless, the Pentagon paid roughly $6 million in successive years for devices that Wilkes and Wade purchased off the shelf for $700,000. The three conspirators didn't put these two wasteful earmarks in successive defense budgets to make the country safer. They did not do it to make U.S. soldiers fighting in Iraq and Afghanistan safer. They did it for one reason: to divert millions of dollars in defense funds from the battlefield to their pockets.

But there were more profits to be made in other programs as well. One of MZM's post-9/11 missions was to reduce the critical shortage of interpreters in Iraq. Because the Pentagon won't discuss MZM's contracts, which are classified, it is unclear whether MZM also earned 850 percent profit margins on its linguistics contracts. But as cultural misunderstandings and language confusion grew and Iraq slipped deeper and deeper into chaos and sectarian strife, it is inarguable that more interpreters and better interpreters would have saved lives and averted some of the grave misunderstandings between U.S. soldiers and Iraqi civilians that ultimately fed the insurgency.

Millions of dollars in earmarked funds also went to Wade to find ways to defeat the deadly roadside bombs sending some U.S. soldiers to Walter Reed and others to Arlington Cemetery and other lasting resting places. Only a few months after revelations in June 2005 that MZM's contracts were born of corruption, the Pentagon secretly increased the size of MZM's contract to counter the hidden roadside bombs, known as improvised explosive devices, or IEDs. The "plus-up" of the IED contract was awarded to MZM at its new facility attached to the army's National Ground Intelligence Center (NGIC) in Charlottesville, Virginia, according to sources working within the facility.

The military won't publicly talk about MZM's IED contract, but if it did, it would almost certainly describe the "plus-up" as having been awarded competitively. However, some of the contractors at the facility privately described it differently. They said they were startled one afternoon when NGIC officials announced that the IED contract was being dramatically increased in value and that they could all bid on it. NGIC's bosses then dropped a hammer on MZM's competitors. Those wishing to bid on the contract needed to have their bids and personnel in place within two working days.

Only MZM could possibly have placed a bid because it was already doing the work and had its IED personnel in place. The other contractors inside the facility believed that MZM, unlike the rest of them, had been given advance notice of the looming plus-up, affording the company plenty of time to tailor its bid to the specific requirements of the contract.

Technically, it might have been an open and competitive process. But in reality, MZM won the contract by default under the rules NGIC had laid down. This rigged award occurred after the Cunningham bribery scandal had broken and the company was being offered for sale. Whether intended or not, it certainly had to be an encouraging signal to anyone thinking of buying MZM. The message was loud and clear: The Pentagon will continue doing business with the company, bribery scandal or not.

The Pentagon's continuing faith in MZM as the scandal raged contrasted sharply with stories trickling out from former MZM officials who spoke privately with reporters after the scandal broke about their own troubling experiences with the company. One came from a U.S. soldier, stationed six thousand miles away in Iraq, who had worked at MZM between February and August 2002. In a series of e-mails, the soldier asked not to be identified publicly because of his continuing military career, but he said he would eagerly talk with FBI agents if any ever knocked on his door.

And he left little doubt about what he wanted to tell the FBI. He even spelled out his potential testimony in this e-mail written June 20, 2005:

I was recruited and hired by [MZM] out of the Army in Feb 02 to come abroad as [job description deleted] for MZM, Inc. I was one of three (such professionals) working for them. I was hired personally by Mitch. He explained to me that he had a background in the CIA and had "the vice-president [Dick Cheney] and some members of congress" in his backpocket. I did not know exactly my role there but was quickly farmed out to work at the DoD Counterintelligence Field Activity. At the time in Feb 02, Mitch was trying to gain a large contract to provide contract personnel, including myself, to work at CIFA.

I was stunned to learn once I started at CIFA that I had no real job. I stayed there from Feb til Aug 02. I can honestly tell you that any advising or work I did for DoD was only the result of my desire not to steal a paycheck. Every two weeks I would receive a check from MZM but in reality I did very little for my money. I questioned Mitch, [deleted], and [deleted] and was told explicitly to keep my mouth shut as I was making them a lot of money. . . .

I had enough by August 02. I was in the Army reserve and volunteered to go to Bosnia to get the hell out of MZM. It was my intention never to go back there. When I told them of my plans, they tried to buy me off to stay. No way, I smelled a rat a long time ago and knew I had to get out of there.

For a group of people that have high security clearances and are supposed to be aiding in the war on terror, they are out of control. . . . There is no doubt in my mind they are dirty. I guarantee you if the FBI comes calling, I am talking as I expect a lot of others will do so.

Both this soldier's lament and that incredible profit on the electronic storage device come to mind every time Cunningham falls back on what has become his now-familiar rationale for his corruption: He had voted only for programs that he believed in and that were good for the country. But the only thing that drove these transactions was profit. The storage device deal could have been what Assistant U.S. Attorney Phillip Halpern was thinking of when he told U.S. District Judge Larry Alan Burns in San Diego on March 3, 2006:

When held up to the light of day, we can see that many of the items supplied by [Cunningham's] confederates were not originally requested by the Pentagon. They were available to be purchased by the government at a fraction of the cost that they were sold. They were not really needed. And, perhaps most tragically, if the funding for these systems was not taken out of the funding of the Pentagon, other programs could have been funded that would have addressed our nation's all too real pressing and urgent needs.

Unfortunately, it will be years—if ever—before anyone knows how much damage Cunningham, Wade, and Wilkes did to national security, how many lives were put at risk or lost on the streets of Iraq, how much money was diverted to their pockets instead of going toward achieving the victory over terrorism that all three men said they desired.

chapter fourteen

CROSSING THE BRIBERY LINE

NOT SURPRISINGLY, WHAT MOST PEOPLE REMEMBER ABOUT THE CUNNINGham case is the bribe menu. Even those who had concluded that Cunningham had abused his office were amazed that any congressman would be reckless enough to commit to paper the specific amounts of bribes attached to his official actions.

But on second glance, it was the detail included in those documents—the many instances in which Cunningham sold himself and his high office—that stunned even veteran prosecutors. For the bribe memo was far from the first time Cunningham had solicited payments. For years long before Wade met Cunningham, the lawmaker was steering earmarks to Brent Wilkes. As early as September 1996, Wilkes had been plying Cunningham with prostitutes, private jet travel, and limousine service. Wilkes gave Cunningham $700,000 in lavish gifts and cash during a decade in which Cunningham steered him tens of millions of dollars in federal contracts. The two men badgered, bullied, and threatened Pentagon officials who stood between Wilkes and the money Cunningham was steering his way.

But Cunningham was under fresh financial pressure in 2000, trying to figure out how to pay for his daughter's Ivy League tuition. "I just sent my daughter off to Yale," he complained on the House floor. "I cannot tell my colleagues how expensive that is."[1] Tuition, room, and board at Yale totaled $32,880 that year, significant even for a member of Congress. There is no way of knowing whether that played a role in his thinking, but it coincided with Cunningham's decision to step up the size of bribes he was taking. And Wade, who had studied Wilkes's dealings with Cunningham, was only too willing to go there, too, with them. Before long, Wade and Wilkes and Cunningham would use phony asset transfers to conceal millions of dollars in bribes.

The first such sham transaction was Wilkes's "purchase" in May 2000 of the *Kelly C* for $100,000. Wilkes wrote two checks to Cunningham, one for $70,000, the other for $30,000. Cunningham deposited the larger check in his account at Union Bank in San Diego and the smaller one in his personal account at the Congressional Federal Credit Union in Washington. Wilkes took over the mortgage payments on the *Kelly C,* a total of $11,116.50 between October 2000 and March 2001. But neither the title nor the registration of the *Kelly C* ever changed hands. Cunningham not only used the boat as he always had but kept it in the very same slip at the Capital Yacht Club.

The net result of the transaction? A $100,000 bribe from Wilkes to Cunningham—the first to be documented from Wilkes.

On November 16, 2001, Wade introduced Cunningham to his favorite antique store in Kensington, Maryland. Onslow Square is a spacious shop in what is known locally as West Howard antiques district. A dozen antique dealers occupy two-story buildings interspersed with auto-repair and auto-upholstery shops. Onslow Square and its owner, Sandra Ellington, were popular fixtures there, drawing such well-heeled customers as Ethel Kennedy and the actor Robert Duvall, who lives in Virginia's horse country, not far outside Washington.

On that maiden shopping trip, Wade used an MZM corporate check to pay for $12,000 in antiques that would be delivered to Cunningham: three nightstands, a leaded glass cabinet, a washstand, a buffet, and four armoires. It was the first of many such visits for the two men. They became regulars, in fact, with Ellington selling them antiques roughly once a month between November 2001 and November 2003. It was not difficult for her to recall those visits because Cunningham—as usual—wanted to be noticed.

Most memorable to Ellington was the first visit from Cunningham. Gruff and walking with what she recalled as a swagger, he gave her a business card, embossed with the congressional seal, identifying himself as a congressman. Then he gave her an autographed photo of himself in his flight suit. "He wanted me to know who he was. He told me about the *Top Gun* movie and he said that it was based on his story," she recalled, still astonished by his brazen self-promotion.

"Mitch Wade had polish. Mr. Cunningham didn't. He was into flash. He liked things that were heavily carved," said Ellington. "He liked the high-end things. He liked things that look like money." And, even though it was not his own money, he also liked to haggle over prices.

"He'd stand in front of a piece and say that the price was too high, that the piece wasn't worth it. Then I'd say, 'Leave it out if it doesn't fit your budget. If you can't afford it, leave it out.'" Cunningham would then walk off dismissively. "But I knew he wanted it, and I knew he'd come back," she said. She thought it odd that the contractor's Jack Russell terrier also was named "Duke."

The furnishings bought on the first excursion were acquired for a new condo Cunningham was about to buy. The lawmaker's wife, Nancy, a career school administrator in San Diego, had gotten a job in Washington. The Department of Education had hired her to serve as acting chief of staff to a department assistant secretary. Her annual salary would be $114,200. At the time, her husband sat on the House Appropriations subcommittee overseeing the Education Department's annual budget—a clear conflict in the eyes of many.

Nancy was unhappy enough about moving to Washington, but she was absolutely insistent that she would not be living aboard a sixty-five-foot, flat-bottom riverboat rocking on the Potomac. So eleven days after Wade took Cunningham antique shopping, the lawmaker bought a fourteen-hundred-square-foot penthouse condominium with a view of the Potomac River in suburban Arlington, Virginia.

Cunningham didn't sell or refinance the couple's California home to pay for the $350,000 condo. He didn't have to—not when he had friends ready to pitch in. Cunningham ended up putting down $200,000 in cash, and he financed the remaining $150,000. The $200,000 down payment came from the New York developer Thomas Kontogiannis. On December 3, 2001, Kontogiannis, a friend of Cunningham's, transferred $200,000 to the company providing the mortgage, Coastal Capital, which was controlled by Kontogiannis's nephew, John T. Michael.

At the time, Kontogiannis—known to some as "Tommy the Greek" and to others as "Tommy K"—was in legal trouble. He was accused in New York City of bilking the Queens public schools of millions of dollars with a bid-rigging, bribery, and kickback scheme. The scheme involved a school superintendent who provided insider information to a company called Business Innovative Technology, allowing the company to get three school district computer contracts worth a total of $6.3 million. In return for that information and other help, the administrator got $925,000 in bribes and three real estate properties from Kontogiannis. Kontogiannis split a kickback exceeding $2.2 million with another defendant. But the New York defendant had a California congressman ready to vouch for him.

On October 19, 2000—less than two months before Kontogiannis took care of Cunningham's mortgage—the prosecutor trying to convict the developer received a faxed letter on congressional stationery informing him that the defendant was being wrongly prosecuted. The letter—sent, incredibly, in the middle of grand jury deliberations on the case—blamed a disgruntled contractor for the

Randy "Duke" Cunningham's war record vaulted him to a seat in the House of Representatives in 1991. His status as a war hero stemmed from a seven-minute dog fight in the skies over North Vietnam on May 10, 1972. Cunningham that day became the first Navy ace since the Korean War by shooting down three enemy MiGs, bringing his total to five. Among the medals he wore on his dress uniform were the Navy Cross, the highest medal the Navy can award; two Silver Stars; fifteen Air Medals; and one Purple Heart (*U.S. Navy*).

Cunningham (second from left) and legendary Coach Don Watson (center) celebrate with members of Hinsdale Central's swim team after winning the 1967 Illinois State championship *(Hinsdale Central)*.

Cunningham and his back-seater, Willie Driscoll, explain their aerial feats to reporters the day after they became the first Navy aces since the Korean War *(U.S. Navy)*.

A happy Cunningham was reunited May 16, 1972, with his two-and-a-half-year-old son Todd and his wife, Sue, upon his homecoming from Vietnam at San Diego's Lindbergh Airport (*National Archives*).

In what he described as the best moment of his triumphal tour of the United States in 1972, Cunningham returned to his hometown of Shelbina, Missouri, to the cheers of his neighbors, a reunion with his parents, and a parade down the main street of town. (*Shelbina Democrat*).

Cunningham shows off the California vanity plates he proudly put on his sports car in 1972 less than three months after returning to a hero's welcome from Vietnam (*Jerry Rife, Union-Tribune*).

Cunningham had a reputation as a ladies man and flirt in the Navy and later when he served in Congress. When he and his wife, Nancy, separated after his legal troubles began, she referred to this side of his personality as "Mr. Fun Ball" and said it was a main reason she moved back to San Diego after living for a brief period outside Washington with her husband in a Penthouse condo that overlooked the Potomac River, which had been purchased with help from defense contractor Mitch Wade and New York developer Thomas Kontogiannis. Kontogiannis has not been charged in the Cunningham investigation but remains under investigation as an unindicted co-conspirator (*Robert Hughes/ ZUMA Press*).

Mitchell John Wade leaves U.S. federal district court in Alexandria, Virginia, February 24, 2006, after pleading guilty to four counts involving bribery, election fraud, and conspiracy. From 2001 through 2005, during a time when Wade was plying Cunningham with $1.3 million in bribes, Wade's company, MZM Inc., went from having no prime contracts to more than $163 million worth, most of them sole source and classified. His sentencing is scheduled for the fall of 2007. Wade's early decision to provide the government with a trove of incriminating evidence helped prosecutors move rapidly in building their case against Cunningham and other co-conspirators. (*AP Images/Susan Walsh*).

The Cunningham scandal broke June 12, 2005, when the *San Diego Union-Tribune* published a Copley News Service article saying the San Diego congressman had purchased a mansion in Rancho Santa Fe for $2.55 million on December 3, 2003, with two mortgages totaling $1.1 million. He was able to buy the mansion when defense contractor Mitchell Wade bought Cunningham's previous house at a $700,000 loss (*Union-Tribune*).

The Cunningham scandal ratcheted up after the *North County Times* published an article disclosing that Cunningham was living aboard a 42-foot yacht called the *Duke-Stir*, which was moored at the Capital Yacht Club not far from the Washington Monument and Tidal Basin. Defense contractor Mitchell Wade had purchased the yacht for Cunningham to use while in Washington (*Union-Tribune*).

Kyle "Dusty" Foggo, formerly number-three official at the CIA, was indicted February 14, 2007, in San Diego on charges of conspiracy, money laundering, and honest-services fraud in connection with his business dealings with childhood best friend, Brent Wilkes. Foggo failed to disclose lavish gifts, expensive dinners, and vacations Wilkes provided him during a time that Foggo was helping Wilkes get intelligence contracts, the indictment alleges. Foggo pleaded not guilty and was awaiting trial at the time of publication (*Union-Tribune*).

Brent Wilkes, founder of Poway-based ADCS, was indicted February 14, 2007, in San Diego on charges that he bribed Cunningham with prostitutes, luxury vacations, limousine service, corporate jet travel, and tickets to a Super Bowl in exchange for tens of millions of dollars in government contracts beginning in September 1996. Wilkes pleaded not guilty and was awaiting trial at the time of publication (*Union-Tribune*).

Cunningham, with his wife, Nancy, at his side, announces at a July 14, 2005, press conference in San Marcos, California, that he will not seek re-election after eight terms in Congress. While he continued to deny any official misconduct, this was Mrs. Cunningham's last public appearance at her husband's side. They later separated (*John Gastaldo, Union-Tribune*).

Cunningham stumbles as he is led by marshals into the federal courthouse in San Diego for his March 3, 2006, sentencing hearing. Giving Cunningham credit for his military service but criticizing his greed and betrayal of his office, Judge Larry Alan Burns sentences Cunningham to the longest sentence ever meted out to a member of Congress—eight years and four months (*Union-Tribune*).

charges against Kontogiannis. Tommy K, insisted Cunningham, was merely an innocent bystander.[2]

And just in case the prosecutor didn't get the hint that this defendant had heavyweight friends, Cunningham attached a separate letter that he had sent to Rep. Henry J. Hyde, the Illinois Republican who then was chairman of the House Judiciary Committee. In his note to Hyde, Cunningham asked the committee to open an inquiry into the matter. He also included the reply from a committee lawyer saying the panel would, indeed, look into the matter, although the committee said later it never did.

If Cunningham intended the three letters to intimidate the prosecutor, the ploy failed. Several weeks later, Kontogiannis, the school administrator, and several others were named in a 123-count indictment returned by the grand jury. In October 2002, the defendants, including Kontogiannis, pleaded guilty to a misdemeanor charge and agreed to pay back $4.85 million to the city. Nobody received jail time. And Kontogiannis has been making regular monthly payments to the city of about $50,000.[3]

That wasn't the first time a lenient plea agreement helped Kontogiannis avoid jail time. In 1994, he and a U.S. consular official in Greece pleaded guilty to charges that they had exchanged bribes for visas. Instead of being sent to jail, he was fined $2,000 and given three months of house arrest and five months of probation.[4]

Kontogiannis, a native of Greece who became a U.S. citizen in 1976, is reported to be worth $70 million, and his family owns more than two dozen businesses. Cunningham admitted in 2005 that he had talked to Kontogiannis about helping him obtain a pardon from President Bush. To other members of Congress, it was an unbelievable breach of ethics even to discuss such help, but Kontogiannis would later say that Cunningham had done nothing more than recommend an attorney.

Cunningham was probably willing to go the extra mile for Kontogiannis because he owed the New Yorker big time for the help on his mortgage. Wade added to the bribe, laundering $50,000 in cash to

Cunningham through Coastal Capital. Wade gave Coastal Capital an MZM check for $50,000, and Coastal Capital then issued Cunningham a check for $50,000, which the lawmaker deposited in his personal account at Union Bank in San Diego.

As 2002 began, Cunningham had some of the furnishings he needed for the new condo—but he wanted more. He called on Wade. On January 24, 2002, Wade used his MZM credit card to buy Cunningham a leather sofa and a sleigh bed. The price tag for the two items: $6,632. Then, on February 5, Wade used an MZM check to buy the couple more antiques: a nineteenth-century Louis Philippe commode and a four-drawer commode made in about 1830. On February 27, Kontogiannis—his school district case still pending— gave Cunningham a check for $10,000, which he deposited in his personal account at the Congressional Federal Credit Union.

So the condo was starting to shape up, in a very dark, ornate sort of way. But how was Cunningham supposed to drive back and forth between the condo and Capitol Hill? Once again, Wade had the answer—and more checks. On April 6, Wade gave Cunningham a personal check for $13,500, which he used to buy an old Rolls Royce that had caught his eye. The Rolls immediately went into the shop for work. Anybody who has a Rolls knows that repair bills can soar. But that's no problem when Mitch Wade is your personal ATM. On May 4, Wade gave the repair shop a corporate check for $17,889.96 to cover the cost of those repairs. Cunningham kept the vehicle in his assigned parking space in a House office building garage, later "selling" it back to Wade for an undisclosed amount without conveying the title.

Next, the congressman wanted a bigger boat. It was a yacht tied up near the *Kelly C* at the Capital Yacht Club. The object of his desires was a forty-two-foot Carver built in 1987. Unfortunately for a congressman often criticized for homophobic remarks, it was called the *Buoy Toy*. On August 30, 2002, Wade wrote an MZM check for $140,000 to cover the purchase of the *Buoy Toy*. But the owner wanted a cashier's check. So Wade left and returned later with a cashier's check. Cunningham moved the *Buoy Toy* into his slip, where the first order of business was to rechristen it the *Duke-Stir.* Asked why he changed the name of the boat, Cunningham was blunt: "I bought the boat, not the lifestyle."

Cunningham was enjoying a lifestyle out of reach for most of his colleagues. Unlike the Senate, where one-third of the members are millionaires, many members of the House struggle to maintain residences simultaneously in Washington and their districts. But these were not Cunningham's role models. He focused more on the millionaires in his midst, both in Congress and in the more affluent areas of his district, places like La Jolla, Del Mar, and Rancho Santa Fe. These were Duke's kind of people, and he wanted what they had.

The *Duke-Stir* was the latest of the lavish gifts Cunningham was accumulating. He had started collecting gifts from Brent Wilkes at least as early as September 1996. And he would continue collecting them for almost another three years, both from Wilkes and Wade. In fact, the deals to come would dwarf the purchase of antiques, yachts, and other gifts Cunningham had collected by late-2002. But the other side of the conspiracy—arguably the darker side—was what he did in return for those gifts, his betrayal of his office and the people who sent him to Washington.

The gifts to him are now well-documented, thanks largely to information Wade and other informants would provide the government. But Cunningham's favors in return—his *quid pro quo* to Wade and Wilkes for those gifts—would be more difficult to track. For that, investigators would need e-mails and other documents culled from the Defense Department and Congress.

Congressional and Defense Department e-mails would prove that Cunningham inserted himself into the appropriations process with a single overriding concern—getting earmarks for Wilkes and Wade, at the expense of real defense programs. And they would show that once those earmarks were approved by Congress, Cunningham was ready to bully, prod, and cajole Defense Department employees who might interfere with his efforts to see that the money he had secretly earmarked actually got into the pockets of Wilkes and Wade.

In late September 2002, the House Appropriations Committee was making final decisions about spending for the upcoming fiscal year. House members had submitted their prioritized earmark requests to the committee in March. Seven months later, in the waning days of September, they were about to hear back about which of those requests the committee would fund and, if so, by how much. Cunningham most likely expected to control roughly $50 million in earmarks. Allotting GOP earmarks is a fluid arrangement that starts with a recommendation from the House Republican Caucus and later is considered—and usually modified—by the Appropriations Committee in a highly secretive process.

So it was nervous time in Cunningham's office on September 27, 2002. Staffers were on edge, waiting to hear how much the committee had trimmed from Cunningham's 2003 requests. At 1:44 P.M. on that Friday afternoon, a staffer sent Cunningham an e-mail:

> Just starting to get word back from the committee on the numbers. They are still confidential so don't say a word to anyone yet. Looks like everything is being chopped to about 60 or 70 percent. Which means that [Wilkes] will get about 7 and Mitch will get a little over 5. Mitch's program guy told the committee that he needed 5 so this is a pretty good number for mitch [sic]. As for [Wilkes], he has a lot of other stuff in the bill so [there] is no way he will be unhappy with 7.

Anyone who knew the situation recognized this as wishful thinking—or committee spin. There was no way Cunningham would countenance a cut to Wilkes's or Wade's money. But Cunningham didn't check his Blackberry throughout the afternoon. Later in the day, the e-mail writer forwarded a copy of the e-mail he'd sent Cunningham to one of the lawmaker's staffers. It drew this reply from the second staffer at 6:02 P.M.: "Thanks. I am under my desk ducking and covering."

At 8:48 P.M., the staffer, now referring to Cunningham in the subject line as "the big chinchilla," reported back:

> He just came in, and he saw it. He stormed into his office pissed, and said he might as well become a Democrat. I thought that was the end of it, until he came out and said he wants to take $1m from some other big ticket item and put it back on Mitch's. He wants it at six. I need to do this ASAP, so if you have something else you need to discuss, please advise ASAP.

In fact, Wade's $6 million earmark ended up being $6.3 million. Not a bad return for an investment of $140,000 spent on the *Duke-Stir*.

Wade, Wilkes, and Kontogiannis continued to ply Cunningham with cash and gifts throughout the remainder of 2002, including:

- A $20,000 check from Kontogiannis on September 18

- A $16,867.13 MZM check for repairs to the *Kelly C* on September 19

- A $2,000 corporate check from Wade on October 17 to cover the cost of hauling the *Kelly C* to Long Island, where Kontogiannis would supervise and pay for its overhaul in a local shipyard

- A personal check from Wade for $7,500 on November 7 to cover Cunningham's Capital Yacht Club slip fees

- A $40,000 corporate check from Kontogiannis

- $21,749.21 from Wilkes to fly Cunningham round-trip between Washington and San Diego on October 4 and October 6

- A bill of $1,119.95 paid by Wade with his corporate American Express card for more work on the Rolls Royce

Wade picked up the bill in June 2003 so that Cunningham could enjoy a luxurious weekend at the sprawling and historic Greenbrier resort in White Sulphur Springs, West Virginia. Wade used MZM corporate checks to pay for Cunningham's lodging and meals as well as a $1,500 gift certificate that Cunningham used to buy Nancy a pair of earrings and $400 for a separate charm necklace.

Wade and Wilkes also were there to pick up the tab for Cunningham at restaurants such as the Capital Grille, where the tab almost always ran to several hundred dollars.[5] And they provided limousine service around Washington for Cunningham and his family.

Wilkes flew Cunningham to at least nine destinations aboard private jets that "cost thousands of dollars to charter," as prosecutors wrote in their February 17, 2006, sentencing memo.[6] "Meals on such chartered jets would be catered, and would include expensive bottles of wine, lobster and other extravagances."

On March 8, 2004, Wade took Cunningham on what prosecutors later called a "yacht-shopping" trip to Miami. Cunningham's room bill at the oceanfront Delano Hotel, which advertises itself as "a casual chic urban resort," was $1,254.50. He had another $846.27 in hotel food charges. The cost of the charter jet that ferried Cunningham to and from Miami was $12,975.23.

Wade even bought Cunningham toys. In July 2003, he bought three Laser Shot shooting simulators, which are used to train law enforcement field agents. Wade had one of the simulators installed in Cunningham's congressional office.

And Wade did not forget Cunningham's family—he was generous with the congressman's two daughters, Carrie and April. He paid Carrie $4,000 for two weeks of relatively menial work at his wife's charity organization, the Sure Foundation, which was based in MZM's headquarters. And he gave April $2,500 as a wedding present. "I know that sounds like a lot of money," Nancy Cunningham explained later, "but the Wades were wealthy. A $2,500 check for them was like a $75 check for anyone else."[7]

Cunningham had so much to be grateful for—and so much to pay back to his benefactors. When the appropriations season for fiscal year 2004 kicked off in March 2003, Cunningham asked the committee for $72.7 million in earmarks. Of that, $47.5 million was specifically designed to go to Wade and Wilkes.

At the other end of the cycle, in December 2003, after the earmarks for 2004 had been enacted, it became clear how closely Cunningham micromanaged the money even after the funds were in the hands of Pentagon contract officers. An exchange of phone calls and e-mails between Cunningham's staff and a Defense Department contracting office provides an illustration. It involved two Cunningham earmarks in 2004, one for $16.1 million and the other for $10.5 million. The two programs were connected to the Counterintelligence Field Activity's Global Infrastructure Data Capture program.

On December 10, 2003, a Cunningham staffer, acting on instructions from the lawmaker, called a Defense Department contracting officer to express concern that the program office was about to release money under the $16.1 million earmark to Wade when it was supposed to go to Wilkes. "I'm hearing stories that I sure hope are not true. Please reply ASAP," the Cunningham staffer said in a voice message left for the official. The defense contracting officer called the staffer back and then wrote this report to his colleagues in an e-mail (emphasis was in the original e-mail):

> I just spoke to [the staffer] who advised t [*sic*] the $16.1 million for GIDC **should got [*sic*] to ADCS and not MZM.** [The staffer] said the funding had gone to Wilkes the previous two years and [the staffer] had been informed that MZM was "trying to take this funding which is not theirs and [the staffer] is very angry about this." MZM is slated to be the recipient of the $10.5M plus-up for [the program].

[The staffer] wants no funding executed for either program—until this gets straightened out—[the staffer] wants to send a message to MZM.

The staffer had a subsequent conversation with Cunningham who said, in an apparent turn around, that the money should indeed go to Wade rather than to Wilkes. Slightly less than an hour after the original conversation, the defense official provided his colleagues with an e-mail update (again, the emphasis was in the original):

[Cunningham's staffer] just called to eat crow—[the staffer] told me [he/she] was given bad information. Bottom line—the $16.1M for (the program) should go to MZM as planned and referenced in [a DoD official's] e-mail. I confirmed that the $10.5M for [the other program] should go to MZM as well. The [first program] funding evidently goes thru MZM to ADCS possibly as a subcontract.

The confusion was understandable, as the deal was designed to go through Wade, but surreptitiously benefit Wilkes.

Remarkably through all these bribes, Cunningham was never challenged by his staff or by any other member of Congress. All professed to be shocked when his behavior came to light. The lone exception came in 2003 when another car deal raised the suspicions of one man—David Heil, who was then his chief of staff.

Heil knew something wasn't right when Wade sold Cunningham a four-year-old Chevy Suburban for $10,000—about $8,000 below market value. Heil confronted Cunningham. His boss slammed his fist on his desk and yelled at Heil to "stay the fuck out of my personal business," recalled the former staffer. Nonetheless, an unidentified member of the staff later doctored the California Department of Motor Vehicle title registration application to reflect what should have been the price—$18,000.

Heil, it turns out, did not have great luck at picking his bosses—he had previously worked for Bob Ney, the Ohio Republican sent to prison for his dealings with lobbyist Jack Abramoff. Heil had wanted to work for Cunningham because he thought the San Diegan came across as "just a regular, down-to-earth guy." But over time, Heil became disenchanted with his boss. "[Cunningham] looks you in the eye and lies to you. . . . But then again, he did that to everybody," Heil told the Capital Hill newspaper *Roll Call*.

In late 2004, after yet another confrontation with Cunningham over his dealings with the defense contractors, Heil threatened to resign if the congressman didn't agree to give up his seat. Cunningham didn't; Heil resigned.[8]

But there was no shortage of staffers willing to work on Cunningham earmarks. And those staffers were well aware that Wade and Wilkes were growing antsy to collect on earmarks that had been approved for them in the fiscal year 2004 defense budget, including one for MZM to create a "collaboration center" at the Counterintelligence Field Activity (CIFA).

On March 8, an MZM employee e-mailed the Defense Department official overseeing the CIFA contract. Attached to the e-mail was a draft of a letter authorizing MZM to begin drawing on the earmarked funds, including immediately billing the government $6 million for a large electronic storage device similar to one MZM had provided under contract in the previous fiscal year. The e-mail suggested that the official sign the letter to trigger the release of the money.

The defense official initially demurred in an e-mail reply:

> I do not believe it is in the best interest to the Government for me [to] sign the letter you provided. The letter states that I, as [the contracting officer], provide blanket approval for MZM to execute over $12,000,000 of government funding with very little accountability or oversight that I can see. I need to know what the government is buying and how it meets the goals CIFA established for the DoD CI Collaboration Center.

The contracting officer's decision was quickly overturned after MZM pressured the officer's bosses, according to court records. And, on April 22, MZM ordered a $6 million electronic storage device from ADCS while simultaneously billing the government $6 million to cover the purchase.

"As before, all equipment was off-the-shelf material supplied by third-party vendors for a fraction of the $6 million—specifically approximately $1.5 million, yielding profits of approximately $4.5 million to Cunningham's co-conspirators," prosecutors wrote on February 28, 2006.

Immediately after the government paid the $6 million, Wade on May 6 sent Wilkes a check for $5,970,000, keeping only $30,000. Wilkes deposited the check on May 7 and it cleared on May 10. On May 11, Wilkes wired $525,000 to Coastal Capital, relieving Cunningham of his obligation under the second mortgage on the Rancho Santa Fe house.

In May 2005, a year later, Wade and Cunningham went on the prowl for some expensive rugs. The lawmaker picked out five and had them sent to his congressional office in Escondido. Neither man had any reason to believe that this might be their last shopping spree together.

That same month, Cunningham put the yacht, the *Duke-Stir*, up for sale, even though he didn't technically own it. He wanted to make room in his slip for the return of the *Kelly C* from Long Island, where Kontogiannis had paid for $100,000 in refurbishments.

Between the time of the *Kelly C*'s departure for Long Island in 2002 and its pending return in 2005, the worlds of Mitch Wade and Duke Cunningham also had received a makeover. MZM went from having no prime government contracts in early 2002 to having $163 million, with more in the pipeline. Wade and his wife were living in a $3,265,000 mansion near Embassy Row in Washington. The manor in the stately Kalorama neighborhood was chockablock with ostentatious antiques and showy works of art. And Wade seemed close to realizing a $100 million profit when he sold his company.

Much of this had been made possible by his friendship with Randy Cunningham. But Wade had never wanted to have his fate tied solely to the San Diego congressman. He had worked hard to win over carefully selected members of Congress on other committees and from other districts. And in Virginia and Florida he had found two other Republicans more than willing to accept his favors.

chapter fifteen

WADE BUYS HIMSELF
A COUPLE OF LAWMAKERS

I T MIGHT HAVE BEEN THE DECLINE OF THE TEXTILE INDUSTRY IN HIS RURAL
Virginia congressional district that drove Virgil Goode Jr. to the
doorstep of MZM, Inc. on a Friday in March 2005. Because of the
textile crash, parts of Goode's rural, south-central Virginia district
had jobless rates several times the state average. Adding to the woes
of the Virginia Republican, the Bush administration's free-trade
policies were seen as hastening the decline. Towns such as
Martinsville—which once proudly called itself the "Sweatshirt
Capital of America"—were desperate to gain a foothold in America's information-age economy. And their congressman was just as
determined to help in any way he could.

Or maybe Goode was brought to MZM's doorstep by the spiral-
ing cost of running for Congress and the constantly increasing pressure to raise political money. Or it might even have been simply that
attending fund-raisers has become reflexive for members of Congress, especially those who, like Goode, sit on Appropriations.

Regardless of the factors that took him there in March 2005 for the second time in two years, Goode (rhymes with mood) entered the federal-style row house serving as MZM's headquarters and purposefully climbed to the second floor. "It was just like any other fund-raiser—stuff to eat, stuff to drink," Goode recalled later. "They had hors d'oeuvres. I made a talk about the importance of our military and having them supplied with good information. It was a pro-defense talk. . . . They had some interesting artifacts there. An old flag, items from past inaugurations."

As routine as Goode made it sound, this fund-raiser has a remarkable story behind it. Like all of Wade's deals, this one started with an idea that percolated up from the world of military intelligence. The idea was to do background checks on foreign companies involved in U.S. weapons programs. It would be called the Foreign Supplier Assessment Center.

To make this deal happen, Wade needed a champion on Capitol Hill. He needed a member of Congress willing to put the proposed Foreign Supplier Assessment Center at the top of his or her annual list of earmark requests. Wade knew Goode's part of Virginia. He knew the rolling hills and farmland. He knew the need for jobs. He knew Goode was on Appropriations. And he knew how to get his attention—with a fund-raiser in 2003 that brought in almost $40,000, making MZM the largest contributor to Goode's 2004 re-election race, by a wide margin. That fund-raiser came as Goode was putting together his list of earmark requests for the upcoming fiscal year. As a member of Appropriations, Goode's allotment of earmarks was bigger than those of most other members of the House.

Around the time of this event, Wade approached the lawmaker with his idea for the Foreign Supplier Assessment Center. The center could improve the security of the country while bringing high-paying jobs to his congressional district, he said. To sweeten the pot, Wade noted that MZM would buy a building in Goode's district to house the center. As it turned out, the city of Martinsville was burdened with a $1 million debt on the shell of a building it had constructed five years earlier in the Clearview Business Park. It had been on the market, but there were no buyers. Wade offered to buy the shell at almost half of the amount of the debt. Goode quickly arranged help from the state to retire the remainder of the debt as long as MZM brought in promised high-paying jobs. MZM now owned the building at a fire sale price.

In November 2003, after the appropriations process was completed, Goode, Wade, and Virginia Governor Mark Warner stood side-by-side as they announced that Congress had earmarked $3.6 million to create the Foreign Supplier Assessment Center. The facility, to be housed in the building in Martinsville, would create 150 good-paying local jobs. The headlines were great for Goode; the earmarked profits even greater for Wade.

Over three years, Goode would get a total of $15 million earmarked for the center, a source of stubborn pride for him even after the scandal. "With regard to the Foreign Supplier Assessment Center, I think that's needed whether it's in Martinsville or Ohio or California or New York or wherever," Goode said in an August 2005 interview. "We definitely need to do that. That is the type of entity that could be outside the immediate Beltway area [of Washington]."

Goode, of course, also stressed the benefits to Martinsville: "My interest in that stemmed not from MZM, but I visited a circuit board maker in my district and they were saying how China was selling so many circuit boards to the military and that was cutting into their business," he said. "And I think we should always be mindful of what we are buying for the military from foreign countries."

But Goode conceded that the assessment center was Wade's idea: "I talked to Mitch Wade. He liked it. He said the Defense Department was looking at it. I think the Defense Department has bought munitions from China. If you buy munitions from China, then we need to assess that."

Goode's voice rose when he was reminded that the Defense Department never requested the program, that it was forced on the Pentagon by the $3.6 million earmark he had inserted in the fiscal year 2004 defense appropriations bill:

Of all the requests I've put in for defense, and for any other area, in agriculture, the Department of Defense doesn't come over and request it. The Department of Agriculture doesn't come over and request it. When I put in the request for water and sewer projects in the Fifth District, when I was on that subcommittee, the EPA never came by and requested it. I don't know where you got that idea from. Now the subcommittee of jurisdiction can ask the agency what they think of it. But nobody from the Defense Department came by on any one or all of them—and I've probably put in over the last five or six years thirty or thirty-five requests. And the Defense Department hasn't come by on a single one and asked me to put it in.

But the Pentagon had a pretty good reason for not viewing Goode and Wade's Foreign Supplier Assessment Center as a particularly wise expenditure of limited federal funds. The explanation was simple. As the Defense Department noted in August 2006 when it refused to renew funding for the Foreign Supplier Assessment Center: "The U.S. government has other entities that provide similar services." It cited four, including the Intelligence Community Acquisition Risk Center.[1]

"If they had somebody doing this work all along, why did we pay for it in the first place?" asked Keith Ashdown of the watchdog group Taxpayers for Common Sense. "This was about politics and not about military need from the get-go."[2]

If Thomas "Tip" O'Neill, the former Speaker, was correct that "all politics is local," then Goode and Wade helped show that almost all earmarks are local as well. Certainly, this one was for Goode. When the center opened in 2004, Goode said, "This expansion of MZM Inc. will be a significant boost to the local economy." But the reality never lived up to the promises made by Wade. Congress earmarked a total of $15 million for the program over three years. That money was supposed to provide for 150 jobs in Martinsville, but only twenty-three people were working at the center when it closed on July 31, 2006. Goode's effort to help Martinsville, its population of fifteen thousand, had backfired. An unknown amount of the $15 million ended up in Wade's pocket or helped underwrite his lavish generosity to members of Congress, their staff members, and defense officials.

Nobody seriously claims that Goode himself did anything obviously illegal. For instance, prosecutors believed him when he said he did not know Wade had used illegal means to raise much of the money that MZM employees had given to Goode. And there is no law against a congressman's providing earmarks to a political supporter. But Goode did not emerge from his dealings with Wade and MZM politically unscathed. MZM employees and its PAC had given him about $90,000 in campaign contributions over three years. Most of the money came out of the 2003 and 2005 fund-raisers at MZM's headquarters. As the fallout from the Cunningham scandal mushroomed in late 2005, the MZM money became politically radioactive. In an attempt to divest himself of the tainted MZM funds, Goode in December 2005 gave nearly $90,000 from his campaign war chest to charities.

When Wade pleaded guilty to bribery and campaign finance violations three months later, on February 24, 2006, he admitted that $46,000 of the money given to Goode had been raised illegally. Although the checks had been donated in the name of MZM employees, Wade had reimbursed the employees. Goode said he didn't know the contributions were illegal. "I was shocked and amazed to learn the details of the plea agreement concerning former MZM CEO Mitch Wade," was Goode's immediate response. "I had no knowledge that any of the contributions by MZM persons to our campaign were illegal."

Roughly a week before MZM's Martinsville plant closed in July 2006, Richard A. Berglund, who had been its director, pleaded guilty to a misdemeanor charge of helping Wade make illegal contributions to Goode. For a politician running for reelection, it was another jolting reminder that Wade was more trouble than he was worth. Goode survived politically, but for the first time since he had switched parties he was held below 60 percent in his very conservative district.

Wade didn't always reimburse employees for their contributions, according to several former MZM officials who said in interviews that he had pressured them and other employees to donate to the company PAC and to members of Congress. "By the spring of '02, Mitch was twisting employees' arms to donate to his MZM PAC," said one former employee. "We were called in and told basically either donate to the MZM PAC or we would be fired." Many companies have PACs, but campaign finance laws prohibit employers from pressuring workers to contribute to them. They are permitted to encourage contributions, but not to compel them.

Another former employee said that Wade used letters to remind employees before their employment anniversaries to contribute a designated amount to the company PAC. The specific amount was based on seniority in the company: Officials with high seniority were expected to give $1,000 each and those with low seniority were expected to give $500, the former official said.

A third former employee described being rounded up along with other employees one day in the company's Washington headquarters; then, with the political recipient standing by, they were told to write a check.

"It is illegal to solicit campaign contributions for the company's political action committee by the use of threats, force or threat of job reprisal," said Larry Noble, the former general counsel of the Federal Election Commission and then director of the Center for Responsive Politics, a nonpartisan organization that tracks the flow of money in politics. "[Employees] are allowed to suggest an amount to give, but they have to say you can give more or less, or nothing at all. And they have to say that there will be no job reprisals for not giving. So even being silent on it and soliciting contributions is, actually, technically a violation of the law."

The congressional district of Florida House member Katherine Harris had little in common with Goode's, whose Virginia district had roots in furniture making, tobacco, and, most recently, textiles. Harris represented Sarasota, a bay-front city along the Gulf Coast with roots in the go-go years of the roaring 1920s. That's when the Ringling Brothers—Charles and John—began wintering their circus there. While the animals rested, the brothers kept busy by launching an architectural tradition of ostentatious super-mansions that have become a hallmark of Harris's affluent, Republican district.

Goode is so little known outside his district that he could be entered in the protected witness program, but Harris's face would be recognized by many from coast to coast. Sarasota is an appropriate political backdrop for Harris, whose Chanel style reflects her moneyed background as the granddaughter of a citrus magnate and Florida land baron. She owes her political emergence to the good fortune of growing up in a battleground state where, as secretary of state, she displayed unwavering partisanship and a heavy hand in blocking Democratic efforts to recount the razor-thin 2000 presidential race before certifying Republican George W. Bush the winner of the state's crucial twenty-five electoral votes over Democrat Al Gore.

Harris, first elected to the House in 2002, was running for reelection in March 2004 when she had dinner with Mitch Wade in Georgetown's pricey Citronelle. The evening was vintage Wade, designed to impress the Republican starlet, then forty-four years old. It succeeded. The thank-you note, written on her congressional stationery, was effusive: "What a special evening! The best dinner I have ever enjoyed in Washington. I especially enjoyed getting to know you better! Please let me know if I can ever be of assistance."[3]

Around the time of the dinner, Wade personally handed Harris sixteen checks for $2,000 each written in the names of MZM employees; fourteen were dated March 23, 2004. MZM employees and the company PAC gave her a total of $50,000 that year to help with her reelection bid. Wade later admitted that he had reimbursed employees for $32,000 of the contributions, making them illegal.

Two months after the March 2004 dinner at Citronelle, Wade plunked down a little more than $1 million for a four-story, stucco-clad office building in downtown Tampa. It sat about fifty miles outside of Harris's district but close to MacDill Air Force Base, head-quarters of the U.S. Special Operations Command and the Central Command, which oversees military activities in the Middle East. The building, which was in disrepair, needed almost $1 million in improve-ments, including thickening some walls to sound-proof them for secu-rity reasons. To defray some of the costs, the state of Florida gave MZM a $320,000 tax break. Tampa and Hillsborough County chipped in an additional $80,000 tax break as an inducement to MZM to buy there. In exchange, MZM promised to generate over the next three years eighty jobs with an average annual salary of $64,634.[4]

By spring 2005, Harris was gearing up to challenge Florida Dem-ocratic Senator Bill Nelson in 2006. The statewide race would be ex-pensive and Harris, like anyone facing a statewide race, was trolling for campaign funds. A year after their 2004 dinner, Wade and Harris dined again at Citronelle. The tab this time was similarly high, $2,800. This time, Wade shared with Harris his idea for a Navy coun-terintelligence program to be attached either to the Special Opera-tions Command or to Central Command. Although the Air Force base was outside her district, it was close enough, he said, that it would make sense for MZM to buy a building in Sarasota, which would bring high-paying intelligence jobs to her district. What he needed from her, he explained, was help getting a $10 million ear-mark for the program. He talked about holding another fund-raiser for her that year to help her in her quest to become a U.S. senator.

Wade was dealing with an inexperienced member of Congress, one not known for her competence. Indeed, Harris joined Randy Cunningham in being dubbed the dumbest members of the House by *Washingtonian Magazine* in 2004, and, as the magazine stated it, "no rocket scientists." Certainly, she was unschooled in the importance of timing on earmark requests. Just as baseball has an annual cycle—spring training, opening day, the all-star break, the playoffs, and the World Series—appropriations bills have an annual sequence as well. The process begins in March. That is when members begin organiz-ing the lists of priorities for funding to be turned over to the various Appropriations subcommittees. And that is when Wade took Harris to dinner. He had every reason to believe that his sales pitch had worked. But somehow Harris failed to include his $10 million earmark for the Navy counterintelligence program on her list of earmarks. When he discovered the oversight, Wade went ballistic, according to two MZM employees involved in handling the earmark.

One of the employees described one of her first conversations with Wade this way:

> I said, "Let's talk about Congress. Do you need me to go out there and attend dinners on your behalf? Do I need to do things? How should we be doing this? It's a corporation, how would you like things billed?" And he said, "I've ordered you an American Express card and I don't care if you wine, dine, or sleep with them, I want my deals done."

Wade also told her of a condo that he had purchased just up the street from the MZM office and invited her to move in, which she declined because his offer had seemed creepy to her.

Another employee said of Wade:

> Mitch had a very old-world view of Congress. He had the view of, "OK, you know, you take 'em out, have some drinks, take 'em to dinner. We'll take 'em to a ball game. And, you know, then we'll get some stuff done." [Later she added] Mitch didn't understand that Congress had deadlines. It was very frustrating for me at times because I had to explain to him that this piece of paper, it had to be into the office three months ago. And he said, "No, just get it done." I said, "No, it doesn't get done that way." That's a good way to infuriate committee staff; to infuriate personal staff; infuriate a member.

But this time, it was Wade who was infuriated. And he made no effort to keep his fury secret. Employees heard his screaming jag and the epithets directed at Harris, including his threat to "never give her another dime."

In April, Harris sent an addendum to the defense Appropriations subcommittee, adding a request for Wade's $10 million counterintelligence program. But she instructed the subcommittee to consider it her third priority. When Wade learned that it was listed third, he hit the ceiling again.[5]

About that time, Wade hired Harris's congressional scheduler, Mona Tate Yost, paying her roughly three times the amount Harris had been paying her. One employee said that Wade directed Tate Yost to go back to Harris on the Hill and pressure her old boss to make his earmark request her top earmark priority. Tate Yost declined to speak publicly about her dealings with Wade, but others said she felt awkward and conflicted about the assignment. This was partly because Yost was in her early twenties and quite junior to Harris and partly because of her fondness and respect for Harris.

Wade "was really using her on the side to bully Katherine Harris and to remind her—and he would put her in absolute uncomfortable situations where she would come to me and she would say, 'He wants me to go call her and tell her she has to do this,'" recalled an MZM employee. "And, you know, the girl would say, 'I can't do that. I can't.'"

In mid-June 2005, the first stories about Wade's bribery of Cunningham broke, shining a bright spotlight on the money Wade also had given Harris and Goode. Many questions were raised about whether Harris and Goode had helped Wade with earmarks. When Congress completed work on the funding bills toward the end of the year, Wade's proposed counterintelligence Navy program was not there. Congress did not fund it.

Nonetheless, Harris was dogged by her dealings with Wade during her quixotic and amateurish campaign for the Senate. When Wade pleaded guilty in February 2006, he admitted to giving Harris $32,000 in illegal contributions. In response, she issued a statement:

Mr. Wade never informed me about the reimbursement of any campaign contributions. I supported a project proposed by Mr. Wade and his company out of a desire to secure jobs and economic opportunities for the people of my district. Had I known of his illegal conduct, my campaign would not have accepted any contributions from Mr. Wade.

Ed Rollins, the veteran political consultant who was serving as Harris's top adviser, did an internal inquiry and joined a chorus of advisers who recommended that she drop out of the race because of the questions that were being raised about MZM's donations to Harris and her efforts to help Wade get an earmark. "But her story kept changing. . . . Our great concern was that you get into trouble when you don't tell the same story twice. . . . Maybe you don't think you did anything wrong, but then maybe you start getting questioned about it and so forth, and you may perjure yourself," Rollins said.[6] Harris rejected Rollins's advice to drop out of the race, and he joined a staff exodus from the campaign.

Harris told an *Orlando Sentinel* reporter on April 19, 2006, that her campaign had "reimbursed" Citronelle for the 2005 meal. When the reporter asked how the campaign could have reimbursed a restaurant for a meal that already had been paid for, Harris abruptly stalked off, leaving the question unanswered. Her press secretary called the *Sentinel* later in the day and asked the paper not to publish Harris's dubious, impromptu claim. The *Sentinel* ran the story on April 20, and the next day Harris released a statement about her second dinner with Wade. (At that point, she still had not publicly acknowledged the first dinner, in 2004.) She wrote:

> At the time I had a meal with Mitchell Wade, I thought that my campaign would be reimbursing my share of the cost. I later discovered that somehow this was not done. I then discussed with my staff the best way to correct this oversight. Neither I nor my advisors ever thought it would be appropriate to reimburse Mr. Wade in the midst of the government investigations into his conduct. Just to resolve any questions, I have donated to a local Florida charity $100 which will more than adequately compensate for the cost of my beverage and appetizers.

The night of our dinner, Mr. Wade purchased several expensive bottles of wine which he took home with him uncorked—this is apparently the reason the bill was so high. I take full responsibility for this oversight and continue to operate under a policy of openness, transparency, and accountability to the people of my district and the state of Florida. While the rules are complicated, as a member of Congress, it is my responsibility to know and obey them. It has always been my intent to conduct myself in an ethical manner, and I regret this oversight.

The relevant rule is fairly straightforward. A member of the House is prohibited from collecting gifts, including meals, worth more than $50. For Harris, this was just one controversy too many. After Governor Jeb Bush disavowed her campaign and other top Republicans ran for the exits, Harris was trounced by Bill Nelson in the 2006 elections, receiving only 38 percent of the vote on the same day another Republican won the governorship.

Like Cunningham, Goode and Harris welcomed Wade's attention and eagerly tried to pay him back with earmarks. But as enriching as Wade found it to have members of Congress willing to do his bidding, he still needed other officials to help complete the deal. It wasn't enough just to have Congress earmark a program; Wade also had to find a way to make sure that the military facility assigned to run the program would choose MZM over other possible contractors. Members of Congress can make recommendations, but Wade wanted government agencies to say they needed what he had to offer. Wade did not want any surprises when the contract was awarded at the facility level.

For these reasons and others, Wade went the extra mile to cultivate allies within the intelligence agencies. MZM's Blanket Purchase Agreement made it easy for an agency to buy Wade's wares. But Wade still needed to grease things within the agency to ensure the smooth delivery of the purchase order.

MZM's first order under its Blanket Purchase Agreement came in October 2002. It was for $193,281 to help with a document-scanning program called FIRES (Facilities, Infrastructure, and Engineering Systems). The work was being done at the National Ground Intelligence Center (NGIC). As the agency's full name implies, NGIC (pronounced in-jick) engages in military intelligence work. Located in Charlottesville, Virginia, it also is within Goode's district, which is how Goode and Wade first met. NGIC, with a staff of nine hundred government employees working side by side with outside contractors like MZM, provides analyses of foreign military forces and strategic global infrastructure, such as digitized blueprints of the Panama Canal.

Many of MZM's contracts would come through NGIC. Wade's guilty plea in February 2006 revealed how he got NGIC to select MZM for so much work. Wade's toehold at the plant was the $193,281 FIRES contract. Eight months before MZM got the contract, Wade hired the program manager's son. Later, Wade hired the manager himself, Robert Fromm.[7]

The U.S. attorney didn't identify Fromm by name at the time of Wade's plea agreement, which caused confusion in news reports. The reason for the confusion was that the Fromms weren't the only father-son tandem Wade hired in connection with NGIC. Two months after MZM began work on the FIRES program in October 2002, Wade hired William S. Rich III, the son of NGIC's executive director, William S. Rich Jr. In September 2003, the elder Rich resigned from NGIC to go to work for MZM as a senior executive vice president for intelligence. MZM hired the wife of NGIC's chief of staff, Robert Canar, as a secretary.[8] By law, government employees are not allowed to discuss possible employment with companies they supervise. More than a dozen NGIC employees migrated to MZM in three years. During that same period, MZM's revenue from the FIRES project soared from $193,281 to several million dollars a year.

Wade's friends at NGIC provided vital and privileged information to Wade that was unavailable to other contractors. Such information was used to tailor proposals in such a way as to gain an advantage over other contractors. Then they recommended MZM over other contractors. And they provided favorable performance reviews of MZM's work.

> These performance reviews were critical to MZM, [read a statement from the office of the U.S. attorney for the District of Columbia]. Notwithstanding the fact that Wade received these purchase orders without competitive bidding as a result of his earlier receipt of the $225 million BPA, MZM could not be assured that they would continue to receive new purchase orders without receiving these type of favorable reviews by Defense Department officials. In engaging in this corrupt activity, Wade deprived the citizens of the United States of their right to the honest services of government—the right of the Defense Department to make decisions free from bias and favoritism.

Brent Wilkes had spread his money and favors far and wide to Republicans. Wade's approach was much more targeted, giving primarily to a handful of lawmakers who could help him with specific projects. A former MZM employee quoted Wade as saying: "The only people I want to work with are people I give checks to. I own them."

But as satisfying as Wade found his dealings with Harris and Goode, he never forgot that special first love, that first member of Congress he had bought. He knew that he would always have Duke Cunningham.

And Cunningham was confident that Wade would be there for him no matter what his needs might be. Cunningham, after all, now was living in a mansion in Rancho Santa Fe and on a yacht in Washington. He had access to other boats, and a Rolls Royce was parked in his assigned spot in the congressional garage. He had access to limousines and jets. He was sitting on the Intelligence Committee in the post-9/11 budgetary world when money was flowing freely into secret intelligence programs. And he sat on the Defense Appropriations subcommittee, which handled the funding for intelligence programs. He was uniquely positioned to influence a part of the federal budget that had little transparency or oversight.

There was no denying it—life was awfully good for Cunningham and Wade in May 2005. They had no idea that the seemingly endless supply—of houses, cars, dinners, earmarks, and obscene profits—was about to run out.

chapter sixteen

THE INTERVIEW

Marcus Stern was a pretty curious kid. Before he arrived as a student at Washington's Woodrow Wilson High School, he had been fascinated with cells, spending hours in the Chevy Chase library reading up on them. So, when his biology teacher made a point that clashed with what he had learned, Marc challenged him and stubbornly refused to drop the challenge. Exasperated, the teacher proclaimed, "Well, regardless young man, they have been teaching it my way for hundreds of years and I will continue to teach it my way." Stern shot back, "That means they were teaching it your way back when they were burning witches in Salem."

Suspension and expulsion quickly followed.

Nothing Stern experienced in the years that followed swayed him from his conviction that it is best to be a contrarian. School and rules were for others; caution and prudence were for sissies. To the core, he was a contrarian. And that was still his mindset when, as a journalist in the Washington bureau of Copley News Service, he found himself placing a call to Rep. Randy Cunningham.

Ironically for a journalist who abhorred pack journalism, the first step to the story that toppled Cunningham was taken because Stern grudgingly joined the Washington herd in chasing a story. As the news editor for Copley's eleven-person bureau, he did what every other regional news bureau in town was doing in mid-May 2005—jump all over a nine-month analysis of privately funded congressional travel. The analysis of five and a half years of trips was done by the Center for Public Integrity, American Public Media, and Northwestern University's Medill News Service; at least twenty-three thousand trips valued at almost $50 million were examined.

The study caused quite a stir because so many of the trips—paid for by defense contractors, special interest groups, and lobbyists—were little more than cushy vacation visits to four-star hotels and resorts and pampered excursions on corporate jets. Neither Copley nor Stern was immune; Stern's reporters were asked to check out the findings on the local members of Congress for Copley papers in California, Illinois, and Ohio. When reporter Dana Wilkie turned in her story on the San Diego delegation, Stern was curious about how Cunningham had explained his acceptance of trips.

Cunningham was by no means one of the more peripatetic members. Between January 2000 and June 2005, he had taken only six trips, valued at only $25,572.04—far down the list and way, way behind the leading junketeer, Wisconsin Republican James F. Sensenbrenner. Sensenbrenner, chairman of the House Judiciary Committee, had taken twenty-two trips valued at $179,814.

The sponsors of Cunningham's six trips were a varied lot, but they included no defense contractors. Ziff-Davis Publishing, owners of several computer magazines, brought Cunningham to Chicago April 19–20, 2000, for a speech. The Serbian Bar Association also flew him to Chicago for an award June 23–24, 2000. Safari Club International, a pro-hunting group, had Cunningham as its keynote speaker at a dinner March 23, 2002. The next year, the American Gas Association sprung for five days in Sioux Falls, South Dakota, to have the San Diego Republican attend an energy seminar from September 28 through October 2.

Nothing in these first four trips particularly interested Stern. But he was intrigued by the fifth and sixth trips: Both were to Saudi Arabia, a country Cunningham had previously displayed little interest in. And—unusual for a trip to a foreign country by a congressman—both were arranged and paid for by a private citizen rather than by the government of the host country. Both were funded by Ziyad Abduljawad, a Saudi native and naturalized American citizen who was chairman of PLC Land Co., located in Cunningham's district. Abduljawad was just "a friend," insisted the congressman's chief of staff, Harmony Allen. But the Saudi native, who now lives in Newport Beach, is also a member of the wealthy Saudi Abduljawads, a family whose tentacles wave throughout the Kingdom.

The first trip was from April 3 to April 8 and was valued at $10,537. In the second trip—December 9 to December 14—Cunningham was joined by his fellow California Republican, Rep. Ken Calvert, and—most interestingly—by a man later listed as a co-conspirator, the New York developer Thomas Kontogiannis. That trip was valued at $10,789.90 by both Cunningham and Calvert. And Cunningham offered identical reasons for both trips: They were taken, he said, "to meet with government and business leaders to promote discourse and better relations between the two nations."

When Stern edited Wilkie's story on June 8 and read that explanation, his reaction was immediate: "I don't believe it."

As the bureau's news editor, Stern had become Copley's "go-to" guy on foreign hot spots. In recent years, he had reported from Iraq three times, Afghanistan twice, Pakistan four times, Haiti four times, and had taken solo trips to Yemen and Saudi Arabia. Now he wanted to know what he called "the real reason" the fun-loving Cunningham had spent those twelve days in a country that prohibits alcohol and the mingling of unmarried men and women. Stern was determined to find a more plausible reason for the trips. His main focus was finding out everything he could about Ziyad Adbuljawad. He also checked legislative and news databases to look for connections between the congressman and the Saudis. But these efforts went nowhere.

In frustration, Stern launched what he called "a lifestyle audit" of Cunningham. That meant checking all available databases to see whether the congressman was showing any upgrades in his lifestyle. The reporter had already hit a dry hole trying to confirm rumors that Cunningham was building a hunting lodge on Maryland's Eastern Shore. But he continued his own hunt for anything out of the ordinary. Many of the databases he checked were San Diego–based. Finally, he saw something interesting, thanks to the national Nexis database on real estate transactions.

There it was—Cunningham had purchased a mansion in Rancho Santa Fe, thirty miles north of San Diego, on November 25, 2003, almost eighteen months earlier. Stern didn't need to look at the selling price to have his news sense ratcheted to a higher level. All he needed was that name—"Rancho Santa Fe." Rancho Santa Fe isn't exactly filled with high school administrators like Nancy Cunningham and husbands who earn $154,700, as Cunningham did in 2003. Rancho Santa Fe is for people with money—real money. Money like residents Bill Gates, the Sultan of Brunei, Joseph Coors, Phil Mickelson, and the singer Jewel. Money like former residents Douglas Fairbanks, Mary Pickford, Joan Kroc, and Howard Hughes. At the time Cunningham was buying this house, *Forbes* magazine had Rancho Santa Fe ranked as the nation's wealthiest spot among communities of more than a thousand households.

So Stern looked deeper into the sale. Cunningham and his wife had bought the Via del Charro property for $2.55 million with one mortgage for $500,000 and another for $595,000, property records showed. Stern estimated that Cunningham likely had put down $1,455,000 and financed $1,095,000—a curiously high down payment and mortgage for an elected official. But suspicions and estimates don't make news stories. It was possible, Stern conceded, that Cunningham had made a killing on the sale of his longtime personal residence in seaside Del Mar Heights. So he checked the real estate records again and found that Cunningham had sold the Del Mar Heights house for $1.67 million. Cunningham had bought that house on January 20, 1988, for $435,000, financing $315,000. Selling the house fifteen years later for $1.675 million would produce a big profit, perhaps enough to make it possible for him to buy the Rancho Santa Fe mansion.

But Stern noticed something else that piqued his curiosity. The buyer of the Del Mar Heights house was not listed, as you would expect, as a Joe and Jan Smith or a Mr. and Mrs. Lopez. The buyer, rather oddly for this strictly residential neighborhood far from downtown San Diego, was something called "1523 New Hampshire Ave. LLC." As a native of the nation's capital, Stern recognized it as possibly a Washington address. Checking corporate databases, Stern found that 1523 New Hampshire Ave. LLC was a company registered in Nevada. The man listed as the president was Mitchell Wade, a name Stern had never before heard and not one associated with San Diego. Wade also was listed as the president of another Nevada-registered company—MZM Inc. And 1523 New Hampshire Avenue was the Washington address of MZM's corporate headquarters.

Stern joked later that the real breakthrough for his story came when he turned to that sophisticated new tool of investigative reporters—Google. That led him to MZM's corporate Web site. To his astonishment, he saw that MZM had become an overnight success in the defense industry, going from no prime contracts to more than $100 million in contracts in two years, roughly the time span of the house sale. There was a link on the MZM Web site to a trade magazine story about how MZM had rocketed from nowhere onto the list of the nation's top one hundred defense contractors since 2003.

It was, Stern told his bureau chief, his "'holy shit' moment"—the moment he realized that all this rummaging through Web sites and databases had led him to a real, potentially significant, story. But there was much more reporting to do.

Stern then looked to see what Wade had done with the house after he bought it. Again, he was astonished to see that Wade had put the house back on the market almost immediately at roughly the same price. On January 5, 2004, it went back on the market for $1,680,000—$50,000 more than he had paid Cunningham for it.

But the house languished on the market for 261 days before selling for $975,000 on September 22, 2004. That the house had sat on the market for eight months before selling at a $700,000 loss was distinctly curious because the San Diego housing market was sizzling and prices were moving up briskly. It was hard to look at the facts and the timeline without concluding anything other than that Wade had substantially overpaid Cunningham for the house.

But sitting in Washington a continent away from San Diego, Stern needed experts and facts to substantiate that conclusion. So he asked Copley's bureau office manager Rosemary Petersen to find a San Diego real estate appraiser to do an appraisal on the property at the time Cunningham sold it to Wade.

Petersen is one of those people so prized in Washington because she knows how to get things done behind the scenes and knows how to persuade often balky bureaucracies to lend a hand. But her famed efficiency was to be tested this time. Because this time realtors and appraisers wanted nothing to do with a possible corruption story about a powerful congressman. Petersen called an appraiser who agreed to appraise the house, assuredly saying it would take no more than a week. Several days later he sent a list of "comparables" for the Del Mar Heights house to the bureau. But the week passed without the requested appraisal. When Petersen called the appraiser to follow up, he said he wasn't going to complete the appraisal. When asked why, he declined to comment. So she called another appraiser. That appraiser was obliging until she told him the address. At that point, the second appraiser ran for the exits. A third appraiser also bolted after hearing the address. When Petersen pressed him on why he wouldn't do the appraisal, he said the association's lobbying office in Sacramento had recommended against getting involved. Petersen called the trade association, but the calls went unreturned.

So Stern decided to get a visual inspection of the house. In the San Diego market it matters if you have a great view of the ocean, and a breathtaking view from Cunningham's house would undercut the notion that Wade had overpaid. When Copley News Service employee Paul Nasri made that visual inspection, it was another nail in Cunningham's political coffin—there was no real view and the overall condition of the house was less than pristine. Stern could now say with certainty that the house's value would have fallen toward the lower range of comparable houses in the neighborhood. There was no way for Wade or Cunningham to deny that Wade had overpaid Cunningham for the house. By paying the inflated price, Wade had made it possible for Cunningham to buy the $2.55 million mansion in Rancho Santa Fe.

Still, an overpayment, while titillating, was far from proof of corruption. Stern knew he had to show that Cunningham had provided a quid pro quo to Wade—something of value that Cunningham had obtained by dint of his influence as a member of Congress. Stern needed to show that Cunningham had betrayed the public trust by using his positions on the House Defense Appropriations Subcommittee and Intelligence Committee to steer military intelligence contracts to Wade's company, MZM.

By now it had been a full month since Wilkie's story on the Saudi trips had roused Stern's curiosity. It was time to go directly to Wade and Cunningham. The first call to Wade did not go smoothly. Stern was put through to a nervous young man who would identify himself only as "Scott." Stern explained that he wanted to speak to Mitchell Wade about a real estate transaction. Scott asked for details. Stern told him he was inquiring about a house in San Diego that MZM had purchased from Cunningham. He noted that it went right back on the market and languished there for months before Wade was able to sell it at a much lower price. Scott put Stern on hold for several minutes.

When he returned to the phone, Scott was not only nonresponsive but blunt: "We don't know what you're talking about. We have nothing to discuss," went the official response. Sensing Scott was about to hang up, Stern added quickly, "No, I want to speak to Mitchell Wade."

"He's not going to speak to you. Thank you for your interest," Scott replied curtly.

When Stern asked for Scott's full name, he refused to give it and abruptly hung up. Immediately, Stern called back and asked to leave a message for Scott. The receptionist put him through to the voice mail of Scott Brummet, one of Wade's assistants. Stern left a message saying that when Scott calmed down they would need to talk, perhaps over a cup of coffee. But Stern assured Brummet that they would indeed need to talk.

Stern then called Cunningham's office, outlined his questions about the house sale to the congressman's press secretary, and requested an interview.

A short while later, Stern got a voice message from Brummet, telling him to call back. He did. Brummet, now in control, apologized for his earlier, rather abrupt reaction, saying that he was new and unfamiliar with the transaction Stern had asked about. Although Wade was traveling and unavailable to talk with Stern by phone, he had talked with Brummet and given him "some insight" into the transaction.

"We were looking at expanding our company presence in San Diego," Brummet explained. "We looked at the property and thought it would work for us. But after we bought it, we realized that it did not meet our security or our corporate needs."

So they sold it. But Brummet insisted, "We purchased it at market price and sold it at market price." Stern noted that the market price appeared to have fallen considerably between the purchase and sale despite rapidly rising home prices in the area.

"We don't have any control over the market," Brummet said, adding that they had obtained the best price they could at both ends of the transaction and that they were still looking for property in San Diego. Stern pushed him back, calling the company's story "pretty weak." He suggested Brummet "go back to the well" and get a better explanation. Brummet turned testy. He replied that MZM was expanding and purchasing facilities all over the United States. Stern pointed out that none of those had been bought from influential congressmen. The call ended with Stern asking whether he might call back if he had any follow-up questions and Brummet answering, "By all means."

It was now early afternoon and the congressman's office was moving this rather unusual interview request up the hierarchy. It wasn't the press secretary who called back. It was the chief of staff, Harmony Allen. And she was very, very curious about Stern's proposed line of questioning for her boss. She guessed that Cunningham had been able to buy a house in Rancho Santa Fe because he had made lots of money on the sale of the Del Mar Heights house. But Stern said he had to know directly from the congressman whether there had been any quid pro quo with government contracts.

All that was left was a direct confrontation between the reporter and the congressman. Two hours later, Cunningham squeezed in a call to Stern during a break in a meeting of the House Permanent Select Committee on Intelligence with the head of the Pentagon's Counterintelligence Field Activity. It was to turn out to be the most important interview of both men's careers.

Indeed, prosecutors would later call this interview the key moment in Cunningham's downfall. Before he talked to Stern there was no investigation of him, no hint of corruption, no sign that this high-flying congressman and war hero was going down.

The interview that was to forever alter his fate and radically change his reputation lasted twenty-five minutes and nine seconds— five times as long as the furious dogfight in the skies over North Vietnam back on May 10, 1972.

Cunningham was unflappable throughout the session, never seeming to break into a sweat or to be fazed by anything the reporter said to him. And Stern was never accusatory or prosecutorial. Despite the high stakes, it was, in many ways, more like a conversation between associates. Stern began by saying, "I just wanted you to help me clarify this so nobody gets any misunderstanding." Cunningham laughed at this; he soothingly replied, "I don't want any either."

Stern laid out the facts of the home sale right away, noting that Wade had paid "a very, very good price" and sold it off for "far, far less." Cunningham was unperturbed. He patiently set out to explain what had happened, casting himself almost as an innocent bystander, a homeowner who just wanted a new house to be closer to his kids and, gosh, he was "trying to get as much as [he could] out of the house" just like anybody else would.

He recalled with a chuckle that he had originally bought the Del Mar house "right after" *Top Gun* hit the theaters. But now "it no longer kind of suited" what he and Nancy wanted. So, he said, he just "told a lot of people" that he wanted to sell. And Mitch Wade just happened to be in a group of people who heard this comment. "And Mitch Wade said, 'Hey, I'm looking for a place.'" He was a tough customer, Cunningham explained—he demanded comps "not just on the block, but, you know, entire Del Mar." At this point, two minutes into the interview, the congressman made his first effort to casually blame the real estate agent, Elizabeth Todd, stating that she "actually set the price" through her firm of Willis Allen Real Estate. "Mr. Wade agreed, accepted. And we sold the house." He added with great confidence that it was now "probably worth more than [he] sold it for." He said this almost in sadness at the thought of how much more money he could have made if he had just held onto the house a little longer.

Stern pressed ever so gently. "Well, it wasn't [worth more] when they put it back on the market less than a month later." He asked Cunningham why he thought Wade had so quickly abandoned his acquisition.

"Marc, I have not a clue on the thing. I was surprised that he sold it or even wanted to sell it after he bought it so quick," replied Cunningham. He said that he had accepted Wade at face value when he had told him he wanted the house because "he was looking for a presence in San Diego and he wanted a place to stay."

At this point, when pressed further by Stern, Cunningham altered his original story a tad. Just two minutes after he said he had been surprised by Wade's interest in the house, he changed that slightly so that now it was Wade who first expressed a desire to buy in San Diego: "I said, hey, I got a house for sale."

Still calm and very much in control, Cunningham again shifted responsibility for the transaction to Todd; he added that it "was none of [his] business" what Wade did with the house. All he knew, he repeated, was that the agent had set "a market price."

Stern agreed with Cunningham that sellers always want to maximize their profits; he then shifted focus to the lucrative contracts MZM and Wade received just at the time of the house sale. Cunningham patiently explained to Stern the ways of Washington: "I don't have anything to do with contracts," he said, even though he was a senior member of the committees that oversee those contracts. He readily acknowledged that he had supported contracts for MZM but said this was no different from his support for prominent defense companies with ties to San Diego, such as Qualcomm, Titan, SAIC, or TRW. All he did was to "write letters of support to all of those groups, saying, hey, I support this program that General Umptiump or Admiral Uptiump supports this program," he said. "But I don't make the decisions on what's going to be funded or not. It's based on what the military wants. National security."

Sitting at his desk on the eleventh floor of the National Press Building, Stern silently said to himself, "Got 'em." Cunningham's voluntary admission that he wrote letters to help MZM secure millions of dollars worth of contracts was the quid pro quo that had been missing.

Stern gently reminded the congressman that members of his committees "always have been [influential] and probably always will be." Cunningham was jocular: "Well, I wish I was more influential. I wanted to be chairman some day and, hopefully, I will be influential." But, now, he said, quietly, he was at the mercy of his chairmen. "I don't really have anything to say about [contracts]," he offered.

Stern pushed him to respond to skeptics who might misconstrue the windfall for the congressman. The answer ended up being the most memorable quote of the day:

Listen, that's a fair question. All I can tell you is, Marc, I think you know me and my whole life I've lived above-board. I've never even smoked a marijuana cigarette. I don't cheat. If a contractor buys me a lunch and we meet a second time, I buy the lunch. My whole life has been above-board and so this doesn't worry me. It's a fair question but I don't know why Mr. Wade sold his property at that expense.

Stern seemed to run out of gas and signaled the end of the interview, "Ok. I appreciate it." The congressman thanked him for the questions and said he would welcome more. "I think you also understand my background and my life and the last thing I would do is get involved in something that, you know, is wrong."

Stern thanked him for his time and said he would "sort of digest this" before following up. But before hanging up he asked: "Are you and Mitchell Wade friends?" That prompted one of the biggest lies of the day. Of a man he later admitted he had been almost inseparable from for years, he now denied being any more friendly with than he was with any other CEO. "I mean, we meet, we have events. I see them in San Diego at chamber events and those kinds of things. I would say it's no different than anybody else."

A minute later, Stern indicated that this really would be the end of the interview now. Questions about MZM's programs yielded little. So, after thirteen minutes of questioning, he thanked Cunningham for his time, noting, "I don't see any reason to hold you up any longer."

Then—out of the blue—Stern turned chatty and started talking about books. "You know, I've just been reading *Charlie Wilson's War,* by George Crile. Have you read that?" Somewhat taken aback, Cunningham quickly warmed to the question, praising the book, which tells the story of the flamboyant twelve-term Texas congressman who combined a ladies' man reputation with a passion for aiding the Afghan mujaheddin in their battle against the Soviets in the 1980s.

Stern wanted to—but did not—note to Cunningham that had he really read this book he wouldn't have tried to diminish the clout of members of the Appropriations Committee. Crile, after all, had skillfully shown how Wilson used his perch on the House Defense Appropriations Subcommittee to hasten the fall of the Soviet empire.

Instead, the two men chatted as if they were old friends, critiquing the book, sharing notes about trips to Saudi Arabia, discussing challenges in U.S.-Saudi relations. He talked passionately about his desire to improve relations with the Kingdom, even offering a rare criticism of the Bush White House for failing to grasp the impact of their policies there.

Stern was now able to ask several questions about the topic that had first fueled his scrutiny of the congressman—those two pesky, still-unexplained trips to Saudi Arabia. He pressed for details on the mysterious Abduljawal. Cunningham offered a full-throated defense of his motives, saying the trips had nothing to do with his businesses. "He has a passion, just like I do with Ireland. I want the English out of Ireland," he said with a laugh. "He wants a relationship back with Saudi Arabia. It's where his heritage is. Like the Irish is mine." Cunningham boasted he had introduced Abduljawal to the Republican caucus and to the Speaker of the House.

For Stern, this did nothing to sate his curiosity about the Saudi trips. He would have to accept the fact that he could prove nothing else about the trips and that Cunningham's explanation could not be refuted by any known evidence. The trips would have to stand as simply the detail that drew him into a story that had taken him in a surprising direction.

Stern tried to conclude the interview once again. But before he could do that, Cunningham added: "Like I say, give me a call if you want to talk to Elizabeth [Todd] or you want to talk to me. This doesn't bother me because I didn't do anything in the blind. It's public record. And I did it through Willis and Allen [sic]. So I feel good about it."

It was, Cunningham almost certainly felt, twenty-five minutes well spent. There was nothing in the tone of the interview to suggest that he was in trouble. He had once again—it seemed—dodged enemy fire. In fact, a news story was set to run in just four days, and it was a story that would change how he would be viewed by history.

chapter seventeen

A FAST-PACED WEEK

SUNDAY, JUNE 12 WAS GOING TO BE A TYPICALLY GORGEOUS DAY IN PAR-adise. Sixty-four degrees and sunny. And Phil Halpern knew as he brought that morning's *San Diego Union-Tribune* into his kitchen at 7:30 that it would be a perfect day to work off the tension of another tough work week with a long bike ride. With friends waiting for him, he didn't even glance at the front page. All he had time for was the sports page, featuring stories about a thrilling ninth-inning walk-off win for the Padres and the dramatic conclusion of the Triple Crown with Afleet Alex handily winning the Belmont Stakes by seven lengths. The rest of the news of the day would have to wait. There were roads to conquer, calories to be burned off.

The compact five-foot-seven, 145-pound lawyer mounted his bike—a Litespeed Vortex with Campagnola Record components and American classic wheels—and headed out on a strenuous five-hour, hundred-mile ride. It was a ride that took him from his house near San Diego's Old Town, past Miramar Marine Air Station, once home of the Top Gun fighter school, up north through Escondido, past Rep. Randy Cunningham's district office, then past the Lawrence Welk Resort to Oceanside, and then, finally, through La Jolla back to Old Town.

When he finally returned home, exhausted, he picked up the *Union-Tribune* he had discarded and glanced at the front page. There it was—"Lawmaker's Home Sale Questioned"—the story that was to dominate his professional life for the next year.

Halpern, a competitive cyclist who has run a 2:36 marathon, had served as an assistant U.S. attorney for the Southern District of California since October 1, 1984. For twenty-one years, Halpern had prosecuted cases in San Diego, many of them high-profile, including the first corruption case against sitting California judges; the largest bribery case ever brought against an IRS agent; prosecution of a food contractor responsible for causing a hepatitis A outbreak; prosecution of an arms smuggling ring supplying Iran with critical F-14 parts; the first federal case involving the distribution of steroids; the largest counterfeit sports memorabilia prosecution undertaken by the federal government; and the first federal case involving the illegal distribution of human growth hormone.

Because of his background prosecuting white collar crime cases, Halpern said he read the story about Cunningham's home sale with enough interest that it kept him "out of the shower for a while." He recognized the potential of the story to become the kind of high-profile public integrity case he'd like to handle. "This is why I do what I do. I think it's why most of my compatriots who remain in the job for more than four or five years do it. Because, you know, this is something that was clearly worthwhile, worthy of investigation," he said. "I want to take on cases that make a difference."

Halpern would later say that never had he begun a prosecution solely because of a newspaper story. But before he read this story there was no investigation of Cunningham, no chance of prosecution. And what transpired over the next seven days left no doubt that Cunningham was dirty and that a San Diego populace normally so blasé about political stories had been aroused by the piece.

First, of course, he had to get himself assigned to the case. And he was not the only prosecutor working for U.S. Attorney Carol Lam who was reading Stern's story that Sunday morning. In fact, the others had gotten a head start on him.

Sanjay Bhandari and Jason Forge also worked as prosecutors in San Diego. Bhandari was in Germany the day the *Union-Tribune* published the house-sale story.

> I was visiting my wife's family there. My wife is German. And I happened to be checking the *U-T,* which I usually do, on the Internet. Read the story, I believe, immediately after it came out. Immediately after I read it, I concluded that it needed to be investigated. You know, the facts speak for themselves. In this market, in San Diego, for that to happen, something has to be very, very wrong. . . . It clearly needed to be looked at. That was obvious upon reading those facts. And so I immediately sent an email to the chief of the section, George Hardy, and said that I thought it should be investigated, gave him some suggestions for some things to do, and asked that when I got back, I could start working on it. And that was something he agreed to.

Hardy, the chief of the major fraud section, had also talked with Forge by the time Halpern walked into his office Monday morning. Hardy sent him down to see Forge. Forge had worked in the Los Angeles U.S. attorney's office before transferring to San Diego. He was a strict vegetarian for moral reasons. "I like animals more than people," he joked, adding that he had adopted a stray pit bull while working in Los Angeles. When Halpern had arrived in Forge's office that morning, he learned that Bhandari also wanted to work the case. The three of them decided to work it together.

In Los Angeles, they might still talk about Cochran, Bailey, Shapiro, and Scheck. But in San Diego, for this case, a new "dream team" of prosecutors had taken shape. It would be Halpern, Forge, and Bhandari vs. Randall H. Cunningham.

Of course, not everybody was excited and intrigued when they picked up the *Union-Tribune* that morning. Some were left almost physically ill by what they read.

Greg Parks's first inkling of the incendiary scandal that was about to engulf Cunningham came when his father called from San Diego and told him, "Your boss was in the paper."[1] Parks, a legislative assistant in Cunningham's office, had no way of recognizing that what his father was telling him over the phone was the beginning of the end for the most corrupt member of Congress ever caught. He couldn't have imagined that within a few months the scandal would leave him and other Cunningham staffers jobless.

Trying to digest what was in the story, Parks found himself scratching his head and immediately reaching the same conclusion that so many other members of Congress and Cunningham's staff reached when they heard about the house sale in the days to come. For all of them, it was the same—"This has to be some kind of misunderstanding."

Parks was an earnest young Republican from El Cajon, California, who thought he might run for Congress one day himself. Cunningham was a father figure, a war hero, and a political mentor all rolled into one. The lawmaker would take Parks and other staffers out for drinks and Mexican food on special occasions, including every May 10—the day they all called MiG Day, the anniversary of that memorable day in 1972. "He would tell these old Navy stories that would crack us all up," Parks said.

In the days ahead, as more revelations came to light, Cunningham privately reassured his loyal staff that he had done nothing wrong. "The first thing he said was he was sorry this was happening and that we all had to go through this," Parks said. "Then he told us that he was innocent. . . . He had that resilient 'Duke' look in his eye, like, 'I'm going to beat this thing.'"

The *Union-Tribune* circulates throughout all of San Diego County, a county so sprawling that it is hard for anyone living on the East

Coast to fully grasp its breadth. It includes seacoast and mountain ranges, deserts and national forest. At more than 4,500 square miles, the county—by itself—covers more land area than the states of Rhode Island and Delaware combined. It is big enough that the *San Diego Union-Tribune* faces some pretty stiff competition for readers the further one travels from downtown San Diego. But on this Sunday morning, the *Union-Tribune* had the big story for North County all to itself. And one of the readers who realized that, ruefully, was William Finn Bennett, a reporter at the competing *North County Times.*

Cunningham's congressional district lay mostly within his paper's circulation area. Bennett's reaction when he picked up the *Union-Tribune* was one familiar to any reporter who's been beaten: "Oh, shit," he thought, trying to figure out how to match it.

Before the next two weeks were over, it would be one of Bennett's stories that would have the competition muttering. But for now, all Bennett or anyone else could get out of Cunningham's staff was a terse statement: "Mr. Wade was interested in purchasing our home. He received comparables from an independent source establishing the value of the home. He made an offer based on that evaluation. Nancy and I accepted that offer. I have no reason to believe the value of the house was inflated then, and I have no reason to think so today."

But for bloggers, citizen journalists, and reporters, the race was on. It seemed that everybody now was starting to tug at Cunningham. In some ways it was as if the house sale was just the first loose thread anyone had spotted in the tapestry that was the congressman. In another era, the story might have gone unnoticed outside his home county. But a bogus house sale by a member of the House Defense Appropriations Subcommittee to a defense contractor was enough to attract the attention of bloggers who wield growing influence in Washington, diggers such as Joshua Marshall of the *Talking Points Memo.* By Sunday afternoon, Marshall already had posted on his blog a summary of the Cunningham story in the *Union-Tribune,* spreading it across the country more effectively than the television networks, which ignored the story. All over the country, people used the Internet to search out and pore over relevant campaign finance reports and property records.

In the days to come, the results would appear in e-mails, blogs, and newspapers. The electronic pack would dig out other lawmakers who had benefited from Wade's campaign contributions. Realtors, real estate appraisers, and even Cunningham's neighbors began e-mailing their own varying assessments of the Del Mar Heights house sale to Stern and other San Diego reporters. Some real estate professionals e-mailed the original offering of the Rancho Santa Fe house from the Multiple Listing Service, which revealed for the first time the grandeur of a house that Mrs. Cunningham much later would disdain as a fixer-upper.

It quickly became apparent that notoriously politics-averse citizens of Southern California were tracking this political story—and they were angry. Tuesday, two days after the original story ran, the *Union-Tribune*'s editorial page was plastered with angry letters from readers. They were stunning in their intensity. This, after all, was a newspaper with a reliably Republican-leaning editorial page that had always endorsed Cunningham in his campaigns. But on this day, there was fury and palpable anger on its op-ed pages.

Wayne Seward of Carlsbad wrote: "As a disabled veteran, I have always hoped that those who serve this country in Iraq and elsewhere are given the best tools they need to win and to protect them from harm. After reading about Cunningham's secret home deal, I worry that where we spend our defense budget is determined by highest bidder on Cunningham's home."

Robert Tormey of Escondido, a retired Air Force major, wrote that he was "stunned" by the disclosure; he added that "a special prosecutor should be appointed to investigate this transaction."

Randy Bull of Carlsbad was more pointed: "The private deal Cunningham made with defense contractor MZM Incorporated stinks to high heaven."

Along with a tough accompanying *Union-Tribune* editorial demanding investigations, the larger message to Cunningham himself was unmistakable—the voters are angry and you're not going to get out of it this time by crying or by citing your war record.

The drumbeat of stories and disclosures continued, further stoking the anger and the appetite for even more disclosures. The Capitol Hill newspaper *Roll Call* weighed in Tuesday, June 14, day three of the scandal, with predictable statements of outrage by Democrats. Of course they were not going to be silent when a Republican gets caught with his hand out. But more interesting was the paper's disclosure that the supposedly independent real estate professional Cunningham had said had set the price on the Del Mar Heights house wasn't so independent. Elizabeth Todd and her husband, records showed, had made $3,000 in contributions to the Cunningham campaign during the 2001–02 election cycle.[2]

Those numbers did not survive unchanged even for three hours. Blogs and newspapers lost no time in updating the figure. Todd, her husband, Whitney, and his father, Richard, had given Cunningham a total of $11,500 between July 1997 and May 2004. "It looks like a bribe from this distance," Bob Mulholland, communications director for the California Democratic Party, told *Roll Call*. "It smells, and hopefully the Congressional ethics committee will take this issue up." Other Democrats lined up to demand investigations.

Not surprisingly, Republicans were there to defend their colleague. But not all Republicans were ready to take this leap. Too many of them were privately horrified by what they read in the *Union-Tribune* story that was being e-mailed from office to office on Capitol Hill. Still, Cunningham could count on the support of at least one influential GOP leader. After all, he had been a generous contributor to

Majority Leader Tom DeLay's defense fund as DeLay fought off the ethical allegations that would soon end his congressional career. De-Lay was there for him, telling reporters, "Duke Cunningham is a hero. He is an honorable man of high integrity."

Others rushed to Cunningham himself to hear what he had to say. Among them was perhaps Cunningham's closest friend and ally in politics, fellow San Diego Republican Duncan Hunter. Hunter was no Cunningham. The chairman of the House Armed Services Committee, he was widely respected. And Hunter was famed for a simple lifestyle, prompting Bob Dornan, his friend and a former congressman, to observe that Hunter "dresses humbly." For the time being, Hunter was reassured by what he heard from Cunningham. "I just saw Duke and he told me, 'I've been totally above-board,'" Hunter said. "That's good enough for me. He's an American hero and should be given the benefit of the doubt."[3]

Others were not so lucky as Hunter; they heard no public comments from the now-beleaguered Cunningham. He was to maintain public silence on the allegations for eleven days as the controversy swirled about him. He surfaced only long enough to wrap himself in the flag—writing an opinion piece in *USA Today* on Flag Day, in support of a Constitutional amendment to protect the flag from desecration. A vote on the matter was pending in the House.

The flag was not grand enough nor were its stripes broad enough to cover this scandal, though. On June 14, William Bennett got a tip. It came anonymously by phone: "Check out the boat." Bennett immediately called all the marinas along the Potomac River, hoping that one of them would say, sure, Congressman Cunningham is on one of our boats. Finally, one did: Kelvin Lee, the dock master of the Capital Yacht Club. But when Bennett asked for the name of the boat and its owner, Lee demurred. He said he could answer only yes or no. After Bennett pleaded, Lee told him that if he got the names of the boat and the owner Lee would confirm them. Bennett called the Harbor Police office nearby; playing a hunch, he asked whether a boat was registered in Mitchell Wade's name. When they said yes, Bennett asked for the name of the boat.

"When they said, 'Duke-Stir,' I almost dropped my teeth. This was too rich. It was like a movie," he said. Then Bennett had that gratifying realization that some reporters and cops live for. "I have him," he said of Cunningham.

Bennett then went back to Lee, who confirmed the information. The next stop was the U.S. Coast Guard, where Bennett requested the documents that provided more details about the boat. From that point forward, neither Lee nor the Harbor Police would talk with Bennett.

Although neither Cunningham nor his staff would talk with Bennett despite numerous calls, the office did send him an e-mail denying any impropriety: "I am putting information and records together so that you will know how much I pay to stay there, and you will see that everything we've done is appropriate," read the brief statement, which was transmitted by Harmony Allen, Cunningham's chief of staff.

Cunningham never produced those records because they would have demonstrated how deep his corruption ran. It was left to the prosecutors to release the information in court documents related to Cunningham's plea agreement. And, of course, they revealed that Wade paid for everything, including Cunningham's Yacht Club membership and slip fees.

Bennett's story ran in the *North County Times* on June 16, setting off a furor, particularly after Josh Marshall posted it on his widely read blog. "I think we're pretty much at checkmate now, aren't we?" he wrote.[4] Later that day, Marshall added to his blog:

> Cunningham appears to be more or less owned by a defense contractor with business before his committee. I mean, when you add up all we know, it seems like Mitchell Wade basically bought or heavily contributed to buying the Duke luxury homes (albeit, one waterborne) in the district and in Washington. And apparently no one noticed. It's right out of the nineteenth century.

The next day, the *Union-Tribune* carried a Copley News Service story revealing that the FBI had begun an inquiry into the Cunningham matter.[5] "We are very interested in what has been reported to date, and we welcome more information," said Dan Dzwilewski, the special agent in charge of the FBI's San Diego office. "Public corruption matters represent one of the highest priorities of the FBI."

The same day, a couple of dozen protesters appeared outside Cunningham's Rancho Santa Fe house, chanting, "Two, four, six, eight, shame on Duke in Mansiongate!" and "Duke, Duke, we deplore, that you profit, from this war!" [6]

The next day the *Union-Tribune* reported that a federal grand jury in San Diego had already issued subpoenas in the Cunningham matter.[7] No one could remember a scandal moving at such breakneck speed. A week earlier, there had been no suspicion, no investigation, no questions. Now FBI agents were swarming over the case and a federal grand jury was issuing subpoenas. But the story was still being driven almost entirely by the two local newspapers, a few national political bloggers, and citizen journalists delivering their scoops by e-mail to interested parties. A grand jury was issuing subpoenas in what would be the largest congressional corruption scandal in terms of the money involved, but few national publications or networks had even tried to catch up.

There would be plenty of time for that, though. Soon, even the president of the United States would be forced to publicly condemn the actions of his fellow Republican.

chapter eighteen

CLOSING IN

C UNNINGHAM COULD NO LONGER WALK THE HALLS OF CONGRESS WITH-
out being dogged by television cameras and shouted questions.
He couldn't travel his district or attend even the most routine event
without the scandal overwhelming the event. His fellow politicians—even many of those who wanted to support him—demanded
that he speak out. Even his own staff was asking him questions but
getting no answers. The pressure was becoming unbearable.

But for perhaps the first time in his public career, the congressman who had an opinion on everything—the politician who loved
to talk—fell uncharacteristically silent.

In retrospect, what could he have said? He had already tried lying
and it had not slowed the onrushing investigators or journalists and
bloggers in the slightest. He had tried charming his first inquisitor,
Stern, and it had failed. Now he was hoping that those pursuing him
would run out of leads and that the story might fade from view and
give him a chance to recoup. But the story just kept growing.

Rep. Darrell Issa, a Republican representing a neighboring district,
had been restrained in his initial reaction to the allegations, stopping

far short of the fulsome praise offered by other Republicans when the story first surfaced. But, still, he wanted to believe Cunningham and was increasingly frustrated by the congressman's silence. "Duke has one thing he prides himself on more than anything and that is his integrity," Issa said during this period of Cunningham's silence. "His word is his bond."[1] Even if it turns out that Mitchell Wade was scheming to get defense contracts, Issa added, "that doesn't mean Duke was in on it." But he wanted to hear Cunningham explain.

Cunningham was also getting pressure from Melanie Sloan, the executive director of a nonpartisan public watchdog group called Citizens for Responsibility and Ethics in Washington and known by its catchy acronym CREW. Her job was to try to shame the Republican-controlled Congress to do something it resolutely did not want to do—launch an investigation of a member. Under the GOP rule, the once-robust ethics process had totally broken down in what became a bipartisan conspiracy. Republicans agreed not to investigate Democrats, and Democrats agreed not to ask for Ethics Committee investigations of Republicans. The ethics wars, which had claimed Democratic Speaker Jim Wright and Republican Speaker Newt Gingrich, were over.

Sloan was determined to break this truce, begging member after member and Democrat after Democrat to demand that the Ethics Committee rouse itself to action. But the truce, though tested by the Cunningham revelations, would hold—to the lasting shame of both parties for looking the other way when confronted with what would turn out to be the biggest crook ever in their midst.

Still, Cunningham had no choice. He had to respond or be adjudged guilty, guilty, guilty by the public. So on June 23, eleven days after the first report of the sham house sale, Cunningham spoke. Well, sort of. He issued a statement but was never seen speaking the words attributed to him. The statement was three pages long—1,662 words. But none of those words contained a real explanation for what had already been disclosed, and they certainly offered no hint of the massive corruption still to be unearthed.

Instead, all he did was acknowledge what had already become abundantly clear from the newspaper stories: He and Wade were very close friends. It would be hard to keep denying that as he had done so stoutly to Stern in that first interview. And he conceded that maybe the house deal was not such a nifty idea after all. It wasn't corrupt, mind you—just an example of "poor judgment." But he was now willing to acknowledge that selling his house to someone doing business with the government, particularly without listing the house on the public market, looked bad—but only, he suggested, to others unacquainted with him.

"I have always felt a duty to this country and its people—a duty that motivated me to volunteer for the Navy, serve in combat in Vietnam, and run for office," he said.

He continued to insist that the transaction wasn't in any way improper just because it looked bad. "I would never put the interests of a friend or a contractor above the interests of my country," he wrote. "I trust the facts will bear out this truth over time. . . . I want my constituents to know that, despite my personal friendship with Mr. Wade, I gave his company, MZM, no preferential treatment." Later, Cunningham reiterated the point, writing, "I categorically reject any suggestion that I secured a contract for Mr. Wade's company or that I supported funding [for an] important human intelligence program because MZM purchased my home in Del Mar Heights."

On his use of Wade's yacht, the lawmaker said he had been living aboard the *Duke-Stir* since April 2004. "Mr. Wade and I agreed that, in return for me staying on the boat, I would pay the monthly dock fees and maintenance costs associated with keeping Mr. Wade's boat at the marina," he said. Cunningham estimated that he had paid "$8,000 in dock fees and well over $5,000 for service and maintenance" during the thirteen months he had lived on the yacht. He indicated that the figures were preliminary and that his attorneys were still gathering information. "There was nothing improper about my arrangement with Mr. Wade because I paid these monthly fees and costs in lieu of rent," he said.[2]

Of course, most of Cunningham's key points were lies; lies that reporters and prosecutors would quickly uncover. The statement did nothing to calm the storm swirling about him or end the feeding frenzy of competing news organizations. There were too many new questions, new disclosures, new revelations, for that.

One of the newest areas drawing scrutiny was Cunningham's ties to another organization run by Wade—the Sure Foundation. Those ties came under attack from CREW. The foundation, whose stated purpose was to help needy children around the globe, was headquartered in the same building as MZM. Wade was the foundation's treasurer and his wife, Christiane, its president. But it wasn't just the Wade family running Sure. There, on the board, could be found Nancy Cunningham and one of the congressman's daughters—April.

"These two men have mixed up their business, social and charitable lives," said CREW's Sloan. "It would be one thing for Mitchell Wade to be Duke Cunningham's good friend, and even for family members to be on the advisory council," she said. But, she added, "it takes on an entirely different cast in light of the fact that Mitchell Wade has business before Duke Cunningham's [congressional] committee."[3]

There were also questions about much smaller ethical transgressions. Although Cunningham's corruption was undeniably grand and sweeping, it was also petty and pinched. When he wasn't misappropriating millions in defense dollars and pocketing hundreds of thousands of dollars in bribes, he was assiduously taking dollars and cents from ordinary Americans who admired his Vietnam war heroics. This money was generated by his Top Gun Enterprises, Inc. Through it, he sold autographed lithographs of himself in a flight suit, copies of his book *Fox Two*, and Top Gun ball caps. The company brought in even more bucks after it went up as a Web site in 2001. Aimed, it said, at "fighter pilot enthusiasts," the site's motto was anything but modest: "Have MiG, Will Travel." It was a modernized version of the 1950s television Western *Have Gun, Will Travel*.

But the site sold only one weapon—a "Randy 'Duke' Cunningham Fighter Ace Kalinga Style Buck Knife." The site described the knife as "displayed in a beautifully stained 13–1/2" long x 2–1/2" deep x 4–1/2 wide hard wood case." "It comes with a certificate of authenticity which verifies that the number of 1000 made exclusively for Randy 'Duke' Cunningham by Buck Knives. . . . Overall length of the knife is 10" with a 5" handle and a 5" blade." Of particular interest to those familiar with U.S. law was what was "etched in gold" on the obverse side of the blade. There could be found three things: the official emblem of the American Fighter Aces Association; a Duke Cunningham autographed flight suit picture; and the official seal of the United States Congress.

And all this for only $595! There was no word whether a lawyer came with each knife. But Cunningham found he needed a lawyer because using the congressional seal commercially is against the law.

Cunningham, of course, wasn't the only one who needed the services of a good lawyer these days. Mitch Wade very quickly lawyered up even as he raced to the exits before the company he had built collapsed under him. The scandal proved devastating to MZM almost immediately.

Less than two weeks after the stories started breaking, Wade secretly stepped down as CEO and turned the company over to one of his lieutenants, Frank Bragg. But Bragg's tenure was short-lived. Within days of taking over from Wade, Bragg quit. Kay Cole James, MZM's senior executive vice president for national security transformation, quit that same day. She previously had been President George W. Bush's director of the U.S. Office of Personnel Management and had joined MZM only one month earlier.

Wade then selected James King, one of his longest-serving and closest associates, to be the company's president and chief executive officer. King, a retired three-star general, notified some employees that Friday evening that his mandate was to find a buyer for the company.[4] That would benefit Wade, for he remained the sole owner of the company.

Then the Pentagon announced it had cut off MZM from getting any more contracts under the Blanket Purchase Agreement that MZM had used to get $163 million in contracts over two and a half years.[5] Pentagon officials denied that the cutoff was connected to the unfolding bribery scandal. They actually seemed surprised that nobody believed that this burst of accountability was simply coincidental with the headlines. A Pentagon official insisted with a straight face that the decision stemmed from a recent review and a ruling that the Defense Department should have received bids from companies other than MZM before awarding the firm a Blanket Purchase Agreement in September 2002.

This was a costly hit at MZM's bottom line. But it was not the most dramatic manifestation of the forces gathering to bring down both the company and the congressman. That came when a federal grand jury in San Diego issued subpoenas to obtain documents from Cunningham in connection with the Del Mar Heights house and *Duke-Stir*. The subpoenas by themselves were dramatic, but the speed with which they had been issued was nothing short of stunning. Nobody could remember any investigation of any congressman in history moving at this kind of breathtaking speed.

Cunningham's lawyer, of course, tried to treat the subpoenas as routine, promising full cooperation. "My client has directed me to comply with the subpoena as expeditiously as possible, and he has instructed his staff to cooperate with these document requests," said K. Lee Blalack in a statement the lawyer released June 28. Subpoenas also were issued to Realtor Elizabeth Todd, who now would be asked to explain her lies in front of a grand jury.

It had been a disastrous fortnight for Cunningham, Wade, and MZM, and the scandal continued to accelerate. On July 1—less than three weeks after Stern's first story about Cunningham's sham house sale—federal agents raided his Rancho Santa Fe house, MZM's corporate headquarters in Washington, Wade's Kalorama residence in Washington, and the *Duke-Stir* in its slip at the Capital Yacht Club. The searches were conducted by agents from the U.S. Attorneys Office in San Diego, the FBI, the Internal Revenue Service, and the Defense Criminal Investigative Service.

At about 10:00 A.M., a dozen federal agents entered MZM and herded employees into the foyer. They collected information from more than a dozen employees in the building at the time, including their names and phone numbers.[6]

In Rancho Santa Fe, about twenty agents showed up in white vans and scoured the Cunninghams' mansion. The raid drew a torrent of media attention, with a gaggle of reporters and photographers on the street in front of the house and the staccato thump, thump, thump of news helicopters overhead. One of Cunningham's attorneys, Mark Holscher, appeared briefly at the scene to protest the raid. He said in a later interview that the FBI had broken into the house because nobody answered the door. "They broke the locks and forcibly broke into his home," Holscher said. "They [the Cunninghams] weren't given any advance notice."

Nancy rushed home and was horrified to see every nook and cranny of her house being gone over by white-gloved agents. When her husband called her on her cell phone, she told him, "Don't come home. They're raiding our house. They're raiding Mitch's office. They're raiding the boat . . . I don't want you anywhere near here."[7]

Three thousand miles away at the Capital Yacht Club on the Potomac River, agents passed through a locked gate and clambered down the wooden dock to where the forty-two-foot *Duke-Stir* was tied up. Meanwhile, a witness in Kalorama reported seeing agents enter the house and leave later with boxes.

Nancy was humiliated; Cunningham's lawyers were furious.

"Today's search of Duke Cunningham's home, based on a secret affidavit, was an appalling abuse of government power," the attorneys Blalack and Holscher said in a statement issued after the searches. "We publicly disclosed this week that the government had issued a document subpoena to the congressman and that he had instructed his staff and lawyers to fully cooperate. Just yesterday [Thursday, June 30] we reiterated privately to the government that Duke was going to fully cooperate and that we would be shortly producing the requested documents. They will apparently not take yes for an answer and have instead opted to use strong arm tactics that were designed to generate headlines." Cunningham "welcomes a fair investigation because he is confident that any such inquiry will eventually clear his good name," the statement said.

But federal agents rarely let searches happen on the timetable of criminals and are loathe to give crooks time to shred evidence. And law enforcement officials had, indeed, received reports of shredding taking place at MZM headquarters. Their decision had been an easy one—move in quickly and decisively before any more evidence can be destroyed.

The Friday, July 2, raids came as Cunningham was preparing to fly to San Diego for his first planned public appearance since the scandal broke. It was to be a pretty friendly venue—the Fourth of July Community Celebration and Pancake Breakfast in Encinitas. Encinitas, an affluent coastal community, is famous as the cut-flower capital of the United States and for its loyalty to Republican candidates. The event's organizer, Lou Aspell, expressed no concern over the controversy marring the event. "It's the Fourth of July and there's a lot of patriotic stories that can be shared," Aspell told the *Union-Tribune*. "If there are people who have an issue with that, and don't want to show up, that's their right, but I have no problems with supporting him supporting our event. He is our congressman."[8]

But the event was canceled. "It is clear from all the advanced publicity that any Fourth of July celebration he is scheduled to attend will become a media frenzy," lamented Mark Olson, Cunningham's press secretary, who added that the congressman did not want "to detract from community events celebrating our country's freedom."

The Del Mar Heights house deal was becoming a bigger and bigger problem for Cunningham. His statement to the press was simply overwhelmed by the evidence the feds were finding. As they confirmed more dates, looked at more canceled checks, and got the truth from Realtor Todd, Cunningham's story unraveled quickly.

Perhaps the first thing investigators saw was that this was not some impulse by Cunningham, something he had not really thought about. The facts now clearly showed that Cunningham took his time looking for his dream mansion and then carefully orchestrated an elaborate sham purchase. His benefactors illegally transferred hundreds of thousands of dollars into an escrow account allowing the lawmaker and his wife to purchase what for them would be the ultimate status symbol, that mansion in Rancho Santa Fe.

The property search began in May or June 2003 when Cunningham approached Todd at a fund-raising event at the seaside Torrey

Pines Golf Course. She was a new realtor at Willis Allen Real Estate and was looking for her first sale. Cunningham knew her because of her family's financial support and decided to use her to his own ends. So he called her and told her that he and his "partner" wanted to buy a condo in San Diego. After some back and forth between the two, Cunningham told her that he and his unnamed partner were interested in purchasing a million-dollar unit with an ocean view at the Seahaus project then under development in La Jolla.

But the Seahaus units would not be available for occupancy for two to three years, and Cunningham wanted something sooner. So in June 2003, Todd showed him other condos in the million-dollar range in La Jolla, downtown San Diego, and on Coronado Island.[9]

But the lawmaker's circumstances changed in July, as his wife, unhappy with her experience in Washington and humiliated about the flirtatious behavior of her husband, decided to give up her job in Washington and return to San Diego.[10] So Cunningham had to change his housing needs.

He told Todd he had $1 million in cash to spend, and he added that if he sold his Del Mar Heights house for $1.5 million, he would be in position to purchase a house in San Diego in the range of $2.5 million. His partner, he added, could put an office in the new house rather than in a condo. When Todd asked Cunningham if she could have the listing on his Del Mar Heights house, he told her he already had a buyer for it. But he said he'd still like to use her to handle the purchase of its replacement. To find a suitable new home, Cunningham turned to a publication, *Dream Homes,* which showcased remarkable residential estates in San Diego.

Eventually, Cunningham settled on the $2.55 million, Mediterranean-style, 7,628 square-foot mansion with terra cotta roof tiles and a turquoise pool on 2.89 acres at 7094 Via del Charro, Rancho Santa Fe. The seller was Douglas Powanda, a former executive with Peregrine Systems Inc. He would be indicted a year later along with seven other Peregrine executives for securities fraud. Powanda had falsified the company's books and unloaded $24 million in company stock before the inflated revenue figures came to light, according to prosecutors.

Now Cunningham had to sell his Del Mar house to Wade. He instructed Todd to draft a sales contract for the house valued at $1.5 million. She complied on November 5 and faxed it to the lawmaker in Washington, who signed it and faxed it on to Wade for his signature. But two days later, Cunningham had second thoughts. He needed an additional $175,000, he had decided. So he had Todd prepare a new sales agreement valued at $1.675 million, which became the final selling price of the Del Mar house.

Cunningham used the $1.4 million in proceeds from the sale of the Del Mar Heights house as a down payment on the Rancho Santa Fe mansion. He financed the rest with two mortgages obtained through New York developer Thomas Kontogiannis's nephew's company, Coastal Capital, one for $595,000 and one for $500,000.

After consulting a tax preparer, Cunningham realized two weeks after the sale had closed that he'd forgotten he would have to pay a hefty capital gains tax on the windfall from the Del Mar house. To compensate for the oversight, he had Wade send a check for $115,100 to Top Gun Enterprises, Inc. Wade cleverly noted on the check that it was for "Public Relations and Communications expenses."

As it turned out, Cunningham had no intention of being saddled with $1,095,000 in mortgages on the Rancho Santa Fe mansion. Instead, he agreed to deliver $6 million in government contracts to Brent Wilkes if he would take care of the $525,000 mortgage. Once Cunningham delivered on the $6 million contract, Wilkes sent a check for $525,000 to Coastal Capital, retiring Cunningham's debt.

Cunningham made a similar deal with Wade to pay off the $500,000 mortgage, although the specific earmark Cunningham delivered to Wade has not been disclosed. Wade wrote out two checks totaling $500,000—one for $329,000 and another for $171,000—and sent them to Coastal Capital, ridding Cunningham of that debt as well. Rather than retiring the second mortgage, Coastal Capital sold it to another company and Kontogiannis assumed the remaining payments.

So Cunningham now effectively owned the Rancho Santa Fe house free and clear. Meanwhile, he had sold the Virginia condominium. In March 2004, he and Nancy moved all their belongings then in Washington to Rancho Santa Fe. As ever, Wade stood ready with a check, picking up the $11,393 tab for the moving expenses. The shipping manifest included slightly more than thirty antiques with a total value of $214,900. Among them were two Bijar rugs valued at $40,000 each.[11]

Details were also starting to surface about those yachts and who had paid the bills to let Cunningham live on the Potomac River while in Washington.

With all the focus on the *Duke-Stir,* scant attention had been given to the missing *Kelly C.* On July 3, Stern got a tip that the boat might be at a marina called Consolidated on Long Island. He went online and found Consolidated Marine in Amityville. He then called Jerry Kammer, who was visiting family in Baltimore. "Can you get up to New York right now?" Stern asked. Kammer cut short his visit and headed to Baltimore Washington International Airport. Without luggage and little more than a notebook and a pen, Kammer was on a Southwest Airlines flight to Islip, Long Island, less than three hours after Stern's call.

Still on the Internet, Stern used satellite photos to guide Kammer to the marina. But there was no *Kelly C.* Kammer continued the search the next morning, finally heading to the island's north shore. At the Glen Cove Marina, his luck turned. There he met marina owner Joe Weiser, who said he was familiar not only with the boat but with Cunningham himself. Met him in the fall of 2002, Weiser said. How could he forget Cunningham? "He gave me a picture of himself in his flight outfit!" he added.

How Cunningham came to be at Glen Cove was a story that was to intrigue prosecutors and drag back into the investigation that New York developer—Tommy Kontogiannis—who had been so helpful in providing mortgages for the Rancho Santa Fe house. For it was Kontogiannis who had called Weiser in mid-2002 to say he needed a slip for a boat he had bought.

But it was Cunningham—not Kontogiannis—who piloted the boat to New York and delivered it. Weiser was unimpressed not only with the congressman but also with the bulky, flat-bottomed boat. "It was," he told Kammer, "a piece of shit."

Kammer then drove the four miles to the Kontogiannis home in Glen Head. A large, handsome structure of tan brick, it occupied a heavily wooded lot and sat at the top of a sweeping driveway scanned by twin surveillance cameras. Kontogiannis wasn't there, so Kammer left his business card and his cell phone number with the young man who answered the door. That night, Kontogiannis called Kammer at his hotel room. It would be the last interview Kontogiannis would give a reporter as the scandal veered from Cunningham and Wade to focus on him.

Kontogiannis's story had an improbable beginning. Although boats, unlike houses, lose value over time, he said he had bought the boat from Cunningham for $600,000—triple what Cunningham had paid for it in 1997. Kontogiannis insisted the price was "a steal" and claimed that an appraisal had put its value at twice that. He said he had paid partly with cash and partly by writing off the two mortgages a family company had provided for Cunningham's purchase of the Rancho Santa Fe home.

Kontogiannis responded smoothly to every question. Why did U.S. Coast Guard records show the *Kelly C* was still in Cunningham's name? Kontogiannis said he hadn't bothered to register it because he knew it was unfit to take out on the ocean. Never mind that any vessel the size of the *Kelly C* must be "documented" by the Coast Guard, regardless of whether it plies rivers, lakes, or the open sea. Why had Cunningham shown up at the Glen Cove Marina a few weeks earlier, mechanic in tow, announcing that he was planning to take the *Kelly C* back to Washington and drawing up a list of needed repairs? Kontogiannis said he had been planning to sell the boat back to Cunningham, but very recently had changed his mind.

Weiser told Kammer that the *Kelly C* was being repaired at Consolidated Yachts, a marina and repair yard across Long Island Sound on City Island. So Kammer hurried to the island, part of the New York City borough of the Bronx. Ignoring the "No Trespassing" signs, Kammer walked through the gate and almost instantly recognized the *Kelly C* from the photo Stern had e-mailed him. Sitting next to the huge lift that had hauled it from the water, it was perched on wood blocks stabilized by metal braces.

Kammer scrambled up a ladder and jumped aboard. Evidence of the $100,000 refurbishing was everywhere, from the door with a stylized "C" etched in the glass to the blue carpeting, brown leather couch, and wooden bar. In the cabin he found maps—all of the Potomac and Chesapeake Bay—and a repair list that called for work on the engine impellers, running lights, anchor lights, and filters.

As Kammer climbed back down the ladder, he was intercepted by consolidated owner Wes Rodstrom, who threatened to have him arrested for trespassing. But Rodstrom was more agitated with Cunningham, who was now denying any responsibility for the boat or its repairs. He said he had called Cunningham a few days earlier, only to be told, "I've got nothing to do with the boat." Rodstrom told Kammer with a tone of bitterness: "I could get stuck with the damn thing."

Federal prosecutors later laid out a detailed account of the *Kelly C* transaction when they charged Cunningham and identified Kontogiannis as an unindicted co-conspirator. They described the sale of the boat as a sham in which Cunningham, after moving on to the *Duke-Stir* courtesy of Mitch Wade, parked the *Kelly C* with Kontogiannis, who then had it refurbished at a cost that Kontogiannis himself estimated at some $100,000.

The prosecutors identified the deal as part of an elaborate conspiracy that moved hundreds of thousands of dollars among the conspirators, including Wade, Wilkes, and a Kontogiannis nephew who ran the mortgage company. In mid-2002, Wilkes wrote a $525,000 check to Kontogiannis to pay off one loan. That was right after Wilkes got a $5,970,000 pay day for supplying the Defense Department with computers and data storage equipment, which prosecutors later stated were never used by the government.

The prosecutors claimed that Kontogiannis and his nephew John T. Michael—co-conspirators numbers 3 and 4 in the Cunningham case—steered hundreds of thousands more dollars to Cunningham, who used some of the cash to pay for his Arlington condominium.

The story that broke on the front page of the *Union-Tribune* the morning of July 5 revealed all the details of the *Kelly C* transactions and the fact that Cunningham had tried to intervene—and even seek a pardon from President Bush—after Kontogiannis pled guilty in the New York bid-rigging case. And, with the tone of editorials toughening and the doubts of other politicians growing, Cunningham desperately needed something positive, some glint of sunlight.

Fortunately for him, there were people in his district more than willing to ignore the morning headlines, brush aside the evidence, forgive what clearly was law-breaking, and tell Duke that he was more than welcome under their roofs. It was not so much that these people were Republicans—though they were. More important, they had been the beneficiaries of some of his earmarks. And if there is one lesson in the whole sad Cunningham saga it is that almost everybody is willing to look the other way if there is federal money in it for them.

On this particular day, the moral blindness was found at an unlikely place—a Rotary Club meeting at the California Center for the Arts in Escondido, a twelve-acre complex in the heart of the North County city. No one would have expected the audience for the noon speech on July 5 to be hostile; it was too Republican and too business-oriented for that. In fact, the reception went far beyond polite—there was no holding back the adulation. Scandal? What scandal?

Mayor Lori Holt Pfeiler, a Republican, probably never even saw the irony in her explanation for the warm reception, which included two standing ovations from the more than one hundred audience members. "He has brought money back to support our water treatment plants, our recycling plant, and Citracado Parkway is very important on his list," she said. "If we didn't have a great representative in Washington, we wouldn't have all the great projects in Escondido."

Ah, the power of earmarks.

The Rotarians even meekly acquiesced when Cunningham's staff ordered them not to ask questions about the scandal. The congressman's only reference to his troubles that day was to try to explain his uncharacteristic public silence about the allegations. "You know me," he said, "I want to come out throwing arrows and stones in a fight like I'm used to doing. Someone swings at you, you want to swing back." Then, sounding like his old feisty self, he added, "When every week you have something coming out on your life, I want to come out and be very, very open, but my lawyers have said, 'Duke, that's not what you want to do when an investigation is going on.' That's why I don't go out to the press and start jabbering."

That was good enough for these citizens—as long as the earmarks kept coming in. As Cunningham nibbled on a slice of white cake, the Rotarians hugged him and sang a paean to him to the tune of "Anchors Aweigh."[12]

> *Here comes Duke Cunningham*
> *He loves to fly*
> *He flew in Vietnam,*
> *Then, came to Top Gun, Miramar*
> *To teach pilots all the tricks*
> *They'd ever need*
> *Now Duke's in Washington*
> *The fifty-eth, our district he does lead.*

After this show of adoration it was no wonder that Cunningham seemed surprised, when, upon leaving, a reporter asked whether he might be thinking about resigning.

"Why should I?" he asked as he climbed into the backseat of a black Chevy Blazer to drive away.

chapter nineteen

BOTCHED COVER-UP

THE COVER-UP ORCHESTRATED BY RANDY CUNNINGHAM STARTED PRECISELY thirty-nine seconds after Marcus Stern asked him the first question about his sham house sale and it continued in fits and starts right up until only twelve hours before he was sentenced and hauled off to prison. As cover-ups go, it was clumsy and amateurish and ineffective. But it certainly was spirited.

It involved all the usual blatant lies and attempts at misdirection— anything that could block the prosecutors path to the truth. Cunningham's little extra touch was to play his hero card—*I'm a war hero, how could you not believe me?*—and to solemnly invoke national security— *I'd like to tell you more about these contracts but you just don't have the right security clearance.*

Oddly, it was also a tad poignant and, particularly to his longtime friends and admirers, very sad. To have this man they thought they knew, and even idolized, look into the faces of his staff, his family, his colleagues, his former comrades in arms—even his nonagenarian mother—and out-and-out lie was ineffably sad.

Even if the cover-up had been more skillfully designed and executed, though, it is unlikely it could have shielded Cunningham from prosecution, conviction, or imprisonment. The evidence was just too overwhelming. This was because Mitch Wade had approached prosecutors on June 28—seventeen days after the first story on the house sale—and offered to confess and cooperate as fully as possible. The prosecutors were only too happy to take him up on the offer, and the information Wade provided them was insurmountable. Once prosecutors got their hands on the "bribe menu," nothing could have saved the congressman. And, thanks to Wade, they knew all about the antiques, what they had cost, and where they were.

Clearly, Cunningham was told by his lawyers that he had little choice but to 'fess up. But, as evidenced by his comments to court officials and his well-publicized letter from prison later, he never really seemed to accept his guilt. He kept telling himself that all he had done was to accept a few "gifts" in exchange for righteous votes. As long as he believed that, he would continue his futile attempts at cover-up.

Certainly, there was nothing half-hearted about the initial steps in the cover-up. Repeatedly in that first interview with Stern, Cunningham urged him to call Elizabeth Todd, assuring him that the realtor would explain how the price was set and the sale handled. His entire initial rationale rested on two pillars—(1) the fact that he was an honest guy so of course he didn't do anything dishonest and (2) Elizabeth Todd set the price. What he didn't say is that he had contacted her after Wade resold the house at a $700,000 loss in November 2004 and asked her to give him a letter with a phony explanation for this loss in case it ever came to light. She balked at doing this, but finally relented. The best she could come up with was trying to link it with a supposed lull in the San Diego housing market—even though prices were still rising at double-digit rates during this supposed lull.

She lied again when Stern called her at Cunningham's urging, going along with Cunningham's cover story. She later told FBI agents that she wrote the note at Cunningham's request and that it reflected his instructions to come up with a benign explanation for the loss rather than the reality of the market. She also lied when she told Stern that she had set the price. Cunningham very clearly set the price, according to prosecutors. He increased the sales price from $1.5 million to $1.675 million at the last minute and had her rewrite the sales agreement to reflect the higher price. And Todd eventually had to admit that she had never even been in the house before the sale to Wade took place—something that would have been necessary for her to set the price.

Stern's call to Todd came on June 9, 2005, three days before the first story appeared in the *San Diego Union-Tribune*. He asked her why the house had taken eight months to sell at a $700,000 loss. There was no doubting that the question made Todd uncomfortable and Stern was convinced that she was feeling her way through the call, armed with talking points from Cunningham but uncertain of their persuasiveness:

> You know, I don't know why it took so long to sell. To be frank with you I just don't know. I just don't know. I mean, I don't know why it took so long to sell. . . . This is a crazy market out here, I'll tell you what. I don't think it was mispriced. I think there was a point here you just put a price on the house and it just sold and it had ten offers. And things have changed. It's not like that as much any more. I mean, I think we still have a good real estate market out here. Frankly, I don't know why it sat for so long.

When pressed on her specific role in the sale, she said, "I actually wasn't the listing agent so much. I was more advising on that whole situation. And we have a bunch of comps in Del Mar to show that definitely is a justified price." She was referring to the $1,675,000 Wade had paid Cunningham. Had the house been put in the Multiple Listing Service? "No." Had it ever been advertised? "I don't know all those details." So this was basically a private deal that you facilitated by providing comps and a price? "Right."

Again, she took a feeble stab at explaining how a house in Del Mar Heights could possibly lose that much in so short a time in a red–hot San Diego housing market. "I don't know why it didn't sell. I honestly don't. I mean it's a house in Del Mar west of I–5 and it's a good-sized house. I honestly don't know why."

But then her talking points from Cunningham took shape:

There was a little bit of a trend change. If you look at the overall numbers, the prices were still good but things were definitely in this area staying on the market for more days. No doubt about it. Whereas, I said earlier, things used to like fly. You'd have ten offers. Now the trend was like things are staying on the market much longer than they used. So that did follow suit with that trend. No listing agent wants to sit there for nine months or ten months or whatever it was.

Stern's sense upon hanging up was that Todd didn't believe her own story but was sticking to it. It was the story she used in the letter Cunningham requested. Indeed, in their Cunningham sentencing memo filed Feb. 17, 2006, with the court, prosecutors wrote:

The realtor was uncomfortable with Cunningham's request, but agreed because she felt as if she had no choice. She therefore drafted a letter to Cunningham in which she attempted to justify the lower price by, among other things, suggesting that in 2004 trends had changed and the market had become more of a buyer's market. After completing the letter, the realtor faxed it to Cunningham's Washington office. the [sic] realtor acknowledges that she followed Cunningham's instructions in writing the in [sic] a manner designed to help out Cunningham, rather than in a way that candidly or accurately reflected the San Diego real estate market during the relevant periods. Although 2004 was somewhat less of a stellar year for home appreciation than 2003, the overall San Diego housing market continued to appreciate at a double-digit rate, fairly priced homes continued to receive multiple offers, and in no sense could the market in San Diego generally, or Del Mar in particular, be fairly called a "buyer's market."

Cunningham's attempted cover-up did not stop with manipulating the actions of Todd. His next step was to draft and sign a phony letter, purportedly sent to Wade, indicating that he was *shocked* to discover that Wade had lost money on the transaction:

I was both surprised and concerned when I found out that you sold the house at a much lower price than you paid for it. Two concerns: first the original intent was to establish a place near MCAS [*sic*] Miramar for temporary residence and a place to conduct business. I know that after the sale we met with DOD to find a place at Miramar, Pendelton, or North Island but I assumed that you would keep the house as a place to stay. I was not concerned when I learned that you placed it on the market since it was for more than you paid for it. Day before yesterday I was told that the houe [*sic*] sold for less that [*sic*] the original price. I checked with the broker and she said the market and sales had declined greatly since the time of purchase and that you instructed her to get rid of it ASAP. I have taken pride in that cars, houses and property were sold fair with full disclosure. That's why I had Elizabeth compile and send you all homes sold in Delmar [*sic*] including two new ones on my block with less footage and no limited ocean view. They were offered at 1.5m. I do not want to lose our long time friendship over money and the sale also creates a perception that is unjust but could lead to political issues in the future.

This is what I would like to do to maintain our friendship and avoid any negative perception.

1. Establish through the broker the value of the house in today's declining market since you let it go in a firesale it would be fair for me to repay to you the difference of that value and the original sales price. Today in good faith I can cut a check for

$50,000. The remaining balance will be paid monthly with inter-
est. Please let me know what you would like to do. Your support
of the nation's security and friendship is far more important than
any dollar amount.

2. I will request a complete acconting [*sic*] from the realtor.

Your friend
Randy Cunningham

The prosecutors saw this letter for what it was—"really nothing
more than a crude attempt to get their stories straight"—and noted
that Cunningham didn't draft the letter "until just before the first
story about this transaction was published." They also disclosed that
"although Cunningham flashed [Wade] a $50,000 cashier's check,
he never actually paid back any money from the Del Mar home
transaction."

But two phony letters and a sham check were still just a start in
the Cunningham cover-up. One of his big problems by this point is
that he could no longer deny most of the booty he had bought with
the bribes. The raids on his house and boat had taken away that defense. Federal agents had found much of the expensive furniture
Wade had purchased for his lawmaker friend. They found the sterling
silver candelabras, antique French commodes, mirrored armoires,
Persian carpets, hutches, dressers, and antique oak doors fitted with
leaded glass panels.

But Cunningham thought maybe he could hide the reality of
who paid for that booty. So one month after the raid, he called Onslow Square, the antique store where he and Wade had purchased
many of the antiques. FBI agents had been to the store during the in-
tervening days. Now, on August 1, an employee answered the phone
to find a very nervous Cunningham on the other end of the line asking whether the store had received any such visitors. Sandra Ellington, the owner, did not take the call, but the employee who did
switched Cunningham over to the speaker phone so that the owner
could listen. When Cunningham heard the click on the line, he

nervously asked what it was. The employee assured the lawmaker that it was only the sound made through switching phones.

Rattled but determined, Cunningham proceeded with the business of the call. He "reminded" the employee that whenever Wade used a credit card to buy antiques to be delivered to Cunningham that Cunningham had always given Wade a wad of cash to cover the payment. Didn't the employee remember it that way? Cunningham asked.

But this employee had no interest in lying for a crooked congressman from a far-away state. Flatly, he denied having seen Cunningham give Wade cash. Cunningham persisted. Finally, the employee noted that Ellington, the owner, had handled the transactions. Later in the day, Cunningham succeeded in getting Ellington on the phone. Again, he began coaching, nudging, "reminding" her of his made-up details of the transaction. He asked Ellington whether she remembered that he had given Wade cash at the time of the sales. No, she told him, she did not recall his giving Wade any cash. Cunningham replied, "Well, I have it written down in my little book."

Ellington, recalling the episode much later, added, "I said, 'Mr. Cunningham, maybe you gave it to him out in the car. But I'm sure I would remember it if you gave him $35,000 cash in front of me.'" She shook her head and, in wonderment at Cunningham's suggestion, she asked, "Do you have any idea what $35,000 in cash is? That's a stack of money!"

Cunningham called Ellington again, right before his March 3, 2006, sentencing. He wanted to know whether he could leave an armoire with her. She declined, explaining that she didn't do storage. Of course, the government would be seizing all the furniture Wade had purchased for Cunningham and selling it at auction. Was Cunningham trying to squirrel away a piece far from the government's eye? Perhaps only Cunningham knows, but it certainly looked like a final, futile effort to cling to at least some of what he had bought with bribes.

After all, those expensive carpets had all been seized. But that didn't mean Cunningham didn't try to confuse the prosecutors and phony up who had paid for some of them. This time, it was a hand-scrawled note and a check for $16,500 that Cunningham sent the rug dealer who sold Wade the carpets Cunningham had picked out on their final shopping excursion. He sent the check and note after the *Union-Tribune*'s first story on the house sale. In the note, Cunningham explained to the rug merchant that he had searched in vain for an invoice and address for the store at the time the carpets had arrived at his congressional office in Escondido. It was just his luck—here he had tried so hard to pay for the rug, but he hadn't been able to find that darned address. Because, you know, his check was in the mail. Really.

In handwriting that was barely legible, Cunningham wrote: "When rugs arrived I called my staff and asked to find invoice [*sic*] They could not and when we rolled them out could not find the normal invoice—COD. I think the # was 16,500. If higher or lower I will make the change."

Cunningham indicated in the note that he previously had sent a check to a wrong address. Prosecutors called the suggestion "preposterous." Based on an interview with the rug dealer, prosecutors wrote in court papers that "it was clear that [Wade] had paid for the rugs; he and Cunningham had no discussions about the price of Cunningham's rugs nor about any money that was owed for the rugs; and the rugs were shipped with packing labels that reflected his store's address—the same address the store had used for over a decade."

Cunningham was still doing odd things right up to the eve of his imprisonment. The night before he was locked up, he dropped several suitcases and two duffel bags in his wife's driveway for her to keep for him while he was behind bars. In one of the duffel bags she found an assortment of dirty underwear and nearly $32,000 in cash. The $20 and $100 bills were wrapped in plastic bags.[1]

James Macy, one of Nancy Cunningham's lawyers, said the congressman had arranged to drop off the bag for his wife to hold as his personal belongings while he was in prison. Macy said he discovered the money when he started to inventory the belongings. Macy notified the U.S. attorney of the cash "so they wouldn't think money was being laundered." When Nancy told Cunningham that she had turned over the money, he was livid. He was not persuaded when she told him that she had no other choice. "But he just doesn't understand," she said. "He claims he's innocent, that he's been railroaded by the government, that he shouldn't be in prison."[2]

The prosecutors are too professional to admit to being amused by the amateurishness of the cover-up attempts. Instead, they noted all the attempts and made sure the judge knew about them. Their filings stated in part:

> Cunningham engaged in obstructive conduct both early and often. Beginning with his false comments to the reporter who first broke the story on June 12, 2005, continuing with his false press release of June 13, 2005 and June 23, 2005, his false notes to the rug dealer and [Wade] in June 2005, and concluding with his witness tampering with the antique dealer and her employee in August 2005, Cunningham consistently demonstrated a willingness to mislead law enforcement and to encourage others to do so as well. Indeed, this is demonstrated as far back as November 2004 when Cunningham pressured the local realtor to help him explain away [Wade's] loss from the resale of Cunningham's Del Mar home. Moreover, Cunningham not only tampered with witnesses who he knew were in contact with the FBI, he directly provided misleading evidence to the United States Attorney's Office. . . .

Prosecutors added that Cunningham had engaged in "repeated and egregious attempts to both fabricate evidence and influence witnesses."

The verdict was simple. Cunningham was going down.

chapter twenty

GUILTY!

A S RANDY CUNNINGHAM STOOD IN FRONT OF THE LIBRARY AT CALIFORNIA State University San Marcos, there by his side was Nancy, his wife of thirty-one years, mother of his two daughters. She neither tried to play the role of the traditional politician's wife with a fixed, adoring gaze nor tried to hide her true feelings. She was angry. Bitter. Seething. What nobody outside the family knew was that this would be the last time she would stand by his side, the last time she felt she was married to the man she later would refer to as "Mr. Cunningham."

It would be months before she would confirm what everybody could see that day. As she later told Kitty Kelley, "I said, 'You need to know, Mr. Cunningham, that we now do not have a marriage; we have a business arrangement.'"[1]

This was a woman who said she once idolized her husband. But at this press conference, that adoration was long gone. In a now famous picture captured by the *Union-Tribune* photographer John Gastaldo, he is turned to her with the supplicating look of a child seeking a parent's forgiveness. But, as her body language made clear, there was no forgiveness coming from her. Nancy stared straight ahead, her lips pursed as sharply as the lapel crease on her pink blazer.

So there he was, staring at a phalanx of television and newspaper cameras, his political career in tatters, his marriage collapsing, and his legal defenses crumbling. Cunningham had only a brief statement to make in a desperate effort to slow the political and legal free fall that was now threatening his career, his reputation, and, indeed, his very freedom.

And yet he continued to deny facts that the prosecutors already knew: "In the last month, serious allegations have been made about my conduct in office. I again want to assure my constituents that I have acted honorably in the performance of my duties in Congress. This truth will be evident in time. I have cooperated with the government's investigation and I am confident that I will be vindicated." He added that "the daily repetition of those charges in the press" had damaged his "standing in this community."

Cunningham went on:

> I fully recognize that I showed poor judgment when I sold my home in Del Mar to a friend who did business with the government. I should have given more thought to how such a transaction might look to those who don't know me. I have spent an entire life building a reputation of integrity and trust. It pains me beyond words that I have jeopardized your trust. . . . I want each of you to know that I did not profit improperly from the sale of my home in Del Mar.

Then he added that the pain of public doubts sown by the house transaction had led him and his wife to decide to sell the Rancho Santa Fe house and give a portion of the proceeds to three local charities. "Nancy and I know that this gesture will not convince the skeptics of our good faith," he said. "My detractors have already made up their minds and this act will not reach them, or in any way end the government's investigation of me." For those doubters and the investigators, Cunningham added a final, dramatic gesture. After representing the district in the House for fifteen years, Cunningham announced that he would not seek a ninth term.

"I can do my work in Washington and I can defend myself against these allegations, but I don't think I can do either of these things effectively in the midst of a political campaign. You know how tough that is," Cunningham said. "Quite simply, right now, I may not be the strongest candidate."

Then the couple withdrew into the library. To avoid questions from the media, they exited by way of a back door to a waiting car. [2]

The announcement set off an immediate scramble among Democrats and Republicans queuing up to run for what would now become a campaign for a vacant seat in 2006. Cunningham's congressional neighbor and closest political friend, Rep. Duncan Hunter, stepped up once again to defend "Duke" by attacking the media. "The media has been unfair," he said. "You've had almost a story a day, some of them fairly creative." Once again, Hunter called on people to remember that Cunningham had been a war hero and therefore deserved the benefit of the doubt.[3]

There were the lamentations and the gnashing of teeth by those who saw only the earmarks he brought into the community. Never mind morality or legality—they just wanted the federal money, damn it. One representative of the San Diego business community, which had benefited so handsomely over the years by playing the earmark game with Cunningham, was beside himself over the loss. They were losing a champion who delivered tens of millions of dollars a year through his seat on the Appropriations Committee. None would ever have said it so bluntly in public, but some must have thought: "He might be a crook but he's our crook."

Julie Meier Wright, the president and chief executive officer of the San Diego Regional Economic Development Corp., put it more artfully: "He has always been a big supporter of the military and medical research and is on key committees. We are losing a man of seniority in Congress."[4]

The reaction of Republicans nationally was quite different. Where once they had put Cunningham forward as their hero and worshiped at the altar of his ability to raise funds for the GOP, now they could not wait to get rid of him. They already were fighting Democratic cries of a Republican "culture of corruption" prompted by the shenanigans of the lobbyist Jack Abramoff. They didn't need another crook. "There is no question about it that Republicans are relieved now that it is over," Charles Cook, who publishes the nonpartisan *Cook Political Report,* told the *Union-Tribune* later that day.[5]

Also relieved, but for much different reasons, were the neighbors at the marina near where Cunningham had lived on that yacht. They would no longer have to suffer through the congressman's loud parties. Indeed, they had watched in bemusement when the *Duke-Stir* was beset by federal agents on July 1. What they didn't know—and what federal agents didn't know—was that they had missed something important in that raid. That wasn't discovered until representatives of Mitch Wade, and possibly Wade himself, visited the yacht to see what was still there after the seizure of items on the boat.

At first, Wade's folks only noticed something left behind that amused them—tubes of K-Y Jelly, everywhere. David Heil, the staffer who had confronted Cunningham over his dealings with Wade and Wilkes before quitting, offered an explanation in an interview much later. He said that K-Y Jelly had some "nautical purpose." And the reason there was so much of it is that Cunningham was a freak for Costco and therefore bought things like K-Y Jelly in high volume.

When questioned further about how he knew that, Heil said another staffer had told him. Asked how the subject had come up, he explained that Cunningham had kept tubes of K-Y Jelly in the bathroom in his Capitol office, too. It was unclear what nautical purpose might have been served in his congressional office. Nobody ever satisfactorily explained the mystery of the K-Y Jelly cache, and it led to some of the less-printable jokes of the whole investigation.

But there was something else—something much more important—that federal investigators had left behind and, initially, could not explain. This was a note so obscure that none of the agents involved in the raid had any idea of its significance. Certainly, they did not grasp that this piece of paper left in the aft cabin of the *Duke-Stir* was the key to the whole investigation. They left it behind when they took away everything they thought might be incriminating.

The scrap of paper was the infamous bribe menu. It was only when Wade brought it to their attention that the investigators realized that this piece of congressional stationery with the two scrawled columns of numbers was what it would take to persuade Cunningham to admit his guilt. Wade eagerly explained its significance to them, for he was much smarter than Cunningham and much quicker to realize that the defendants who talked first would get the best deal. He had immediately recognized the columns of numbers as the bribe menu sketched out by Cunningham on that day at the Daily Grill in Georgetown. He saw it as his ticket to a shorter sentence, and that was why he had his attorney turn it over to the government with a full explanation of what it was and how it had come about.

Only later did Cunningham and his attorneys became aware that Wade had double-crossed his old friend. As the first co-conspirator to approach the government for a plea agreement, Wade's strategy was to portray himself as a hapless fly caught in the web of a corrupt and greedy politician. Under this theory, the defense contractor was just trying to make America safe in the post-9/11 world, and the price he had to pay for his patriotic endeavors was plying Cunningham with campaign contributions, favors, and bribes. Cunningham had *demanded* them. Cunningham was the spider, Wade the fly.

The problem with the theory is that nobody who dealt with Wade during the making of MZM has compared him to anything quite so hapless as a fly. Scorpion is more like it. Words such as cunning, manipulative, predatory, and controlling come up constantly. So maybe Wade was the spider, Cunningham the fly. The problem with that scenario is that it's hard to see Cunningham as the quarry of any predator. After all, he had learned to hunt as a child and had shot down five MiGs as an adult. Relishing the use of brass-knuckle rhetoric in his attacks on Democrats, he had played hardball in the political arena for more than fifteen years. His colleagues might have questioned his intellect, but he was neither pliable nor naïve. He was in no way a hapless fly.

So the legal system probably had it right when it labeled the two men as co-conspirators. Wade didn't much care what people thought of him. He wasn't out to impress anybody. He was born of modest means and huge ambitions. He didn't want to be just comfortable. He liked countryside estates with open, rolling grassy hillsides and long curving driveways; he favored oversized antiques and traditional oil paintings. And, of course, his taste in Scotch and wine could best be summed up as pretty much anything expensive. Since Wade hadn't been born with these things, it was hugely important that he acquire them. And that required naked ambition and cold-blooded resolve. Wade was a man on the make, pure and simple.

Cunningham, on the other hand, wanted to be admired; in fact, he needed to be admired. He needed constant affirmation of his greatness reflected in the eyes of those around him. His grandiosity fed his sense of entitlement. His sense of entitlement, never sufficiently satisfied, oxidized into envy. And the festering envy left him vulnerable to Wade—the master manipulator. Cunningham had arrived in 1991 in a town that has always drawn people with unbridled ambition, outsized egos, and well-masked character flaws. When voters put Cunningham in Congress, they placed his hand on the national purse strings. It wasn't hard for Wilkes and Wade to coax him to place that hand inside the purse for their benefit. And from that point on, it became a slippery slope all the way to the courthouse steps on November 28, 2005.

That Monday morning, reporters scrambled to the U.S. District Court in San Diego as rumors spread of a previously unannounced court hearing in the Cunningham case. After a four-month public lull in the scandal, word of the hearing set off unchecked speculation that the government was about to indict Cunningham. The indictment of a sitting member of Congress would be hot news in any city, but it would be especially so in San Diego, where local corruption scandals seemed rampant at the beginning of the twenty-first century.

Inside the courtroom that Monday morning, Cunningham assumed a hang-dog air, clasping his hands in front of him and quietly offering concise replies to questions posed by U.S. District Judge Larry Alan Burns. They were short, terse answers, but their impact was huge—they would send the congressman to prison, brand him as the most corrupt person ever to serve in Congress, and forever tarnish a reputation he had spent decades trying to shape.

"Between the year 2000 and June of 2005 in our district, you conspired to accept bribes in exchange for performance of official duties. Did you do that?" Judge Burns asked Cunningham.

"Yes, your Honor."

"Did you take both cash payments and payments in kind?" Burns asked.

"Yes, your Honor."

"Did you follow up by trying to influence the Defense Department?"

"Yes, your Honor."

Outside the courthouse, addressing the press, Cunningham would offer no more denials. Before television and newspaper cameras, he put on a performance of two minutes and twenty-seven seconds that erased any image the public might have had of him from his glory days as a Navy fighter pilot. With the sun spotlighting the right side of his face and photographers' camera flashes lighting the left, Cunningham gave his last, brief press conference, one worthy of a man known to draw on emotion when he speaks. But the emotion wasn't the usual bravado, bluster, and indignation. If Cunningham had failed previously to show candor and remorse, it was now on copious display.

He now had to admit that he had lied that day in front of the campus library in San Marcos—as on so many other days:

When I announced several months ago that I would not seek re-election, I publicly declared my innocence because I was not strong enough to face the truth. So, I misled my family, staff, friends, colleagues, the public—even myself. For all of this, I am deeply sorry. The truth is—I broke the law, concealed my conduct, and disgraced my high office. I know that I will forfeit my freedom, my reputation, my worldly possessions, most importantly [here Cunningham paused for five seconds, bit his lip and resumed in a quavering, cracking voice] the trust of my friends and family.

Trying but failing to regain his composure, Cunningham explained in a still quavering voice that "some time ago" he had notified U.S. Attorney Carol Lam that he "would like to plead guilty and begin serving a prison term." The court hearing that morning, he said, had been the culmination of that process.

"In my life, I have had great joy and great sorrow. And now I know great shame. I learned in Vietnam that the true measure of a man is how he responds to adversity. I can't undo what I have done. But I can atone. And now"—here he paused for seven seconds, using the fingers on his left hand to lift his glasses out of the way so he could brush tears from his eyes—"I am almost sixty-five years old and as I enter the twilight of my life, I intend to use the remaining time that God grants me to make amends. And I will.

"The first step in that journey is to admit fault and apologize. And I do apologize. The next step is to face the consequences of my actions like a man. Today I have taken the first step and, with God's grace, I will take the second. God bless you."

As he turned from the cameras, someone could be heard calling out, "Why'd you do it?"

The question went unanswered. Most likely, even Cunningham did not know the answer. And today was not a day for more lies. Today, he had come clean. Finally.

chapter twenty-one

SENTENCING DAY

S HARPSHOOTERS STOOD POISED ON THE ROOFTOPS LOOKING DOWN ON Front Street as Randy Cunningham took his last car ride as a free man. Other security officials were scattered through the crowd that had massed in front of the Edward J. Schwartz Federal Court House. It was March 3, 2006—time for Randall H. Cunningham to find out how long he would serve in federal prison, how severely he would be punished as the most corrupt member of Congress in its long history.

Back in November, when he was last at the courthouse, he was still a sitting member of Congress and was accorded special privileges that permitted him to avoid the crush of reporters and camera crews outside by driving into a secure area beneath the building.

But U.S. Marshal David Bejarano had ordered that Cunningham be given no special treatment this day. After all, the ex-congressman had pleaded guilty to conspiracy and tax evasion charges. Today, he was just another perp here to face the music. So it fell to Dave Dallaire, Bejarano's supervisory deputy federal marshal, to oversee a security plan that would take Cunningham safely from the curb to the court room through the throng gathered outside. He would have to use the sidewalk and enter through the front door. It was a daunting challenge, and Dallaire's worries were shared by K. Lee Blalack, Cunningham's lead attorney. When Dallaire's cell phone rang, it was Blalack calling from inside the sedan now approaching the courthouse plaza. "He was very concerned about [Cunningham's] frailty and how he was going to get through the crowd," Dallaire recalled.

Blalack's concern was well placed—even more so after the driver overshot the curbside location where Dallaire and other marshals were waiting. Instead of stepping out into the arms of marshals, Cunningham and his attorney Mark Holscher stepped out of the right side of the sedan, only to be immediately engulfed by television cameras and reporters. Blalack, who exited the sedan's left side door, recalled: "By the time I got around to them, it was already a madhouse." Holscher grabbed Cunningham's right arm to support him. Dallaire muscled his way over and cupped Cunningham's left forearm in his right hand. The trio then began the slog forward. The sharp shooters on the nearby roofs continued to scan the chaos below. They were there, Dallaire said, "just in case some wacko came" with the intent of adding bloody mayhem to the chaos by attacking Cunningham.

The scrum had barely begun to move when a backpedaling cameraman tripped over a concrete planter on the sidewalk. He tumbled backwards, just in front of Cunningham, who sagged into him. Dallaire and Holscher had to haul him back to his feet. Dallaire was struck by Cunningham's glass-eyed gaze, overall weakness and unbroken silence. "He didn't say anything. And he never looked up—not once," Dallaire said. "He just kept looking at the ground and walking straight ahead."

Dallaire could not get over how much Cunningham had changed in the three months since his tearful guilty plea and resignation from Congress. "Back then he still looked physically strong," said Dallaire. "But this man was beaten." Cunningham's public and private lives had imploded. He had plunged into a black hole of depression that was quite literally consuming him. His old friend Dan McKinnon wrote to the court that Cunningham's weight had plummeted from 262 pounds to 185 pounds. Estranged from Nancy since the FBI had raided their home, Cunningham had moved into McKinnon's ranch bunk house. There, he found refuge with friends who, McKinnon wrote, had gotten him "walking, chopping wood, and digging weeds." The man who had once exuded the swagger of the fighter pilot now was "totally and utterly disgusted with himself." McKinnon added: "He's a mentally tortured man."

Now, not only was Cunningham dazed by the mob surrounding him and demoralized by the sentence about to be meted out to him, he also was heavily medicated when he showed up to face the judge. There was a fear of suicide, and the psychiatrists treating him were taking no chances and sparing no drug: Zoloft for depression, Ativan for anxiety, Ambien and Trazadone for insomnia. He was on them all. And it showed. He moved as if in a trance. His suit hung from his gaunt frame like a bedsheet. The situation grew more tense with every step. "The marshals got pretty aggressive making space and that made the reporters hostile," Blalack recalled. "You could hear the expletives flying between the TV cameramen saying something about the First Amendment and the marshals saying, 'Get the hell out of the way.' It was a serious moment."

Dallaire agreed. "I've been a marshal twenty-one years, and I've never seen anything like it," he said. "It was a stampede, trying to get in there. I told him, 'Just stay with me, Mr. Cunningham. Stay with me.'" To the mob, Dallaire repeatedly barked the same command: "Make a hole! Make a hole!" The crowd kept pressing in, cameramen determined to capture the image, reporters straining for a quote. The shout of one reporter pierced the din—"Why did you do it, Mr. Cunningham? Why did you do it?" It was the great unanswered question of the whole Cunningham affair.

Finally, with a concluding surge aided by the burly San Diego policemen who waded in to help, they made it to the camera-free refuge of the courthouse. Inside the building, it did not get much easier for the former congressman. No longer did he have to face the horde of photographers; but for a proud man now humiliated by his current predicament and by the things he had confessed doing, it was worse—much worse—to have to look into the faces of the friends already gathered inside the largest courtroom in the Southern District of California. It was one thing to admit you had betrayed the voters in your district; they, after all, were faceless and anonymous. But many of the people in this courtroom had names and faces. With them, there was no masking the shame he felt and the deep personal hurt he had caused them. There, in the twenty seats Blalack had set aside for friends of the defendant, were reminders of a past that had featured so many high points, so many standing ovations, so many awards, so much glory. Even the building itself was such a reminder—only twelve years earlier, Cunningham had been instrumental in naming this courthouse after Edward Schwartz. And now he was there in the docks. And there as well were his fellow aviators in North Vietnam—his backseater Willie Driscoll and Top Gun Pete Pettigrew. There were the two men most responsible for his election to Congress—Rep. Duncan Hunter and Dan McKinnon. There was one of his mentors, retired Congressman Clair Burgener, now frail and only months away from his death. And there was Father Joe Carroll, easily the best-known priest in San Diego, made famous for his good works with the homeless.

Pointedly—and poignantly—none of Cunningham's family members were there. He said he had asked them to stay away, but it is unlikely that his estranged wife Nancy would have come regardless of what he wanted. Her anger was quite clear in the letter she had included in the packet sent by Blalack to Judge Larry Alan Burns. All the other letters expressed varying degrees of warmth toward Cunningham and bewilderment at his actions while pleading for leniency in the sentence. But there was no warmth in Nancy's letter.

It was only 156 words long, barely five for each year of her marriage to the man she now coldly referred to as "Mr. Cunningham." When questioned later about this frosty way of addressing her husband, she said, "It's a mental distancing. As far as I'm concerned, he no longer really exists."[1] And in this letter, it was clear that he existed only in how he related to their two daughters. The letter suggested that if Cunningham spent the rest of his life in prison, she cared not at all—except that would hurt their daughters. "I know the children feel and hope that . . . they will sometime in the future be able to spend time with their father, free of a prison setting."[2]

The tone was much softer—indeed, was achingly sad—in the other letters from family members included in the submission to the court. One was the three pages of careful scrawl, written on American flag stationery by the ninety-one-year-old Lela Cunningham, showing a mother's love for eldest son. Her two boys, she wrote, "loved their God" and "lived in a Christian home."[3]

Cunningham's daughters, Carrie and April, seemed dazed by the sudden upheaval in their lives and the impending imprisonment of their father. There also was no doubting that he had not really been there for them in their youth. "He had expressed many times his regret at not being around more when we were growing up and his desire to make this up to us in the future," wrote Carrie. Noting the "tremendous stress" in the family, she said her father had "betrayed the values and ethics" by which she and her sister had been brought up and now would not be there to see her graduate from college or to attend her wedding.[4] April wrote similarly of a youth with an absentee dad: "My father was often not with my family throughout my childhood," she said, adding, "I have made sacrifices all along so that my father could be a public servant. I have struggled to maintain a father-daughter bond despite distance and difference." She asked the judge for leniency: "If you will give my father a shorter sentence rather than a longer one, I can work on building a relationship with my father as he is now—significantly changed by the damage of his decisions and the trauma of the last several months."[5]

Todd, Cunningham's adopted son from his first marriage, had also written a letter. So had Robert F. Cunningham—Rob, the younger brother who idolized big brother Randy. Rob spoke of how the family was adapting to the newfound shame. "Our family has always been quick to share his fame and let others know that Randy 'Duke' Cunningham is our son, father, brother, uncle, cousin, etc.," he wrote, noting they had also claimed that John Wayne was an actor but Duke

Cunningham was the real thing. "Now, we all share his pain, shame, and ridicule every day in the papers, on television, and through personal conversations."[6] Todd left no doubt that Randy Cunningham—his dad—understands how he has affected the family. "He is very down right now, and his remorse is overwhelming him at times."[7]

That was Cunningham's state when he entered the courtroom and saw his friends. As a priest, Father Joe—as he is known to San Diegans—is accustomed to counseling broken men. But even he was taken aback by the sight of his old friend as they embraced and Cunningham wept. "He was a broken man . . . crying, barely able to stand," Carroll said. "And to see this guy you thought of as a Top Gun pilot, ace of the Vietnam war, all of this image of hero worship. And he basically was very sorrowful, very broken."[8]

That was obvious even to others who were in the courtroom to chronicle the proceedings and not to comfort the guilty man. Several dozen reporters sat at the rear of the courtroom, craning to hear what was being said. There were fourteen more in the jury box, a dramatic touch that struck Blalack as appropriate, given the role of the press in exposing Cunningham's corruption. "I thought that was very fitting," he said later. "It made a nice metaphor for the entire enterprise."

One person who was not there physically but whose presence was very much reflected in the evidence against Cunningham was Mitch Wade. Without the evidence supplied by Wade, Cunningham might not have found himself pleading guilty and standing here this day. Less than two weeks earlier, Wade himself had pled guilty to four counts: conspiring to bribe Cunningham, including evasion of taxes; use of interstate facilities to promote bribery; conspiring to deprive the Defense Department of the honest services of its employees; and election fraud. Under the terms of the agreement, Wade faces up to 135 months of incarceration. But he still had several months to go before he would find out how long he would spend in prison.

Cunningham, however, would find out his own fate in just a few minutes. Two sketch artists focused intently on the sad, shrunken figure who sat between his two attorneys facing the bench. Behind them sat FBI agents who were still working the case and assistant U.S. attorneys who wanted to catch the climactic moment in one of the office's biggest cases in years.

But the center of attention, the man in control was the judge—Larry Alan Burns, a widely respected former prosecutor with a reputation as hard-nosed and by-the-book. Only fifty-one years old, Burns had been a U.S. District Court judge only since President George W. Bush appointed him to the bench in 2003. He had presided over other big cases, but this, without doubt, was the most important case of his brief judicial career.

As the hearing got underway, CNN's Wolf Blitzer, hosting *The Situation Room,* told a national audience that reporter Jen Rogers was in the courtroom. "The instant she learns the outcome, she is going to come outside and bring us a live report," he said. After all this waiting, all this anticipation, Cunningham—and the world—were about to learn his sentence.

Citing "numbing betrayal, on an epic scale," the prosecution had urged the maximum sentence: ten years. The defense lawyers, urging consideration of Cunningham's military service and civic and charitable work, said six years would be appropriate, especially since doctors had estimated that Cunningham's successfully treated prostate cancer nonetheless gave him a life expectancy of about seven years. But they were not optimistic. Having spoken to local attorneys familiar with Burns's work on the bench, Blalack had reason to fear the worst. "Everything I had heard of Judge Burns was that he was very stern in his sentences," he said. "People told me point blank, 'You know you're going to get ten years, don't you.'. . . I had talked with Duke about that. I wanted him to be ready."

One central question involved federal sentencing guidelines, which use a point system to evaluate the gravity of a crime and assign a sentence. But Judge Burns made note of a Supreme Court ruling that the guidelines were advisory, not mandatory. The Cunningham hearing would turn on Burns's subjective determination of what justice required in the case of this man who had risen so high and then fallen so low. Burns had read hundreds of pages of pre-sentence filings and reports and letters. He acknowledged from the bench that on many recent nights the responsibility had followed him to bed.

First, he would hear from the defense. Standing at the podium in the center of the courtroom, Blalack began his pitch by acknowledging that his client's "deplorable crimes . . . warrant a very stiff sanction." But he attacked the notion, advanced by the prosecution, that Cunningham would be getting off easy if he didn't receive the stiffest possible sentence.

"Your honor, this man has been humiliated beyond belief by his own hand," Blalack said. "He's estranged from those he loves and cares most about. He's living away from them and has been for some substantial time. All of his worldly possessions are gone, for the most part. He will carry a crushing tax debt until the day he dies. On top of that, he is going to go to jail, under any scenario, until he's seventy years old, assuming he lives that long." As he spoke, Cunningham wept quietly and wiped the tears from his eyes.

Blalack, a former U.S. Marine and a combat veteran of Operation Desert Storm, had a warrior's respect for Cunningham. "There are men in this courtroom today who are walking around and breathing because Duke Cunningham put his life at risk," he told the judge. Burns knew that was no idle claim because the stack of letters he had received from Cunningham allies included one from Willie Driscoll, stalwart as ever in his defense of Cunningham, and another from Brian Grant, Duke's wingman in Vietnam. "I am able to write this letter, and [am] alive today, solely because of the selfless heroism and skilled airmanship of Mr. Cunningham," Grant wrote.

Blalack pointed to Cunningham's charitable work, which, again, was cited in many of the letters, including one from Peter Yarrow, the front man of Peter, Paul, and Mary. Yarrow asked that the judge take into account "the many decent, ethical and caring aspects of [Cunningham's] character." Blalack insisted that the shame Cunningham had brought upon himself didn't change the "evidence from people who were touched by him where there was no greed."

He added that "it was purely motivated by a desire to help someone in need."

Blalack closed by acknowledging the public pressure for Burns to slam Cunningham. "The newspapers have called for the maximum sentence. We've got an enormity of reporters out front with cameras. There's no doubt that taking the guidelines calculation and looking at the plea agreement and selecting a ten-year sentence is the easy course. But it's not the just course."

Next up was prosecutor Jason Forge, who was born in 1968, the year after Cunningham entered the navy. Forge was intense, purposeful. His hard work on the case had been fueled by an outrage that grew as the depth of Cunningham's corruption became apparent. Just as Blalack was moved by Cunningham's heroism, Forge was disgusted by his venality. He cited the public stake in the sentence: "When the public sees the man who makes the laws is the same man who breaks the laws," the sentence "should reflect that very special and very significant harm that he has caused to society."

Forge attacked the defense claim, laid out by the Beverly Hills psychiatrist Saul J. Faerstein, that Cunningham's fighter pilot training and his prowess in dog fights had fostered "a sense of grandiosity." Faerstein said Cunningham had come to Washington "with an outsized ego and a mantel of invulnerability." He concluded that Cunningham had developed a "sense of invulnerability to any harm" that allowed him to rationalize his behavior; it "blinded him to the corruption it entailed, and led him to behave in ways totally antithetical to his life history, his family background and his moral and religious values."

But Forge was not persuaded. He bristled at this psychiatric warmth for cold-hearted criminality. "Rephrased in plain English, Mr. Cunningham was able to rationalize his illegal conduct because he felt he could get away with it." He dismissed Faerstein's explanation that Cunningham's military accomplishments might have "planted a subconscious sense of entitlement which fed his rationalization to accept these gifts for his sacrifices." Forge scorned that as so much psychobabble. "He did not accept gifts. He actively solicited bribes," he thundered. "He solicited those bribes because he thought he could get away with it."

Forge also rejected Cunningham's claims to have accepted responsibility for his crimes. He reminded Judge Burns of the staffer who had stood up to him and told him to resign. He reminded him that Cunningham had "spent the summer falsely denying" that he had done wrong, "misleading his friends and family members and obstructing our investigation." Not until "he finally realized we weren't going away" did he face up to his criminality.

Then it was Phillip Halpern's turn. The prosecutor weighed in with an old quotation in which Cunningham strutted his determination to restore integrity in Washington: "I first ran for Congress because I was fed up with politicians who took advantage of our trust and put powerful special interests ahead of those who elected him [sic]."

Intensely focused and also outraged at what he saw as Cunningham's monstrous betrayal, Halpern held aloft a clear plastic bag that held the bribe menu. Halpern looked directly at Cunningham, who cast his eyes down. "It is this memo where the defendant specifically memorialized the price of his betrayal," intoned the prosecutor.

Cunningham had not only undermined public trust in government, he had weakened national defense, Halpern said. He had used his position "to bully and to threaten any official who questioned either the need or the value of these programs which he pushed for his own interest." Halpern added: "Bluntly stated, the defendant simply failed to put the nation's interest ahead of his own greed." That greed had drained resources from honest contractors providing legitimate programs that served legitimate needs. "So while the congressman was living the good life in his estate in Rancho Santa Fe, sailing on the Potomac in his luxury yacht, driving his Rolls Royce, enjoying his French provincial furniture, he was performing those acts, squandering precious tax dollars for, among other things, systems the military didn't ask for, didn't need and frequently didn't use."

As Halpern returned to the prosecution table, the judge turned to Cunningham: "Mr. Cunningham, you have the right to address the court, and I'm happy to hear from you today. Anything you want to say on your own behalf, you may do so at this time."

Cunningham rose—tentatively, shakily—to take the podium. His voice was thin and reedy at first but would grow stronger as he continued. "May I bring water?" he asked meekly. "Yes, of course," responded the judge.

Cunningham offered an alternative view of himself, the same view that he had urged upon friends and family. He wanted to be seen as guilty not only of bribery but also of naïveté and excessive trust in friends who turned out to be fakes and who had turned him away from a long path of rectitude.

"I recently saw a bumper sticker that said, 'You're going the wrong way but God allows U turns,'" he said. "After years of service to my country and going the right way, I made a very wrong turn." Using a term from floor debate in the House of Representatives, he turned to the prosecution table and said, "I yield to my colleagues on the other side."

There is, of course, plenty of evidence that Cunningham's corruption, far from an abrupt U-turn, was the ultimate extension of the self-glorification and self-gratification that had long been evident. But his capacity for self-delusion became even more apparent as he insisted that he had begun to turn away from his corruption even before it was exposed in mid-June on the front page of the *Union-Tribune*.

> I would tell your honor, no man has ever been more sorry, not just in the June time frame, but even prior to that, in the things that were going through my own mind. . . . I have, for what I have done, accepted responsibility for those wrong decisions not because I was about ready to be indicted. I spoke to my attorney a long time before that and said, "I need to make amends. I want to do the right thing and clear these issues up."

The facts, of course, suggest otherwise. In May 2005, the month before being confronted by Copley News Service, Cunningham had put the squeeze on Mitch Wade once again—as Jason Forge had noted not ten minutes before Cunningham's painful walk to the podium. Cunningham called Wade and "demanded and received over $15,000 in Indian and Persian rugs." And even after Stern's article appeared, Cunningham flatly denied wrongdoing: "I have always done this job in the interest of my nation and my constituents . . . and I will continue to work to earn their respect and endorsement," he declared.

Cunningham then spoke of his current circumstances and physical frailty:

> Some days, your Honor, I didn't know how I would get through the day. I never thought that I would take my own life, but I wondered how I could cope with the pain from the moment I woke up in the morning until the evening when I went to sleep.
>
> If you look at the rest and the earlier parts of my life, that's the way I've lived my life, your honor. I've tried to do the right thing.

He pledged to make repentance a lifelong process and asked the judge to recognize his fundamental goodness. He cited his own naïveté. "I think I'll trust people less, your Honor, so I won't make those same wrong U-turns." He made one final reference to his Vietnam heroism. "I didn't jump into a pack of twenty-two MiGs because of ego. I did it because it was the right thing to do and to save my friends' lives."

He vowed to spend the rest of his life "seeking to atone and seek forgiveness." Then he made his most concise and honest admission: "I have ripped my life to shreds due to my actions, to my actions that I did myself. Not because someone else did it to me. I did it to myself. I made those decisions. I could have said no and I didn't. It was me, Duke Cunningham. It was wrong."

All eyes followed Cunningham's stiff-legged return to the defense table only to quickly shift to the bench for the climactic moment. Although the statements of the defense and prosecution and Cunningham himself had added to the public record, they had no influence on the judge's decision. He had written it out beforehand and carried it to the bench with him. He had, however, run it by Dave Dallaire, an old and trusted courthouse friend, just before the hearing. "He said, 'This is where I'm going with this—eight years and four months. What do you think?'" Dallaire recalled. "I just said it sounded about right to me."

Burns launched into a methodical, almost melancholy assessment of Cunningham's crimes, which he summarized as the expression of—he had clearly searched for the right word—"avarice."

"The word avarice is an antiquated word. It means reprehensible. But antiquated as it is, I think it applies here." It was one of the seven deadly sins, he noted, along with pride, envy, wrath, sloth, lust, and gluttony.

Burns rejected Faerstein's and Cunningham's U-turn metaphor. "It wasn't a single U-turn. You made the U-turn, and you continued in the wrong direction for a period of five years. And I wonder today how much farther you would have gone in that direction but for the intervention of the government agents and the newspapers that tipped them." He noted the cost to taxpayers and to the national defense: "The government ends up in this case with things that maybe it doesn't need. . . . I dare say that I think we paid a lot of money for some things we don't need as a result of your intervention."

He expressed surprise at the "bullying of [Cunningham's] staff and low-level and mid-level people at the Department of Defense." He wanted to see such conduct as an aberration. "I don't really think that represents you. I looked at your life and you seem to be a fairly humble guy despite all these accomplishments." Yet he made clear his disgust with Cunningham's threat to have someone fired for resisting his earmarks. "I just think that's beyond the pale."

He wondered why Cunningham hadn't become a lobbyist if money was his goal. In an apparent reference to former Rep. Bill Lowery's success as a lobbyist, he said, "If this fellow made two and a half million [annually] I think you could have easily doubled that."

And he very pointedly contrasted Cunningham's behavior with that of the drug dealers and other criminals who come before his bench so often driven to crime by their poverty or personal desperation. "So I look at you and I contrast you with other defendants I see," he said. "And I think to myself you weren't wet, you weren't cold, you weren't hungry, and yet you did these things. And I think that's a very aggravating aspect of this case, I'll be honest with you, Mr. Cunningham."

It seemed, at this point, to be a prelude to the toughest possible sentence. Logan Jenkins, a *Union-Tribune* columnist, later observed that at the midpoint of the judge's remarks he suspected "everyone in the courtroom was certain [he] would hand down a perfect 10—or possibly even a stiffer sentence." But then the judge demonstrated that a sentence not constrained by federal guidelines can be shaped as much by a judge's own life experiences as by his evaluation of the crime.

Judge Burns told his own story of the Vietnam War. "Mr. Cunningham, in May of 1972, when you shot down those MiGs in defense of our country, I was a high school senior. I was sweating it out because we still had a draft lottery then."

Burns was never called to serve. But he voiced gratitude that Cunningham had: "I think your country owes you a debt for that." Sitting at the defense table, Blalack felt a surge of relief. The judge was clearly not inclined to deliver the maximum blow. Blalack was struck by what Logan Jenkins would call the "restrained eloquence" of the judge's comments. "I saw what appeared to be a tear in his eye," Blalack said.

Burns continued,

We talk about messages that need to be sent. I agree wholeheartedly that a message needs to be sent to people in politics that we demand their honest services. But another message ought to be sent, and that is if you served in the Armed Forces of the United States and you served with great dignity and honor, that will be taken into account at some point, too. Today is that day. I take that into account.

Burns then sentenced Cunningham to one hundred months—eight years and four months. With the 15 percent reduction he could earn through good behavior, he could be out in eighty-five months. Blalack reflected that eighty-five months corresponded to what the doctors had said was Cunningham's life expectancy. "I thought the judge was giving Duke a chance to end his sentence and rejoin his family," said Blalack. And he realized that if Cunningham cooperated fully with prosecutors, he could be in line for an even further reduction.

Blalack was thrilled. He leaned toward Cunningham and told him so. "I basically expressed my belief that this was a better-than-expected outcome. I told him that he now had an opportunity, if he continued on the path he had said he wanted to follow, to reduce his sentence further and to make good on his promise to atone for what he had done."

Burns also ordered Cunningham to pay back taxes on his bribe income: $1,804,031.50. Cunningham would have to pay $1,500 a month during his incarceration, an amount that would be deducted from the congressional pension he would receive despite his betrayal of his office. Once he was released, the amount would be reduced to $1,000 per month.

Burns denied Cunningham's request for time to visit his mother in Texas before turning himself in. And then it was over. Burns's gavel fell. There would be no big crowds to wade through as there had been when he arrived. He would, instead, exit the courtroom through the back door in the custody of marshals. He was fingerprinted, photographed, handcuffed, and then held in the San Diego Metropolitan Correctional Center until he could be moved to a federal prison.

Two days later, when Dallaire saw Cunningham next, he reported that he was a much more subdued man. "I told my buddy Charlie, 'God, he's a beaten man.' Charlie said, 'Yeah, he's beat. He finally realized what's happened to him.' I told him, 'Mr. Cunningham, you beat 'Nam, you can beat this.' But it was like talking to a wall. He had no expression. He just looked up at one point and said, 'Thank you for your kind thoughts.'"

On Thursday, March 9, 2006, six days after he was sentenced, Prisoner No. 94405198, wearing a standard-issue prison uniform, shuffled aboard "Con Air," the airline run by the U.S. Marshals Service to transport prisoners. No more lobbyist-owned private jets or Phantom F-4s for Cunningham. He was shackled and kept in place with a waist chain until the plane landed in Oklahoma City.[9] From there he would be flown to a prison chosen by the Federal Bureau of Prisons.

A new life had begun.

epilogue

THE SCANDAL CONTINUES

Randy Cunningham's pledge to Judge Burns that "repentance will be a lifelong endeavor" didn't last all that long. Less than an hour after proclaiming in open court that "no man has ever been more sorry" and declaring that he had "accepted responsibility" for his illegal actions, the disgraced former congressman struck a much different note in his jail cell at the San Diego Metropolitan Correctional Center. Dave Dallaire, who was overseeing his security now that he had been taken into custody, heard Cunningham backpedal. "He said this was a misunderstanding and he thought he was being ram-rodded into this," recalled the deputy federal marshal.[1]

All that contrition and regret voiced just a few minutes earlier in the courtroom had morphed into the lament so familiar from convicts everywhere. It was a variation of "I didn't do it; I don't belong here" that Dallaire had heard from so many others before.

To those insiders who had dealt with Cunningham during the legal process, and to members of Cunningham's inner circle, this was no surprise. They knew that in private he was still rationalizing and defending his actions even while issuing apologetic public statements.

No one saw this more clearly than Nancy Cunningham, who received frequent phone calls from her estranged husband after he was taken to prison in Butner, North Carolina. "He claims he's innocent, that he's been railroaded by the government, that he shouldn't be in prison. He says he signed the plea agreement under duress," Nancy told Kitty Kelley in 2006. "He even thinks he will be pardoned by President Bush," she added, incredulously.[2]

As for Cunningham's lawyers, they had found their client resistant to their best advice and slow to accept the government's overwhelming case. Sources intimately familiar with the situation said they frequently learned damning details of the congressman's corruption not from their client but from the prosecutors. And Cunningham was reluctant to accept a deal, never really believing that he had done anything more illegal than succumb to naïve behavior.

In an emotional handwritten letter Cunningham sent to Marcus Stern from Butner prison on September 15, 2006, the former congressman put the blame almost solely on Mitchell Wade. "Wade is the absolute devil and his lawyer is trying to save his donkey," wrote Cunningham. "I should have said no to the gifts."[3]

In court, Jason Forge, the assistant U.S. attorney, argued that Cunningham had felt no twinge of conscience before the story that exposed the house sale in June 2005. "The tears and the remorse are attributed to getting caught, not to committing the misconduct," he said. But not even the prosecutors denied that the fall of Duke Cunningham was a true American tragedy. "He was a man who had just about everything, but demanded more," said Forge. "He was a military hero admired by millions, but that wasn't enough. He had a family that loved him, but that wasn't enough. He counted among his friends politicians, musicians, physicians, clergymen, veterans. All of these people were not enough. In fact, they were so woefully inadequate that he committed crime after crime after crime because he wanted more."[4]

Humiliated and bitter at the news coverage of his case, Cunningham wrote in his letter to Stern that each story "hurts my family and now I have lost them along with everything I have worked for during my 64 years of life." He added, "I am human, not an animal to keep whipping. I made some decisions I'll be sorry for the rest of my life. I hurt more than anyone could imagine."[5]

Not even the most ardent political foe of Cunningham, nor even anyone who has borne the brunt of his bullying over the years, could fail to be moved by the sight of a man who flew so high now brought so low. In many ways, this was a joyless case. It was particularly painful for the brave pilots who served with him in Vietnam. Many of them are left with conflicted thoughts. They are saddened by the fall of a man with whom they shared moments forever seared into their memories, but they are angered that he brought shame to the Navy they love and to the brotherhood of pilots. Over and over again, they note that they all did things in their youth that were reckless, foolish, or arrogant. But they grew up and they wonder why their friend Duke never seemed to mature and move beyond his wartime heroics.

"In my opinion, Randy stopped developing as a person on 10 May, 1972," said Jack Ensch. "He was frozen in time, and he never advanced from there. . . . I always say it was part of my life, it wasn't my life. With Randy it became his life. And you could say it was the end of his life."

The pain of the scandal is so great that many of Cunningham's closest friends and political allies still refuse to discuss it. But for the sake of history and for the sake of good governance, it is imperative to study the Cunningham case, identify the systemic flaws that permitted his corruption, and assess the blame so that remedies can be applied. Failing that, more Randy Cunninghams are likely to emerge in the future.

Assessing blame in this scandal, of course, starts with Cunningham himself. His greed and sense of entitlement left him open to the blandishments of lobbyists and contractors. Other members of Congress resisted the temptations; Cunningham did not. Even his lawyer acknowledged that he belongs in prison. But this drama also has a stellar cast of characters who were enablers, who allowed Cunningham to career recklessly down the path that today has him sharing a dormitory with a hundred other minimum-security prisoners at a federal prison in Tucson.

The list is long. Start with the Navy and its reaction to the dog-fight of May 10, 1972. Top admirals were so starved for heroes that they embraced their new ace and let him get away with anything and everything. "He always went back to the moment that exploded him onto the scene. He used that moment," said retired Admiral Pete "Viper" Pettigrew. "But in a way, he was also used. He was used by the Navy. And society used him too, in a way. He was basically just a nor-mal guy, and if 10 May had not have happened he probably would have gotten out of the Navy and none of this would have happened."[6]

Then there was his wife, Nancy. Longtime friends—and even Cunningham's own mother[7]—are convinced that Nancy's desire for the nice things in life was a constant pressure on the congressman to acquire more. She lived up to her nickname among her husband's pilot friends: "Mrs. Bling." Despite her efforts to claim complete ig-norance of her husband's shenanigans, here was a highly educated, sophisticated woman who well knew the limits of a congressional salary and the costs of the material things he was accumulating. "Nancy fueled it," said McKeown. "She would say Dennis Hastert drives this and what do you drive?"[8]

Several well-known names in Washington were big-time enablers for the ex-aviator. Some were his close friends, such as Rep. Duncan Hunter. Largely responsible for Cunningham's entry into politics, Hunter did little to guide him through the ethical shoals of official Washington. When the scandal broke, Hunter emotionally defended Cunningham, but told other congressmen he had had no inkling of his best friend's lifestyle, boats, cars, women, and trips. Two other men played key roles in Cunningham's bribery: Newt Gingrich and Den-nis Hastert. Both were Speakers of the House; both could have stopped the corruption before it grew; but both encouraged—and rewarded—the culture in which that corruption thrived.

Gingrich and Hastert don't talk about Cunningham. It was Gin-grich who refused to heed warnings from senior Republicans and who vaulted Cunningham over more worthy Republicans to those invaluable committee positions. It was Gingrich who put him on the Appropriations Committee over the objections of then–Chairman Bob Livingston of Louisiana. And it was Gingrich, and then Hastert, who emasculated the House ethics committee, all but eliminating even the most perfunctory ethics oversight functions. Increasingly, under these two speakers what mattered most was how much money one could raise for fellow Republicans.

Gingrich and Hastert exacerbated the situation by making the House "family friendly" for members, permitting them to spend less time in Washington and more time raising money and campaigning back home. "They took the idea of staying home to be family friendly to *ad absurdum* and they never were here," said Livingston. Now out of Congress, Livingston said the Congress no longer was performing oversight. "The members didn't know their programs because they weren't having hearings. That empowered the chairmen . . . and that empowered the staff and they became arrogant and a lot of things happened because of this nonfeasance."

But the staffers abdicated their responsibility concerning Cunningham as well. Neither the members of Cunningham's office staff nor the staffers on his committees blew the whistle on the corruption. Only one staffer—David Heil—is known to have taken on Cunningham, but he did it privately and to no effect. With the evidence now revealed as overwhelming, the staff should have known. But either willingly or unwillingly, they failed to do their jobs and watch out for the taxpayers and the troops in harm's way who were counting on them.

Reporters eventually disclosed the corruption, but only after more than a decade of press coverage focused almost entirely on his wartime heroism, at-times buffoonish behavior, and outrageous statements.

Finally, the legal system rose to the occasion and moved with breathtaking speed to build cases and collect guilty pleas. In San Diego, U.S. Attorney Carol Lam gave freedom to a strong team of prosecutors, headed by Phillip Halpern, Jason Forge, and Sanjay Bhandari. In Washington, U.S. Attorney Kenneth L. Wainstein built the case against Mitchell Wade. The U.S. attorney's office in Los Angeles took a hard look at the links between earmarks and lobbying.

The Justice Department was less than enthusiastic in its support for these prosecutors, though, never explaining why they took an unusually long time in approving the indictments of Cunningham,

Foggo, and Wilkes. And, in a controversial move, the Justice Department and the White House fired Lam in early 2007, prompting congressional demands to know if she was punished for going after the three Republicans.

The biggest unknown is how Congress will respond to this stain on its reputation. Voters in November 2006 offered an early grade of "Failing," telling interviewers outside polling places that corruption was second only to the Iraq war as the driving force behind their rejection of Republican candidates. The party had tried to sell the notion that Cunningham was just an anomaly, just one rotten apple. That was always a tough sell because of the evidence. But it became an impossible sell when Reps. Bob Ney of Ohio and Mark Foley of Florida became mired in their own scandals close to the election.

The pressure now is on the Democrats, who used Cunningham as Exhibit A in their portrayal of a Republican "culture of corruption" during the 2006 congressional races. Reformers want them to prove they can be different from the Republicans. But the initial returns are not encouraging. Too many Democrats privately concur with Rep. Jim Moran, the outspoken Virginia Democrat. Almost precisely on the one year anniversary of the story breaking the Cunningham scandal, Moran looked forward to using his seniority on the Appropriations Committee to bring things to his Alexandria district, saying, "I'm going to earmark the shit out of it." He later tried to quell the media uproar by stating that he had been joking.

But thanks to the Cunningham scandal, few are laughing at the appropriations process and the explosion of earmarks in recent congresses. Keith Ashdown, a longtime crusader against earmarks from his position with the watchdog group Taxpayers for Common Sense, said that Cunningham altered the debate over wasteful spending and earmarks. "Before Cunningham, it was more of a budget wonk thing. It wasn't anything that grabbed you by the throat and made you pay attention. A lot of people thought that earmarking was just something that congressmen are supposed to do," he said.

"But then the Cunningham story came out in Technicolor on a wide screen. If you care about the way our government works, it kicked you right in the gut. It affected me far more than the Abramoff scandal." Jack Abramoff got more headlines than Cunningham. But according to Ashdown, he was primarily an "influence peddler." In contrast, "the Cunningham story is this amazing illustration of how money flows in a big circle in Washington," he said. "Money coming in from campaign contributions and outright bribes and fees for lobbyists translates into earmarks which lead to more money coming back in to grease the wheels of Congress."[9]

Before Cunningham, the political abuse of earmarks was blatant. Jim Dyer, the longtime staff director on the Appropriations Committee, recalls orders from top House leaders to steer earmarks to vulnerable Republicans. "It was very common to have leadership come in and talk about their endangered species lists, for members who were under 55 percent in the polls and needed extra help to push them across the finish line," said Dyer, who has left his committee position to become a lobbyist.

After Cunningham—and the 2006 election—even Gingrich was forced to concede that the system he helped foster had careened out of control and done great damage to the party it was supposed to help. Comparing the Republican abuse of earmarks to the British behavior that triggered the American Revolution, the former speaker acknowledged that "we tolerated corruption in a way that was totally unacceptable to our base."

Until the Cunningham scandal, most of the work of battling earmarks was shouldered by watchdog groups such as Taxpayers for Common Sense and Citizens Against Government Waste. One of the few consistent congressional critics of earmarks was Rep. Jeff Flake, who saw public outrage over Cunningham as an opportunity to wage guerilla warfare on the House floor in mid-2006. Flake infuriated the House Republican leadership by ridiculing earmarks for community swimming pools and museums and using every occasion to challenge earmarks in appropriations bills. His colleagues voted him down time after time.

"They wanted to make sure their own earmarks stay in the bills, so no one complains," said Flake, who added that Republican leaders of the House Transportation Committee in 2005 bought votes for the highway bill by promising each member of the committee at least $14 million to earmark as he or she saw fit.[10]

There were some encouraging developments as the new Congress convened in 2007 under Democratic leadership. The strongest action came in the House, which adopted new rules to bring sunshine to earmarks by requiring that they be clearly disclosed and that their sponsors be identified. "They had the guts to do what we didn't," said Flake, who should have felt vindicated by the election but instead was punished by his own party because his warnings had proved correct. The new Republican leader, John Boehner of Ohio, stripped Flake of his seat on the Judiciary Committee while rewarding the embattled and free-spending Jerry Lewis by letting him continue as the ranking Republican on the Appropriations Committee.

The reform hailed by Flake was championed by David Obey, the Wisconsin Democrat and new chairman of the Appropriations Committee, who expressed alarm at the situation, blasting the status quo before the 2006 election as "internal bribery."[11] But Obey and the Democrats showed less appetite for truly tough steps after that election left him in the chairman's seat. Even as members were congratulating Obey on his requirement that sponsors of earmarks be identified, they privately acknowledged that this would work only if the publicity embarrassed those sponsors. Since most members put out press releases boasting about earmarks, it was likely that few would be shamed into spending less.

And Obey's zeal for reform noticeably faded when it came to uncovering the extent of Cunningham's corruption. Suddenly, he found himself agreeing with Lewis, his Republican predecessor. Like Lewis, Obey failed to order an investigation into how Cunningham had abused the committee's processes, deeply disappointing outside critics. "At some point you need to step back, figure out what happened, and take steps to make sure that it doesn't happen again," said Norman Ornstein of the American Enterprise Institute, an expert on how Congress operates.

But few in Congress really want to figure out what happened. Congressional secrecy and arrogance combined with personal greed to create this scandal after all. Under public pressure, Peter Hoekstra, chairman of the Intelligence Committee, hired a special counsel— Michael Stern—to investigate whether there was complicity or culpability on the part of the committee staff. Hoekstra did not include the conduct of members of the committee within the scope of the investigation, except, obviously, for Cunningham. Then, when Stern turned over his findings, Hoekstra kept the information secret.

Rep. Jane Harman of California triggered an angry public protest from Hoekstra when, frustrated at this Republican effort to hide the results from the public, she released a five-page executive summary just before the 2006 congressional elections. The five pages that Hoekstra had tried to keep secret revealed that the Intelligence Committee had approved $70 million to $80 million in Cunningham defense and intelligence earmark requests that benefited his co-conspirators. It concluded that the staff had carried out Cunningham's wishes despite "numerous 'red flags,'" concerns that taxpayer money was being wasted and suspicions about the character of Cunningham and his lobbyist friends. The original report, completed in May 2006, was fifty-nine pages and classified. In July 2006, a twenty-eight-page unclassified version was submitted to members of the committee.

But only the five-page unclassified executive summary released by Harman was disclosed, despite the Democratic takeover of the House.

Similar stonewalling continued with the other major investigation underway in Washington involving Cunningham. Court records and the Stern report indicated that the corruption would not have been possible without the assistance of procurement officials in the Defense Department. Problems included the lack of transparency, oversight, and meaningful competition in the procurement process; the secret influence of members of Congress over defense officials; the flood of money into the secret "black budget"; and the revolving door between the Defense Department and the defense industry. The

Defense Department had refused to discuss its investigation, even a year after Cunningham's sentencing.

It was as if the Pentagon, the White House, and the Congress all hoped that with Cunningham out of sight no more embarrassing details would emerge and that everybody would just forget the scandal and move on. But even more than a year after that story exploded into public view, the Cunningham saga continues to unfold, the legal, political, governmental, and personal dramas still being far from the final act. Cunningham himself sits in prison, where he is being treated for his many physical ailments. He is hoping for a presidential pardon and—to the dismay of many critics—he qualifies for a government pension estimated at $64,000 a year from his Navy and congressional service. Nancy Cunningham has announced that she will be filing for divorce to end her marriage to the former congressman. And both Cunninghams face a crushing debt to the Internal Revenue Service.

Even in the face of obvious public revulsion at what Cunningham had done, local officials in his California district were embarrassingly slow to break with a fellow Republican who had brought them earmarks. And U.S. Attorney Lam, who might have expected praise from her bosses for the coolly efficient and professional way her office conducted the investigation, instead found herself a victim of politics. She was unceremoniously dumped from office. With the Justice Department believed to be under congressional pressure, she was asked to resign amid rampant speculation that she was being punished for going after Republicans. Cunningham, after all, had been a staunch supporter of President George W. Bush, and Wilkes was a Bush "Pioneer" in 2004, which meant he raised at least $100,000 for the president's reelection campaign.

By February 2007, Lam was out of a job. But in one of her final acts she oversaw more Cunningham-related indictments, guaranteeing further legal challenges for the four men listed by the government as Cunningham's co-conspirators.

Brent Wilkes, co-conspirator number one, pleaded not guilty on February 14, 2007, to charges of bribery, wire fraud, and money laundering. His trial is expected later in 2007. And it may provide the most legal fireworks of the entire scandal. For Wilkes has implied that he will not go quietly. In a feisty statement to reporters after his indictment, Wilkes announced: "I never bribed Duke Cunningham or anyone else." He also blasted Lam for waging a "vendetta" against him, blaming her for the destruction of his businesses and stress in his family. "Over the last 18 months," he wrote, "my life has been made a living hell. The investigation and its accompanying deliberate leaks of false rumors has destroyed my reputation and inflicted critical wounds on all my business interests."

Mitch Wade, co-conspirator number two, pleaded guilty on February 24, 2006, to charges of bribery and election fraud. He is awaiting sentencing and continues to cooperate with the government.

Tommy Kontogiannis, co-conspirator number three, avoided for the time being, at least, the legal troubles facing the other co-conspirators. He has not been charged with anything, but he remains under investigation.

The New York mortgage banker and Kontogiannis nephew John T. Michael, co-conspirator number four, pleaded not guilty on February 14, 2007, to obstruction of justice charges after allegedly lying to a grand jury. His trial is expected later in 2007.

And what about former CIA Executive Director Kyle "Dusty" Foggo? On February 14, 2007, Foggo pleaded not guilty to charges that he had denied the government his honest services by accepting lavish favors from Brent Wilkes in exchange for using his influence as the number three official at the CIA to steer an agency contract to Wilkes. In his statement broadside, Wilkes described Foggo as "my best friend since childhood, a man as close to me as a brother" and lamented that he "has been dragged into this sordid 'investigation' solely because we are friends."

Rep. Jerry Lewis also drew unwanted public attention on the periphery of the Cunningham scandal. Lewis retained his seat as the ranking Republican on the Appropriations Committee, but his ties to both Wilkes and the lobbyist Bill Lowery are still under investigation by the U.S. attorney's office in Los Angeles. Subpoenas were served on some private companies and Southern California municipalities in

2006 seeking information on Lewis and Lowery's dealings. By the end of 2006, Lewis had spent nearly $800,000 on his defense.

No matter what happens in those investigations and prosecutions, the case of Randall Harold Cunningham—the Duke—will be remembered. It will be remembered on one level as the personal tragedy of a man. Some will remember the unprecedented sight of a congressman's furniture being auctioned off; that happened March 23, 2006, in a warehouse in Rancho Dominguez, south of Los Angeles. The auction brought in $94,625, and the proceeds were split among the federal agencies involved in the investigation. But, more important, it will be remembered for what it showed about the American system of governance and a deeply flawed appropriations process. Even before all the investigations were concluded, prosecutors had seen enough to declare that Cunningham's criminality "is unprecedented in the long history of Congress" and that "it is a numbing betrayal, on an epic scale." And, in a reprimand that stung Cunningham personally, even the president of the United States pronounced his judgment on Cunningham. Once he had bantered with Cunningham, praising him and kidding him; now Bush called his conduct "outrageous" and recommended that he "pay a serious price."

But Bush never addressed the underlying issues in the scandal, nor did he acknowledge the role his party had played in permitting it to fester. It is a scandal that occurred because of one man's greed. But it also occurred because the system lacked transparency and because too few were paying attention. "Corruption snuck in because nobody knew what was going on," sadly concluded Bob Livingston.

Now, in the wake of the scandal, there is no excuse not to impose the reforms that guarantee more people—members of Congress, staffers, reporters, even voters—can know what is going on when public money is spent. If, for either political or selfish reasons, needed reforms are once again shelved, then one thing is certain—Duke Cunningham will not long be known as the most corrupt member of Congress in history. For without fresh reform and renewed public vigilance it is only a matter of time before someone wrests that title from him.

NOTES

PROLOGUE

1. Kitty Kelley, "Ace in the Hole: Duke Cunningham's Wife Tells All," *New Republic Online,* August 17, 2006.

CHAPTER TWO: MAY 10, 1972: THE DAY THAT MADE DUKE

1. Cunningham interview with *USA Today,* January 18, 1991.

2. Robert K. Wilcox, *Scream of Eagles* (New York: Pocket Star Books, 1990), 210.

3. Interviewed for the History Channel documentary *Dogfights: The Greatest Air Battles.*

4. Wilcox, *Scream of Eagles,* 208.

5. Ibid., 212.

6. Page 4 of February 13, 2006, letter from Saul J. Faerstein, MD, to U.S. District Judge Larry Alan Burns.

7. Interview with Jerry Kammer, November 6, 2006.

8. Randy Cunningham and Jeffrey Ethell, *Fox Two: The Story of America's First Ace in Vietnam* (New York: Warner Books, 1984), 93.

9. Jeffrey Ethell and Alfred Price, *One Day in a Long War: May 10, 1972, Air War, North Vietnam* (New York: Random House, 1989), 27.

10. Cunningham and Ethell, *Fox Two,* 48.

11. Interview on *Dogfights: The Greatest Air Battles.*

12. Page 14 of February 13, 2006, letter from Willie Driscoll to U.S. District Judge Larry Alan Burns.

13. Don Hollway, "Showtime for a Top Gun," *Aviation,* March 1994.

14. Ethell and Price, *One Day in a Long War,* 110.

15. Interviewed for the American Public Television documentary *Legends of Airpower.*

16. Ethell and Price, *One Day in a Long War,* 116.

17. Brad Elward and Peter Davies, *U.S. Navy F-4 Phantom II MiG Killers, 1972–73* (Oxford, U.K.: Osprey Publishing Limited, 2002), 42.

18. Page 5 of February 13, 2006, Driscoll letter to Judge Burns.

19. Interview on *Dogfights, the Greatest Air Battles.*

20. Ibid.

21. Cunningham and Ethell, *Fox Two,* 107.

22. Interview on *Legends of Airpower.*

23. Wilcox, *Scream of Eagles,* 278–279.

24. Interview on *Legends of Airpower.*

25. Cunningham and Ethell, *Fox Two,* 110.

26. Ethell and Price, *One Day in a Long War,* 189–190.

27. Alex Roth, "Shooting Down Cunningham's Legend," *San Diego Union-Tribune,* January 15, 2006.

28. Elward and Davies, *U.S. Navy F-4 Phantom II MiG Killers,* 44.

29. Interview with Jerry Kammer, November 17, 2006.

30. Ibid., November 15, 2006.

CHAPTER THREE: THE BOYS OF HILLTOP HIGH

1. *Landa v. Sears et al.,* San Diego Superior Court, Civil Case No. 394997, March 4, 1977.

2. Michael A. Graham, "Honored Policeman Who Quit Force Misses City, But Not Job," *San Diego Union,* March 9, 1980, B-1.

3. Stephen Kinzer, "Our Man in Honduras," *New York Review of Books,* September 20, 2001.

4. Ken Silverstein, "Dusty Abroad: Foggo's Travels in Honduras," a column printed by Harpers.org, the Web site of *Harper's Magazine,* http://harpers.org/sb-dusty-foggo-21-20060513.html, May 13, 2006.

CHAPTER FOUR: HOMECOMING . . . AND FINDING POLITICS

1. Randy Cunningham and Jeff Ethell, *Fox Two: The Story of America's First Ace in Vietnam* (New York: Warner Books, 1984), 114.

2. Stewart Kellerman, UPI story from Saigon, May 11, 1972.

3. Interview with Jerry Kammer, January 2007.

4. Ralph Blumenthal, "First 2 Air Aces of Vietnam War Are Here for Treat," *New York Times,* May 25, 1972.

5. Cunningham and Ethell, *Fox Two,* 128.

6. Dani Dodge, "Disgraced Lawmaker's Wife Intensely Private, Protective of Her Family," *San Diego Union-Tribune,* February 12, 2006.

7. Kitty Kelley, "Ace in the Hole: Duke Cunningham's Wife Tells All," *New Republic Online,* August 17, 2006.

8. Interview with Dani Dodge of the *San Diego Union-Tribune,* 2006.

9. Ibid.

10. Kelley, "Ace in the Hole."

11. Gerry Braun, "Cunningham Called Subpar Navy Officer," *San Diego Union-Tribune,* February 1, 1996.

12. Gregory L. Vistica, *Fall from Glory: The Men Who Sank the U.S. Navy* (New York: Simon & Schuster, 1995), 235–237.

13. Interview with Jerry Kammer, November 6, 2006.

14. Cunningham and Ethell, *Fox Two,* 130.

15. Survey of financial disclosure forms by new members, *Roll Call,* November 19, 1990.

16. Kelley, "Ace in the Hole."

CHAPTER FIVE: MR. DUKE GOES TO WASHINGTON

1. Interview with George E. Condon Jr., September 8, 2006.

2. Barry M. Horstman, "Cunningham Is Flying High in Washington," *Los Angeles Times,* February 17, 1991.

3. *Congressional Record,* January 4, 1995, E34.

4. Lois Romano, "Cunningham Friends Baffled by His Blunder into Bribery," *Washington Post,* December 4, 2005.

5. *Congressional Record,* May 11, 1995, H4838.

6. Lois Romano, "The Reliable Source," *Washington Post,* October 6, 1992.

7. *Congressional Record,* October 1, 1992, H10204.

8. "Heard on the Hill," *Roll Call,* June 24, 2004.

9. Dana Wilkie, Copley News Service, "Cunningham Version of Weekend Confrontation Disputed," September 8, 1998; Associated Press, "Cunningham Exchanges Angry Words with Constituent," September 6, 1998.

10. Wilkie, "Cunningham Version of Weekend."

11. *Congressional Record,* June 15, 1994, H4522.

12. Comments to history class recorded by students and printed in the October 8, 2004, edition of the San Dieguito Academy's *Mustang.*

13. *Congressional Record,* October 4, 1992, H11299.

14. Ibid., May 26, 2005, H4079–H4081.

15. Interview with George E. Condon Jr., November 21, 2006.

16. Laurie Kellman, "Shove-and-Shout Fray Hits House," *Washington Times,* November 18, 1995.

17. Romano, "Cunningham Friends Baffled."

18. *Congressional Record,* October 2, 1998, H9286.

19. Ibid., March 29, 2000, H1527.

20. Interview with Jerry Kammer, 2006.

21. Hearing of the House Government Reform Committee on prostate cancer, September 23, 1999.

22. Interview with Jerry Kammer, September 6, 2006.

23. Interview with Jerry Kammer, November 18, 2006.

24. Copley News Service, "Cunningham Runs for GOP Leadership Post," June 13, 1997.

25. Jim VandeHei, "Numbers Don't Add Up in Secretary Race," *Roll Call,* July 14, 1997.

26. Interview with Jerry Kammer, November 20, 2006.

27. Interview with Jerry Kammer, October, 2006.

28. *Congressional Record,* February 23, 1999, H696.

29. Interview with Jerry Kammer, 2006.

30. Jim Vande Hei, "Money Talks in Race for a GOP Leadership Post," *Roll Call,* June 6, 1997.

31. *Buchanan and Press,* MSNBC, May 1, 2003, 6:00 P.M. EST.

CHAPTER SIX: THE EARMARK—INVITATION TO CORRUPTION

1. Taxpayers for Common Sense, earmark database for HR 3, final version as signed by the president of the United States on August 10, 2005.

2. Newt Gingrich, speech to GOPAC, November 9, 2006.

3. Ken Silverstein, "The Great American Pork Barrel," *Harper's,* July 2005, 33.

4. "The Favor Factory: How a Top House Appropriations Aide Didn't Have to Wait to Lobby," *Washington Post,* July 31, 2006.

CHAPTER SEVEN: SEEDS OF A SCANDAL

1. *District Business Conduct Committee for District 2 v. Marvin I. Friedman,* National Association of Securities Dealers, Complaint No. C02960023, July 29, 1996.

2. California State Assembly Bill 840, introduced February 25, 1993, passed by Assembly May 27, 1993, passed by Senate September 2, 1993. The legislative counsel's digest, which is part of the bill, says the bill "requires" Caltrans to apply for federal funding. The language of the bill says that Caltrans "shall apply" for federal funding.

3. Peace's letter is quoted by Bill Burns, "Dept. of Defense Woos & Gets Audre, an Intelligent Move," *San Diego Daily Script,* April 14, 1993.

4. David Johnston and David D. Kirkpatrick, "Deal Maker Details the Art of Greasing the Palm," *New York Times,* August 6, 2006.

5. *Securities and Exchange Commission v. Barry Nelsen and Ellis J. Tallant,* U.S. District Court for the District of Columbia, Civil Action No. 1:97cv00798.

6. In interviews, Brent Wilkes has implied that his lobbying in 1992 involved an earmark for Audre rather than for Evergreen. But Tom Casey says that, to his knowledge, Wilkes did no lobbying for Audre in 1992 and that Audre received no earmark that year. Barry Nelsen says that the lobbying was related to a $500,000 pilot project for Evergreen which, he says, was granted in late 1992 or early 1993 by the Department of Commerce.

7. Ibid.

8. John Moore and Elana Varon, "Lobbying Blitz Pays Off for CALS Vendor," *Federal Computer Week,* November 7, 1994.

9. Ibid.

10. Joe Murray, "A Fun Bunch of Guys: When the (Poker) Chips Are Down, Depend on Your CIA to Be There," *Atlanta Journal Constitution,* May 20, 1994.

CHAPTER EIGHT: DUNCAN VS. DUKE

1. Deposition of Richard Gehling, April 27, 2000, 25–27, 52. Gehling was being deposed during Audre's bankruptcy case as he was suing for back pay. This and other portions of the deposition quoted in this book are found in Exhibit C of the *Declaration of Ian Kessler in Support of Motion for Summary Judgment,* filed May 14, 2001, in the bankruptcy case of *Audre Recognition Systems Inc.,* Bk. No. 95-10045-B11, in the Southern District of California.

2. John Moore, "Report Criticizes ADCS Project," *Federal Computer Week,* January 23, 1995, 4.

3. Confidential Audre Memo, April 14, 1995. This and other Audre memos quoted in this book are found in Exhibit E of the *Declaration of Tom Casey in Support of Motion for Summary Judgment,* filed April 17, 2001, in the bankruptcy case of *Audre Recognition Systems Inc.,* Bk. No. 95-10048-B11, in the Southern District of California.

4. Confidential Audre Memos, March 31, 1995, and May 12, 1995. See note above.

5. Office of the Inspector General of the Defense Department, *Evaluation of Automated Document Conversion Implementation,* Report No. 96-153, June 10, 1996, signed by Robert J. Lieberman, assistant inspector general, for auditing pages 4, 6, and 11. The report does not mention Port Hueneme by name but says that "only one service" wanted Audre technology. Interviews with Pentagon and congressional sources confirm that the service in question was Port Hueneme.

6. Deputy Undersecretary of Defense (Logistics), *Automated Document Conversion Raster-to-Vector Evaluation, Interim Report,* April 5, 1996, iii.

7. Ibid., ii–iii.

8. Dana Wilkie, "Cunningham in the Wings on Contract for a Donor," *San Diego Union-Tribune,* December 15, 1997.

9. *U.S. v. Brent Wilkes and John Thomas Michael,* 07-CR–0330 LAB, U.S. District Court for the Southern District of California, Indictment, February 13, 2007, 9.

10. Ibid.

11. ADCS Press Release, "ADCS Wins $1 Million Contract," April 14, 1997. The Cunningham quote also appears in an ADCS pamphlet, "About ADCS: Providing the Latest in Image Conversion Technology."

12. Ibid.

13. Deposition of Richard Gehling, April 27, 2000, 48.

14. Ibid., 51.

15. Ibid., 59–60.

16. The quotations from Donald Lundell and Randy Cunningham both come from Dana Wilkie, "Cunningham in the Wings on Contract for Donor," *San Diego Union-Tribune,* December 15, 1997.

17. *Congressional Record,* 105th Cong., "Gulf War Veterans' Health," July 11, 1997, S7259.

CHAPTER NINE: OUR MAN IN PANAMA

1. Deposition of Brent Wilkes, September 6, 2000, 423, *ADCS Inc. v. MSCI Technologies et al.,* CA-99-1978-A, U.S. District Court for the Eastern District of Virginia.

2. Transcript of telephone conversation between Gail Cotton and Ann Barnes, June 22, 1998, obtained from the Veterans Affairs Department through the Freedom of Information Act (FOIA).

3. The Wilkes and Kimbrough quotations are from the minutes of an August 4, 1998, meeting between Brent Wilkes, Rollie Kimbrough, and other executives of ADCS and MCSI, included as an exhibit in *ADCS Inc. v. MCSI Inc.*

4. These calculations come from Gail Cotten's handwritten notations on the MCSI invoice, obtained from the Veterans Administration through the FOIA.

5. *U.S. v. Cunningham,* U.S. District Court, Southern District of California, Case No. 05cr2137-LAB, Government's Objections to Presentence Report, Exhibit 13, February 28, 2006. Exhibit 13 contains minutes from an interview between federal investigators and an official identified only as Government Official B. Paul Behrens confirms that he was the Government Official B.

6. *U.S. v. Cunningham,* Government's Objections to Presentence Report, Exhibit 14, February 28, 2006. Exhibit 14 contains minutes from an interview between federal investigators and an official identified only as Government Official D. Sources close to the investigation say that Gary Jones was the Government Official D.

7. *U.S. v. Wilkes,* Indictment, 11.

8. Department of Defense, Office of the Inspector General, *Audit Report: Fiscal Year 1999 Automated Document Conversion System Program,* Report No. D-2000-119, May 2, 2000, 6.

9. Ibid., 11. 1. *U.S. v. Wilkes,* Indictment, 18, 21.

CHAPTER TEN: LIVING LARGE

1. U.S. v. Wilkes, Indictment, 18, 21.

2. Ibid., 25, 26.

3. Ibid., 25.

4. Kelly Thornton and Onell R. Soto, "Two Cunningham Figures Indicted Over CIA Deal: Feds Allege Web of Bribery, Debauchery," *San Diego Union-Tribune,* February 14, 2007.

5. David Johnston and David D. Kirkpatrick, "Deal Maker Details the Art of Greasing the Palm," *New York Times,* August 6, 2006.

6. Foggo e-mail to Wilkes, September 16, 2004, cited in *U.S. v. Kyle Dustin Foggo and Brent Wilkes,* Case No. 07-cr-00329, LAM, U.S. District Court for the Southern District of California, February 13, 2007, Indictment, 10.

7. *U.S. v. Foggo,* Indictment, 5–6.

8. Foggo e-mail to Wilkes, September 10, 2003, cited in *U.S. v. Foggo,* Indictment, 6.

9. Foggo e-mail to Combs, January 7, 2004, cited in *U.S. v. Foggo,* Indictment, 7.

10. *U.S. v. Foggo,* Indictment, 8.

11. Katherine Shrader and Allison Hoffman, "Water Deal Exposes Secret Iraq Contracts," Associated Press, February 6, 2007.

12. *U.S. v. Foggo,* Indictment, 9.

CHAPTER ELEVEN: THOUGHTS BY A LAVA LAMP

1. Kitty Kelley, "Ace in the Hole: Duke Cunningham's Wife Tells All," *New Republic Online,* August 17, 2006.

2. Dana Wilkie and Marcus Stern, "Cunningham's Waterfront Crusade: Local Congressman Steers Cash Toward His D.C. Neighborhood," *San Diego Union-Tribune,* November 15, 1998, B1.

3. Colbert I. King, "The Duke of D.C., Unhorsed," *Washington Post,* December 3, 2005, A23.

CHAPTER FOURTEEN: CROSSING THE BRIBERY LINE

1. *Congressional Record,* September 13, 2000, H7565.

2. Charles R. Babcock, "Lawmakers Ties to N.Y. Developer Investigated," *Washington Post,* July 26, 2005.

3. Bryan Virasami, "Paying on Time for His Crime," *Newsday,* November 30, 2005.

4. Joe Cantlupe, "Ex-Congressman's Friend Emerges as Mystery Man," *San Diego Union-Tribune,* April 15, 2006.

5. Government Sentencing Memo, *U.S. vs. Randall Harold Cunningham,* U.S. District Court, Southern District of California, February 17, 2006.

6. Ibid.

7. Kitty Kelley, "Ace in the Hole: Duke Cunningham's Wife Tells All," *New Republic Online,* August 26, 2006.

8. John Bresnahan and Tory Newmyer, "Former Aide Confronted Cunningham Over Corruption," *Roll Call,* February 28, 2006.

CHAPTER FIFTEEN:
WADE BUYS HIMSELF A COUPLE OF LAWMAKERS

1. Walter Pincus, "Pentagon to Scrap Site Connected to Scandal; Rep. Goode's Earmark Led to Contract Award," *Washington Post,* August 1, 2006.

2. Laurence Hammack, "Military Center to Close Monday," *Roanoke (VA) Times,* July 29, 2006.

3. Anita Kumar, "Harris Letter Thanked Contractor for Dinner," *St. Petersburg (FLA) Times,* July 8, 2006.

4. Michael Fechter, "MZM Held Out for Big Tax Break," *Tampa (FLA) Tribune,* March 21, 2006.

5. According to MZM employees present at the time.

6. Adam C. Smith, "Briber Paid for 2nd Meal for Harris," *St. Petersburg (FLA) Times,* May 21, 2006.

7. Charles Babcock, "Contractor Pleads Guilty to Corruption; Probe Extends Beyond Bribes to Contractor," *Washington Post,* February 25, 2006.

8. Walter Pincus, "Intelligence Center, MZM on Cozy Terms," *Washington Post,* July 17, 2005.

CHAPTER SEVENTEEN: A FAST-PACED WEEK

1. Alex Roth, "Staffers Believed Cunningham Right Until the End," *San Diego Union-Tribune,* May 21, 2006.

2. John Bresnahan, "Democrats Eye Cunningham Deal," *Roll Call,* June 14, 2005.

3. Logan Jenkins, "House Sale Opens Door to Duke's Undoing," *San Diego Union-Tribune,* June 16, 2005.

4. Joshua Micah Marshall, "Living Large, Free of Charge," *Talking Points Memo,* June 16, 2005.

5. Marcus Stern and Joe Cantlupe, "Ties Between Contractor, Congressman Questioned," Copley News Service, June 17, 2005.

6. Dani Dodge, "Subpoenas Issued in Cunningham Case," *San Diego Union-Tribune,* June 18, 2005.

7. Kelly Thornton, "Subpoenas Issued over Cunningham Deal," *San Diego Union-Tribune,* June 18, 2005.

CHAPTER EIGHTEEN: CLOSING IN

1. William Finn Bennett, "Issa Defends Cunningham—Embattled Lawmaker Turns Away Requests for Interviews," *North County Times,* June 20, 2005.

2. Marcus Stern, "Cunningham Says Sale Showed Poor Judgment," Copley News Service, June 24, 2005.

3. Jerry Kammer, "Cunningham's Ties to Charity Attacked," Copley News Service, June 24, 2005.

4. Marcus Stern, "Firm in 'Duke' Controversy Might Be Sold," Copley News Service, June 28, 2005.

5. Renae Merle and R. Jeffrey Smith, "Pentagon Ends New Work on D.C. Firm's Contract," *Washington Post,* June 28, 2005.

6. Renae Merle and R. Jeffrey Smith, "Agents Search Homes, Yacht of Contractor, Congressman," *Washington Post,* July 2, 2005.

7. Kitty Kelley, "Ace in the Hole: Duke Cunningham's Wife Tells All," *New Republic Online,* August 17, 2005.

8. Joe Cantlupe, "Agents Raid Cunningham Home, MZM Office and Yacht," Copley News Service, July 2, 2005.

9. Government's Sentencing Memo, February 17, 2006, 7.

10. Kelley, "Ace in the Hole."

11. Government's Sentencing Memo, February 17, 2006, 14.

12. Dani Dodge, "Congressman Chats with Some Friendly Rotarians," *San Diego Union-Tribune,* July 6, 2005.

CHAPTER NINETEEN: BOTCHED COVER-UP

1. Kitty Kelley, "Ace in the Hole: Duke Cunningham's Wife Tells All," *New Republic Online,* August 17, 2006.

2. Ibid.

CHAPTER TWENTY: GUILTY!

1. Kitty Kelley, "Ace in the Hole: Duke Cunningham's Wife Tells All," *New Republic Online,* August 17, 2006.

2. John Marelius and Dani Dodge, "Eight-Term Congressman Says Probes Would Make Campaigning Difficult," *San Diego Union-Tribune,* July 15, 2006.

3. Ibid.

4. Dani Dodge and Craig Gustafson, "Some Disappointed Over Cunningham's Not Running," *San Diego Union-Tribune,* July 15, 2006.

CHAPTER TWENTY-ONE: SENTENCING DAY

1. Kitty Kelley, "Ace in the Hole: Duke Cunningham's Wife Tells All," *New Republic Online,* August 17, 2006.

2. Nancy D. Cunningham letter to Judge Larry Alan Burns, February 17, 2006.

3. Lela Cunningham letter to Judge Larry Alan Burns; undated.

4. Carrie M. Cunningham letter to Judge Larry Alan Burns, February 14, 2006.

5. April Cunningham letter to Judge Larry Alan Burns, February 12, 2006.

6. Robert F. Cunningham's letter to Judge Larry Alan Burns, February 10, 2006.

7. Todd Cunningham letter to Judge Larry Alan Burns, February 12, 2006.

8. Interview with George E. Condon Jr., September 8, 2006.

9. Onell R. Soto, "Con Air Picks up San Diego Passenger," *San Diego Union-Tribune,* March 11, 2006, 5. Marelius and Dodge, "Eight-Term Congressman."

EPILOGUE

1. Interview with Jerry Kammer, 2007.

2. Kitty Kelly, "Ace in the Hole: Duke Cunningham's Wife Tells All," *New Republic Online,* August 17, 2006.

3. Cunningham letter to Marcus Stern from the Low Security Correctional Institution in Butner, North Carolina, September 15, 2006.

4. Transcript of the sentencing in U.S. District Court, Southern District of California, March 3, 2006, 33.

5. Letter to Stern.

6. Interview with Jerry Kammer, 2006.

7. Ibid.; Kelly, "Ace in the Hole."

8. Interview with Dani Dodge, *San Diego Union-Tribune,* 2006.

9. Interview with Jerry Kammer, 2007.

10. Interview with Jerry Kammer, 2005.

11. Interview with Jerry Kammer, 2007.

ACKNOWLEDGMENTS

THERE WOULD HAVE BEEN NO BOOK, INDEED NO RUN OF AWARD-WINNING stories, without the unflagging support of our editors and bosses both at Copley News Service and the *San Diego Union-Tribune*. That starts—always—with David C. Copley who was a rock from the very first Cunningham story and who was unwavering in his simple but important mandate to follow the story wherever it led regardless of which political party or what private interests might be embarrassed. Similar support came from Charles Patrick, Hal Fuson, and Glenda Winders at Copley and editor Karin Winner at the *Union-Tribune*. They were the ones who had to take any calls of complaint and who kept pushing us to keep digging to find out more about Cunningham's dealings. Few other reporters—or authors—are lucky enough to have such supportive bosses.

But there were so many others who played important roles in the reporting and writing of this book. Many cannot be publicly thanked because of their continuing work in the Defense Department, Central Intelligence Agency, Department of Veterans Affairs, Congress, and private industry. It is our biggest regret that more of Cunningham's friends and supporters did not talk with us to help flesh out a full portrait of the troubled congressman. But that does not in any way diminish our sincere gratitude to those who did not want to surrender the field to his critics and were instrumental in steering us away from caricatures of complex people.

It is traditional for authors to talk about the drudgery of the book-writing process, using colorful imagery about bleeding over every line. The truth, though, in this case is that there was little drudgery in putting this book together. From talking to the kind people of Shelbina, Missouri, to poring over campaign finance reports, to debating systemic changes with congressional reformers, this book was a joy to write. Not because there was any joy in the fall of a legitimate war hero; but because we kept learning more about the scandal and more about Congress as we proceeded. And for that joy, we must thank a great many people. There are those good government sentries who monitor congressional ethics and raise the alarm when wrong things are being done; people like Keith Ashdown and Norm Ornstein, Tom Mann, Winslow Wheeler, and Nathan Facey. And there was Gordon Imrie who shed light on the pre-war Cunningham, and Kathleen Wilham, president of the Shelby County Historical Society, who volunteered so much of her time and assistance.

There are our colleagues in Washington who helped in both our daily coverage of the scandal and in this book, most notably Rosemary Petersen, who kept us focused; and Finlay Lewis, who taught us the difference between writing for newspapers and writing for books; and Otto Kreisher, who patiently made sure we knew our MiGs from our Phantoms and was our military expert. We also benefited from the work of Joe Cantlupe, Dana Wilkie, Toby Eckert, and intern Kelly Bennett, all members of the Pulitzer team. And good advice came as well from the always-insightful Rudy Murillo, who reminded us that even when writing a book there still is a baseball season. And we can't forget the ever-capable Kay Torpey who went from transcribing the remarks of the president of the United States to laboring through hours of tapes of interviews for this book. At the National Archives, we benefited from the cooperation offered by Archivist Specialist Rutha Beamon. And in Cleveland, one of us benefited from the daunting example of the senior George E. Condon, who managed to gracefully complete two books at age ninety while we were working on just this one.

In San Diego, the list is even longer and more varied. In the *Union-Tribune* library, valuable help was given by Anne Magill, Merrie Monteagudo, Denise Davidson, Michelle Gilchrist, Erin Hobbs, Danielle Cervantes, Cecilia Iñiguez, Peter Uribe, and Beth Wood. In the photo department, we benefited from the long memory of Jerry Rife and the great photos and assistance of Robert York, James Skovmand, Nelvin Cepeda, Rick Nocon, Reenie Shea, Crissy Pascual, K. C. Alfred, and John Gastaldo. In the newsroom, Dani Dodge, who helped cover the Cunningham story, shared her unpublished notes and interviews. And always helpful were Alex Roth, Susan White, Onell Soto, Bruce Bigelow, and news editor Lora Cicalo, who together were a big part of the team that secured the Pulitzer that gave birth to this book. Also supportive was business editor Jim Watters. And we would be remiss if we didn't recognize the valued input of other journalists who graciously gave freely of their time and thoughts to help us through the process. That would include too many to mention, but would be headed by William Finn Bennett and Mark Walker at the *North County Times*, Charles R. Babcock, Walter Pincus of the *Washington Post*, and bloggers Josh Marshall, Laura Rozen, Ken Silverstein, and Jason Vest. And we're grateful to Hans Ericsson who out-foxed a lot of other photographers to get the best shot of the *Duke-Stir.*

All of these people—and others who cannot be named—contributed too much for us to properly acknowledge. They are responsible for so many of the anecdotes and details that made writing the book so much joy. They saved us time after time from over-simplifications or mistakes. It is our hope that neither made their way into the finished product. But if they did, they are solely the responsibility of the authors.

Also, we certainly cannot let go unheralded the founder and editor-at-large of PublicAffairs, Peter Osnos, and our editor, Lindsay Jones. No publisher ever showed more confidence and no editor ever showed more bravery than when this intrepid team agreed to let four newspaper reporters tackle the very different challenge of writing this book. That three of these aspiring authors had never before written a book should have sent Osnos and Jones running for the exits. Add in the fact that the topic of the proposed book—the Duke Cunningham scandal—was getting nowhere near the headlines of the Abramoff scandal, and no one could have faulted them had they politely declined the project.

But they didn't. They believed in the book's importance; they believed that the multi-hyphened monster that is Stern-Kammer-Calbreath-Condon could produce a coherent and cohesive work; and they believed, most importantly, that here was a story worth telling. They believed that here was a book that could both serve history and spin an interesting yarn. It was this belief that infused our work and carried us through the writing process. They also provided us with top-notch editors who guided us ably—Laura Stine and Jennifer Blakebrough-Raeburn. For all that they did, our thanks go to Osnos and Jones—though they must share top billing with Deborah Ritchken of the Sandra Dijkstra Literary Agency, the San Diego–based agent who was the first to see a book in the Cunningham drama being laid out in daily stories from Copley News Service and the *San Diego Union-Tribune*. She conceived the project and breathed life into it.

Finally, we must thank those who allowed us to put so many of our daily responsibilities on hold for months to meet our book deadlines while still dealing with those pesky duties of our day jobs. Our families managed to get by with absentee husbands and fathers. We hope they know the depth of our gratitude.

Washington, D.C.
March 17, 2007

INDEX

PublicAffairs is a publishing house founded in 1997. It is a tribute to the standards, values, and flair of three persons who have served as mentors to countless reporters, writers, editors, and book people of all kinds, including me.

I.F. Stone, proprietor of *I. F. Stone's Weekly*, combined a commitment to the First Amendment with entrepreneurial zeal and reporting skill and became one of the great independent journalists in American history. At the age of eighty, Izzy published *The Trial of Socrates*, which was a national bestseller. He wrote the book after he taught himself ancient Greek.

Benjamin C. Bradlee was for nearly thirty years the charismatic editorial leader of *The Washington Post*. It was Ben who gave the *Post* the range and courage to pursue such historic issues as Watergate. He supported his reporters with a tenacity that made them fearless and it is no accident that so many became authors of influential, best-selling books.

Robert L. Bernstein, the chief executive of Random House for more than a quarter century, guided one of the nation's premier publishing houses. Bob was personally responsible for many books of political dissent and argument that challenged tyranny around the globe. He is also the founder and longtime chair of Human Rights Watch, one of the most respected human rights organizations in the world.

For fifty years, the banner of PublicAffairs Press was carried by its owner Morris B. Schnapper, who published Gandhi, Nasser, Toynbee, Truman, and about 1,500 other authors. In 1983, Schnapper was described by *The Washington Post* as "a redoubtable gadfly." His legacy will endure in the books to come.

Peter Osnos, *Founder and Editor-at-Large*